"十四五"普通高等教育会计专业精品规划教材

会计英语

KUAIJI YINGYU

主　编　蒋海晨　黄钟颖
副主编　廖　实

苏州大学出版社
Soochow University Press

图书在版编目(CIP)数据

会计英语 / 蒋海晨,黄钟颖主编. —苏州:苏州大学出版社,2021.8(2024.7 重印)
"十四五"普通高等教育会计专业精品规划教材
ISBN 978-7-5672-3617-2

Ⅰ.①会… Ⅱ.①蒋… ②黄… Ⅲ.①会计-英语-高等学校-教材　Ⅳ.①F23

中国版本图书馆 CIP 数据核字(2021)第 131932 号

会计英语

蒋海晨　黄钟颖　主编

责任编辑　沈　琴

苏 州 大 学 出 版 社 出 版 发 行
(地址:苏州市十梓街1号　邮编:215006)
广东虎彩云印刷有限公司印装
(地址:东莞市虎门镇黄村社区厚虎路20号C幢一楼　邮编:523898)

开本 787×1092　1/16　印张 13.5　字数 321 千
2021 年 8 月第 1 版　2024 年 7 月第 4 次印刷
ISBN 978-7-5672-3617-2　定价:45.00 元

苏州大学版图书若有印装错误,本社负责调换
苏州大学出版社营销部　电话:0512-67481020
苏州大学出版社网址　http://www.sudapress.com
苏州大学出版社邮箱　sdcbs@suda.edu.cn

"十四五"普通高等教育会计专业精品规划教材

编委会

顾　问　冯　博
主　任　王则斌
副主任　罗正英
委　员　周中胜　权小锋　俞雪华　张雪芬
　　　　龚菊明　陈　艳　郁　刚　蒋海晨
　　　　倪丹悦

前言 Preface

经济国际化、市场全球化、资源共享化已是当今社会经济发展的大势所趋。中国融入世界经济大格局的程度越来越高,速度也越来越快。在此背景下,社会和企业的发展对人才的培养也提出更高的要求,需要大批精通专业同时熟练掌握外语的国际化人才。于个人而言,专业技能与外语能力缺一不可,外语能力的欠缺或将限制个人发展。基于此,本书旨在用地道的英语讲解专业财会知识,帮助学生使用英语流畅阅读,交流会计专业的基础知识与相关理论,并逐步提高阅读英语会计文献和使用英语处理常规会计业务的能力。

本书以财务活动为主线,内容涵盖财务会计、财务管理、管理会计、审计、会计信息系统等几大方面。在编写上,本书采用单元模块编写法,全书共 8 个单元,每一单元包含若干章节,其内容布局为:

- ✓ 学习目标(Learning Objectives):明确本章学习重点。
- ✓ 对话(Warm-up: Dialogue):熟悉与本章内容相关的口语表达。
- ✓ 课文内容(Text):循序渐进、重点突出地阐述专业知识。
- ✓ 单元小结(Chapter Round-up):总结本单元的知识重点与难点。
- ✓ 词汇(Glossary):汇总本单元的专业词汇。
- ✓ 课后练习(Review Questions, Exercises and Group Activities):包括书面练习、课堂演示、小组讨论、案例分析等多种形式,有助于学生复习巩固本单元知识要点,同时有助于提高其口语表达能力,提升英语交流水平。
- ✓ 补充阅读(Supplementary Reading):与本单元知识点紧密相关,原汁原味的英文文献选读,帮助学生通过阅读原版英文资料加深对专业知识的理解,同时拓宽其专业视野,启发其专业思考。

此外,书后还附有各单元课文内容的参考译文,有助于学生更好地理解和掌握课文内容。

本书的编写立足于财会专业学生,兼顾会计专业知识和英语学习的双重要求。本书难度适中,条理清晰,内容充实,语言地道,贴近实际,适合高校会计、审计、管理等专业的双语教学,亦可作为涉外企业商务人士的自学或培训用书。

编　者

目录 Contents

Unit One   Introduction to Accounting

Learning Objectives   / 1

Warm-up: Dialogue   / 1

Text   / 2

Chapter Round-up   / 8

Glossary   / 9

Review Questions   / 9

Exercises   / 10

Group Activities   / 11

Supplementary Reading   / 12

Unit Two   Accounting System and Process

Learning Objectives   / 15

Warm-up: Dialogue   / 15

Text   / 16

Chapter Round-up   / 29

Glossary   / 30

Review Questions   / 31

Exercises   / 31

Group Activities   / 34

Supplementary Reading   / 34

Unit Three Financial Accounting

Learning Objectives / 37

Warm-up: Dialogue / 37

Text / 38

Chapter Round-up / 52

Glossary / 53

Review Questions / 54

Exercises / 55

Group Activities / 56

Supplementary Reading / 57

Unit Four Financial Reporting and Financial Analysis

Learning Objectives / 61

Warm-up: Dialogue / 61

Text / 62

Chapter Round-up / 73

Glossary / 74

Review Questions / 75

Exercises / 75

Group Activities / 78

Supplementary Reading / 80

Unit Five Managing Financial Resources

Learning Objectives / 83

Warm-up: Dialogue / 83

Text / 84

Chapter Round-up / 92

Glossary / 92

Review Questions / 93

Exercises　/ 94

Group Activities　/ 95

Supplementary Reading　/ 95

Unit Six　　Management Accounting

Learning Objectives　/ 99

Warm-up: Dialogue　/ 99

Text　/ 100

Chapter Round-up　/ 106

Glossary　/ 107

Review Questions　/ 107

Exercises　/ 108

Group Activities　/ 110

Supplementary Reading　/ 110

Unit Seven　　Auditing

Learning Objectives　/ 113

Warm-up: Dialogue　/ 113

Text　/ 114

Chapter Round-up　/ 128

Glossary　/ 129

Review Questions　/ 129

Exercises　/ 130

Group Activities　/ 131

Supplementary Reading　/ 132

Unit Eight　　Accounting in Information Systems

Learning Objectives　/ 134

Warm-up: Dialogue　/ 134

Text　/ 135

Chapter Round-up / 139

Glossary / 139

Review Questions / 140

Exercises / 140

Group Activities / 141

Supplementary Reading / 142

Translation / 144

Glossary / 200

References / 206

Unit One

Introduction to Accounting

 Learning Objectives

When you have studied this chapter, you should be able to:

* explain the role of accounting and identify the different areas of the economy in which accountants work;

* understand the definition of accounting;

* identify the main branches of accounting and the potential users of accounting information;

* outline the common structure of business entities;

* understand the accounting assumptions, basic rules and qualitative characteristics of accounting information.

 Warm-up: Dialogue

Emily: Hello, Kevin. It's nice to meet you. We are looking to hire an accountant. What did you take in university?

Kevin: Nice to meet you. I have a bachelor's degree in commerce and majored in finance and management in the business school.

Emily: That sounds very interesting. Please tell me more about your programs in university.

Kevin: In my programs I studied financial accounting, management accounting, financial analysis, auditing, taxation law, corporation law, and so on.

Emily: Sounds good. Have you got any professional certificate?

Kevin: Not yet. But I'm working on the examinations of CPA now.

Emily: Have you got any working experience related to accounting?

Kevin: Yes, I have been working as an accountant assistant for two years in a local accounting firm.

Emily: That's good. We hope to hire an accountant who can become a partner in our firm in the future.

 Text

Section 1 Accounting as a Profession

Accounting has developed as a profession over the past hundred years or so, attaining a social status equivalent to that of law and medicine. Different countries have different professional accounting bodies, which represent the interests of their members by lobbying governments, and provide the framework for self-regulation. There exist some major professional accounting bodies in the world, such as American Institute of Certified Public Accountants (AICPA), the Association of Chartered Certified Accountants (ACCA), the Certified General Accountants Association of Canada (CGA-Canada), CPA Australia, the Hong Kong Institute of Certified Public Accountants, etc. Entry to the professional accounting bodies requires a number of conditions to be satisfied. Mostly, people seeking entry must normally hold a degree, successfully complete certain programs or examinations and have appropriate working experience.

Accountants generally practice their profession in three main areas: public accounting, commercial accounting and not-for-profit accounting.

Public accountants offer their professional services to the public for a fee. Owing to the sophistication of today's business structure and increasing regulations by government, public accountants tend to specialize in one of four general services: auditing, taxation, management advisory services, or insolvency.

Many accountants are employed in business entities. The entity's senior accounting officer, or the controller, has overall responsibility for directing the activities of the accounting staff, who serves the function of general accounting, cost accounting, budgeting, taxation accounting, internal auditing and accounting information systems.

Another area is not-for-profit accounting. City councils, state governments and the federal government collect and spend huge amounts of money annually. Government accounting is concerned with the efficient usage of its resources and in consistency with the provisions of city, state and federal laws and regulations. Other not-for-profit organizations, such as churches, charities, hospitals and private educational institutions, follow accounting procedures similar to those used in government accounting.

Being a language of business of modern society, accounting is applicable to all types of economic entities, including profit-seeking organizations and not-for-profit entities, which engage in the using of economic resources and the making of economic decisions.

Section 2 Accounting Defined

Definition of Accounting

Accounting, which is often called the language of business, uses its own special words and symbols to communicate financial information for economic decision made by managers, shareholders, creditors and many others. As a matter of fact, accounting is a service provided for those who need information about an entity's financial positions and performance.

Accounting has been defined as the process of identifying, measuring, recording and communicating economic information to permit informed judgments and decisions by users of the information (Figure 1-1).

Identifying involves recognizing economic events and determining which of those events represent economic activities relevant to a business. For instance, the selling of goods to a customer, the provision of services to a client and the payment of wages to employees are all economic activities, which are named by accountants as transactions and events.

Measurement must occur before the effects of transactions can be recorded. In our economy, business activity is measured by prices expressed in terms of money, which serves as both a medium of exchange and as a measure of value. Accounting transactions are therefore measured in terms of dollars and cents.

Recording is the process of systematically maintaining a record of all transactions which have affected the business entity after they have been identified and measured. Therefore, Recording provides a history of the economic activities of an entity. Technically, the recorded data must be classified and summarized to be useful in making decisions.

Being the final step of the accounting process, communication can be described as the procedure of preparing and distributing accounting reports to potential users. Identifying, measuring and recording will be pointless if the financial information contained in accounting records cannot be communicated to the potential users. Once the users of accounting information have access to appropriate reports, they are able, after analyzing and interpreting the reports, to make relevant economic decisions.

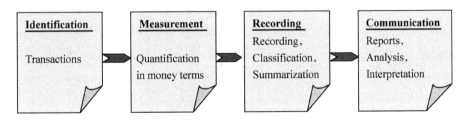

Figure 1-1 Accounting Process

II. Users of Accounting Information

The ultimate objective of accounting is to provide information in reports which can be used by external and internal decision makers, or external users and internal users.

External users are those who are outside a business but have direct interest in it, such as investors, creditors, government agencies, suppliers, customers and the public. They make decisions concerning investing, the granting of credit, the purchasing or sales of goods and services, complying with tax laws as well as other regulatory requirements, and so on.

Internal users include management and employees. Among them, managers must have financial data for planning and controlling the operations of the business entity. Managers need answers to such questions as: What resources are available? How much is owing to outsiders? What is the most efficient production process? What will be the effect of increasing or decreasing selling prices? Employees must also be an important user group of financial information, because they need some assurance about the stability and profitability of the company.

III. Classification of Accounting

Modern accounting serves a wide range of users who have various economic interests in business entities. Accordingly, accounting is categorized into two basic branches: financial accounting and management accounting. Financial accounting is related to the preparations of financial reports for users mainly outside the business, while management accounting mainly provides information to internal management for decision-making.

Section 3 Accounting Assumptions and Rules

I. The Structure of Business Entities

The three most common structures for profit-seeking entities are sole traders or single proprietorships, partnerships and companies.

A single proprietorship or, sole trader, is a business entity owned by one person. Many small service enterprises, retail stores and professional practices are operated as single proprietorships. The owner of a single proprietorship business supplies cash and other assets to the business, is entitled to all profits, and is legally liable for its debts. From an accounting standpoint, however, the business entity is treated as an entity separate from its owner, and accounting is done only for the affairs of the business entity and the owner's personal affairs are kept separate from those of the entity.

A partnership is a business owned by two or more persons acting as partners. No special legal requirements need be met to form a partnership. All that is necessary is an agreement among the people joining together as partners. Although the partnership agreement may be oral, a written agreement is preferred in order to facilitate the resolution of disagreements which may arise between partners. The partners supply the resources and share the profits and losses.

Partnerships are not separate legal entities. Consequently, the individual partners are personally liable for the debts of the partnership. From an accounting viewpoint, however, partnerships are treated as entities separate from their owners. Like single proprietorships, partnerships are widely used for small service enterprises, retail stores and professional practices.

A company or corporation is a separate legal entity formed under the Corporations Law. Its owners are called shareholders, because their ownership interests are represented by shares in the company. Because a company is a separate legal entity, shareholders in a limited company are not liable for the company's debts once the shares held have been paid for in full. This feature is known as the limited liability principle.

Separate legal entity status enables a company to conduct its business affairs in its own name as if it were a legal person. Thus, a company can buy, own and sell property; it can sue or be sued in its own name; and it can sign contracts with others. In essence, a company is treated as a legal entity with all the rights, duties and responsibilities of a person. Shareholders are free to sell all or part of their shares at any time. This ease of transferability of ownership, coupled with the limited liability for company debts, generally adds to the attractiveness of investing in company shares. Profits are distributed to shareholders in the form of dividends.

The comparisons between single proprietorship/partnerships and corporation are listed in Table 1-1.

Table 1-1 Comparisons Between Single Proprietorship/Partnerships and Corporation

	Single proprietorship/partnerships	Corporation (Limited companies)
Formation	Simple and cheap to set up.	Complex and expensive.
Capital structure	* Owners provide capital only. * No shares can be issued. The life of the business is usually limited. * Owner has total liability for debts.	* Large potential membership to provide capital and resources. * Ownership is transferable by selling shares, so the life of the company is theoretically unlimited. * Shareholders' liability is limited to the amount of their contribution.
Management	Owners themselves are involved in management.	CEO/Professional manager is responsible for daily operation.
Profitability	Profits are distributed only to the owners.	Profits can be distributed to shareholders as dividends or retained in the business.
Tax inference	Tax advantage (Tax shield).	Dual tax.

Accounting Assumptions

1. The accounting entity assumption

If the transactions of an entity are to be recorded, classified and summarized into financial statements, the accountant must be able to identify clearly the boundaries of the entity being accounted for. Under the accounting entity assumption, the assets, liabilities and business activities of the entity are kept completely distinguishable from those of the owner of the entity as well as from those of other entities. A separate set of accounting records is maintained for each entity, and the financial reports prepared represent the financial position and performance of that entity only.

2. The going concern assumption

The going concern assumption states that the entity will continue in operation in the foreseeable future and there is no intention to put the entity into liquidation or to make drastic cutbacks to the scale of the operations. In the event that the management is planning the sale or liquidation of the entity, the going concern assumption and the cost assumption are set aside and the financial reports are prepared on the basis of estimated sales or liquidation values. When this occurs, the reports should identify clearly the basis upon which values are determined.

3. The period assumption

Users of financial information, however, need timely information for decision-making purposes. Accountants must therefore prepare periodic reports on the performance, financial position, financing and investing activities. There are also statutory requirements for entities to determine periodic profit figures, e.g. for taxation. Such things require the division of the life of the entity into arbitrary equal time intervals, which is known as the period assumption. As a result of this assumption, profit determination is often referred to as a process of matching the revenues recognized during the period with the expenses incurred in that period.

4. The monetary assumption

The monetary unit assumption requires that only those things that can be expressed in money are included in the accounting records. Accountants assume that data expressed in terms of money are useful in making economic decisions and that the monetary unit represents a realistic value that can be used to measure net profit, financial position and changes in financial position. Any events which cannot be quantified in terms of money cannot be listed in the entity's accounting information system. However, this does not preclude the reporting of non-monetary information in footnotes to the financial reports, if such information is relevant to economic decision-making.

Ⅲ Other Accounting Rules

1. Historical cost principle

It requires that assets are recorded at cost when they are obtained or the expenditures incurred on acquisition rather than fair market value. This principle provides reliable information, which removes the opportunity to provide subjective and biased market value.

2. Accrual principle

It means that revenues and expenses are recognized in the accounting period in which they are earned or incurred, even though the cash receipts or payments occur at another time or even in another accounting period. It is the use of accrual principle that accomplishes much of the matching of revenues and expenses, because most transactions involve purchases and sales at one point in time and cash payments and receipts at some other points.

3. Matching principle

It requires that all expenses incurred in generating revenues during a period of time be deducted from the revenue earned. In other words, all the expenses related to given revenue should be matched with and deducted from that revenue for the determination of periodic income. This results in an accurate measure of the net income or net loss for the period.

4. Full disclosure principle

It means that the financial statements and notes or explanations should include all necessary information to prevent a reasonably astute user of the financial statements from being misled. Under this principle, all the information necessary for the users' understanding of the financial statements must be disclosed. For example, certain provisions of leases, significant amounts of purchases commitments, and notices of pending lawsuits or settlements should be disclosed in the notes to the financial statements.

Ⅳ Qualitative Characteristics of Accounting Information

1. Reliability

Information is reliable if: users can depend on it to represent what it is supposed to represent and it reflects the substance of the transactions that have taken place; it is free from bias and material error and is complete; and it has been prudently prepared.

2. Relevance

The information provided should be that which is required to satisfy the needs of information users. In the case of company accounts, clearly a wide range of information will be needed to satisfy the interested parties already identified.

3. Materiality

It is concerned with the magnitude of financial information to assess whether it may be omitted, misstated or not disclosed separately without having the potential to affect adversely the economic decisions made by users of a particular set of general-purpose financial reports. The materiality of an item may depend not only on its relative amount but also on its nature. For example, the discovery of a $10,000 bribe is a material event even for a large company. Accountants make judgments based on their knowledge of the company and on past experience, and users of financial statements generally rely on the accountants' professional judgments.

4. Substance over form

The accountant would be concerned more with the economic substance rather than the legal form of a transaction. For example, certain types of equipment leases are handled in the accounting records as if the entity had purchased the items rather than acquiring them under a lease. In substance, the transaction is treated and reported as a purchase of the item even though legal ownership of the item may never be contemplated.

5. Comparability

Information should be produced on a consistent basis so that valid comparisons can be made with information from different periods and with information produced by other sources (for example, the accounts of similar companies in the same line of industry). Comparability is more effective when different entities use the same accounting practices, including the same measurement and reporting standards.

6. Prudence

In selecting between alternative procedures, or alternative valuations, the one selected should be the one which gives the most cautious presentation of the business financial results or position. In other words, more confirmatory evidence is required about the existence of an asset or gain than is required about the existence of a liability or loss.

7. Understandability

Information needs to be capable of being understood by users who have a reasonable knowledge of business and accounting and are willing to study the information provided with reasonable diligence.

8. Timeliness

The usefulness of information is reduced if it does not appear until long after the period to which it relates, or if it is produced at unreasonably long intervals. What constitutes a reasonable interval depends on the circumstances: management of a company may need very frequent information to run the business efficiently; but shareholders are normally content to see accounts produced annually.

Chapter Round-up

- Accounting has played an important role in modern society. The main purpose of accounting is to provide financial information to a variety of users to make economic decisions.
- Accounting is defined as the process of identifying, measuring, recording and communicating economic information.
- There are mainly two groups of accounting information users: external users and internal users. Consequently, accounting can be split into two branches: financial accounting and management accounting.
- There are a couple of basic assumptions and rules underlying the conceptual framework for the purpose of establishment of financial reports.
- The accounting information is expected to possess a number of qualities when expressed in financial reports.

Glossary

accounting	n.	会计,会计学
accountant	n.	会计师,会计人员
framework	n.	框架,构架
taxation	n.	课税,征税
insolvency	n.	破产,无力偿还
business entity	n.	企业单位,业务实体
budgeting	n.	预算
not-for-profit	adj.	非营利的
profit-seeking	adj.	营利的,追求利润的
shareholder	n.	股东
creditor	n.	债权人
measurement	n.	计量,测量
transaction	n.	交易
financial	adj.	金融的,财政的,财务的
management	n.	管理,管理层,管理部门
stability	n.	稳定,坚定
profitability	n.	赢利能力,收益性
assurance	n.	保证,担保
proprietorship	n.	独资企业
partnership	n.	合伙,合伙企业
ownership	n.	所有权
limited liability		有限责任
dividend	n.	股息
capital structure		资本结构
assumption	n.	假定,假设
accrual	n.	权责发生制
matching	n.	匹配,配比
disclosure	n.	披露,揭示
materiality	n.	重要性
prudence	n.	谨慎

Review Questions

(1) Describe the steps in the accounting process.
(2) What are the main services offered by public accountants?

(3) Who are the main users of accounting information?

(4) What are the different uses of accounting information for investors and creditors?

(5) What are the advantages and disadvantages of single proprietorships, partnerships and companies?

(6) What are the basic four accounting assumptions? And describe their importance in the preparation of financial reports.

(7) What are the qualitative characteristics the accounting information should carry in the financial report?

(8) What happens if relevance conflicts with reliability?

(9) How to make the judgment about materiality?

(10) What's the meaning of accrual principle? Give an example of accounting practice to illustrate the use of accrual principle.

Exercises

1. True or false

(1) Accounting is the information system that identifies, records, and communicates the economic events of an organization to interested users.

(2) Management accounting provides financial information mainly to external users for decision-making.

(3) Commercial accountants tend to specialize in one of four general services: auditing, taxation, management advisory services, or insolvency.

(4) Accounting entity assumption is an assumption that requires the activities of the entity be kept separate and distinct from the activities of its owner and all other economic entities.

(5) Matching principle means that revenues and expenses for a period are equal.

(6) Accrual concept means that all expenses incurred in generating revenue for the period are subtracted from those revenues to determine net income.

(7) The division of the life of the entity into equal time intervals is called the period assumption.

(8) Full disclosure requires all facts necessary for the users' understanding the financial statements must be disclosed.

(9) The going concern concept of accounting assumes that a business will continue in operation for an indefinite period of time.

(10) Materiality principle permits a firm to expense separately the costs of such items as small tools, pencil sharpeners, and waste paper baskets when acquired because they are "immaterial" in amount.

2. Match the items in Column I with the appropriate descriptions in Column II

Column I (User group)	Column II (Questions asked)
Employees	How do its prices compare with its competitors?
Customers	Has it enough money to pay my wages?
Governments and their agencies	Can the company pay its taxes?
Suppliers and other creditors	What's the dividend like?
Public	Will I get my interest paid?
Investors	Is the company likely to stay in business?
Lenders	Will we get paid what we are owed?

Group Activities

(1) Suppose you have a sum of money and want to establish a business. Considering the amount of money, features of the business and the nature of the industry, explain in details which form of the ownership you will choose. Give the reason.

(2) Several independent situations are described below.

a. The owner of the business included his personal dental expenses on the entity's profit and loss statement.

b. The weighted average inventory method was used in Year 1, FIFO in Year 2, and weighted average in Year 3.

c. Depreciation expense was not recorded because to do so would result in a net loss for the period.

d. The cost of three small files (cost $1.20 each) was charged separately to expense when purchased even though they had a useful life of several years.

e. A major lawsuit has been filed against the company for environmental damage, and the company's solicitors believe there is a high probability of losing the suit. However, nothing is recorded in the accounts.

f. Land was reported at its estimated selling price, which is substantially higher than its cost. The increase in value was included in the profit and loss statement.

◆ **Required:**

Indicate for each situation the accounting principle(s) or reporting characteristics (if any) that are violated.

Supplementary Reading

Development of Accounting Concepts and Standards in Australia

Accounting has evolved through time, changing with the needs of society. As new types of transactions evolved in trade and commerce, accountants developed rules and practices for recording them. These accounting practices came to be known as Generally Accepted Accounting Principles (GAAP). GAAP consist of rules, practices and procedures, the authority of which stems from their general acceptance and use by the accounting profession and the business community. They have evolved from the experiences and thinking of members of the accounting profession and influential business-people.

In spite of the gradual development of GAAP in the profession, a need for the development of more rigid accounting standards was recognized. This need had its beginnings with the growth of industrialized society in the nineteenth century. During this time, the company form of organization was born and with it the separation of owner-ship from management. Management was appointed as an agent of the owners (share-holders) of the company to conduct the day-to-day operations with a view to earn profits for the owners.

As business organization became more complex, different levels of management came into existence. Consequently, financial reporting became important, so that lower levels of management could report to higher levels (internal reporting) and top management could report on the entity's progress to the owners (external reporting). In particular, external users of information had to rely on the honesty and integrity of management in the use of their money; but, for various reasons, corporate secrecy was considered to be acceptable behavior. Consequently, share investments gained the reputation of being risky investments, and shareholders were, to some extent, at the mercy of potentially unscrupulous management.

After a series of company liquidations in the late 1950s and early 1960s, which have caused many shareholders to lose considerable savings, much criticism was directed towards the content of externally reported financial statements. This led to the formation of the Australia Accounting Research Foundation (AARF) and the attempt by professional accounting bodies to establish a set of accounting standards for presenting external financial reports. However, compliance with these accounting standards was hard to achieve, as many companies chose merely to ignore them. Consequently, in 1984, the Australian government stepped in to the standard-setting process to approve accounting standards and to ensure compliance with them. This was achieved by establishing an Accounting Standards Review Board (ASRB), which was replaced in 1991 by the Australian Accounting Standards Board (AASB). The Australian government is active today in the standard-setting process, and the responsibility for the development of accounting standards rests with the Treasurer who, in 1999 reorganized the standard-setting process by establishing the Financial Reporting Council (FRC) to provide strategic directions for the AASB.

The AASB has responsibility for developing accounting standards relating to the preparation of financial reports. The work of the AASB has given rise to the AASB series of accounting standards, or AASB standards. The AASB also has the responsibility of developing statements of accounting concepts.

The development of accounting standards in Australia has been greatly influenced by developments overseas. By far the most influential group is the Financial Accounting Standards Board (FASB) of the United States, which has issued a large number of accounting standards since it was established in 1973. In the United Kingdom, the Accounting Standards Board, representing the various accounting bodies in that realm, has issued a number of statements of standard accounting practice (SSAPs) and, more recently, financial reporting standards (FRS), some of which have also influenced standards established in Canada and in New Zealand.

Ethics and Accounting

In the 1990s, ethics and moral behavior in business have received a great deal of attention from the media, professional associations and regulatory bodies, particularly those concerned with the operation of companies and the conduct of company directors. The 1980s in Australia saw the collapse of many large business and financial institutions, causing huge monetary losses and hardship to shareholders and owners. Many dishonest and unethical dealings by senior management of these institutions were exposed at this time. This has led to very strong moves by the community at large to improve the ethics of all people working in business. Most professional bodies have laid down some form of code of ethical and moral behavior.

Most businesses today appreciate the importance of ethical behavior in all their business dealings. In order for a business entity to function effectively, all people working in the entity have to be honest, abide by the rules and do the right thing. If managers' owners, employees and customers regularly deceived one another, told lies, falsified records and did not conform to the rules, the entity must eventually collapse and cease to exist. A high standard of ethical behavior is thus in the long-term interest of business entities. It is sound economic police to have a business highly regarded by the whole business community for its reputation for honest and straight dealings, quality and service. Most of the highly successful businesses today are noted generally for their high ethical standards of business. Financial reports are one of the many control mechanisms designed to control management's behavior and protect the interests of parties who have an interest in the performance of a particular business entity. The reports enable an evaluation to be made of a company's management performance, and provide information on the establishment of contracts, business dealings and resource allocations. The audit function of accounting also represents a controlling influence in maintaining ethical behavior in business entities.

The standing of the profession and individuals within the profession depends on the highest level of ethical conduct by members. The professional accounting bodies in Australia have recognized this and accordingly have set down rules of professional conduct for members. These rules are mandatory for all members, and severe penalties, including expulsion, are imposed on members who break these rules. The Australian Society of CPAs and the Institute of Chartered Accountants have issued a Joint Code of Professional Conduct (CPC) to provide an authoritative guide to members on acceptable professional behavior. The aim, among other things, is to prescribe high standards of practice and professional conduct for members, and to maintain observance of such standards by members and those who work with the members. The CPC covers many aspects of professional accounting activities including competence, compliance with the law and accounting standards, confidentiality of client information, fees charged, advertising and publicity, solicitation of business, and independence.

Critical Thinking Questions:
(1) What's the responsibility of AASB?
(2) What's the meaning of GAAP? And what's the function of GAAP?
(3) Why is professional ethics required in accounting? How to conduct the ethical behavior as an accountant?

Unit Two

Accounting System and Process

Learning Objectives

When you have studied this chapter, you should be able to:

* identify different groups of accounting elements;

* understand the nature of the accounting equation and the effects of business transactions on the equation;

* explain the nature of, the purpose of and the basic format of ledger accounts;

* understand the rules of debit and credit used in double-entry accounting and how to apply these rules in analyzing transactions;

* explain the purpose and format of the general journal, and know how to record transactions in the general journal and how to transfer the information to the general ledger (posting);

* understand the purpose of and how to prepare a trial balance.

Warm-up: Dialogue

Annie: I'm glad to be taking this accounting course. It's quite helpful. Please explain balancing again.
Brook: Okay. I'll start by telling you about debits and credits.
Annie: I know. They are the most important part of accounting.
Brook: That's right. There's a thing that is called the general ledger in the accounting system.
Annie: Yes. Every entry you make in the general ledger must have a debit and a credit.
Brook: Sure. When you do one, you always do the other. That's the rule of debits and credits.
Annie: So, whenever I record a credit I must record a debit. I see. That's how you balance.
Brook: That's right. The books must always balance. All debits must equal all credits.
Annie: If they don't equal each other it means the books are not balancing.
Brook: Absolutely. Out of balance entries means that the whole record system is out of balance.

Section 1　Accounting Elements and Accounting Equation

Accounting Elements

The conceptual framework has provided definitions of accounting elements, which refer to the basic classification for accounting objects and the specification of accounting calculation objects. They are used for the purpose of reflecting financial situation and determining the operating results of a business. Basically, there are five groups of accounting elements: assets, liabilities, owner's equity, revenues, and expenses.

Assets are future economic benefits controlled by the entity as a result of past transactions or other past events. This definition identifies three essential characteristics: (1) Future economic benefits must exist. (2) The entity must have control over the future economic benefits in such a way that the entity has the capacity to benefit from the asset in the pursuit of the entity's objectives, and can deny or regulate the access of others to those benefits. (3) The transaction or other event giving rise to the entity's control over the future economic benefits must have occurred. Mere possession of an asset is not equal to controlling it. For example, an agent who possesses goods received on consignment cannot treat the goods as his or her own asset because the agent does not have control.

Assets can be subdivided into current assets and non-current assets. Generally, assets include cash, accounts receivable, notes receivable, inventory, investments in other businesses, equipment, buildings, vehicles, patents, copyrights, land, etc.

Liabilities are the present obligations of an entity arising from past transactions and events, the settlement of which will result in the outflow of economic benefit from the entity. Hence, a liability must result in the sacrifice of economic benefits which requires settlement in the future. The entity has little, if any, discretion in avoiding this sacrifice. This settlement in the future may be required on demand at a specified date or on the occurrence of a specified event.

Liabilities can also be subcategorized into two groups: current liabilities and long-term liabilities. Examples of liabilities are accounts payable, notes payable, interest payable, wages payable, long-term loans, long-term payables, etc.

Owner's equity is the residual interest in the assets of the entity after deduction of its liabilities. It mainly falls into two parts: paid-in capital (owner's investments) and retained earnings (earnings accumulated through operation). Owners who have investments in the business have ultimate claims on the assets.

Revenues are inflows or other enhancements, or savings in outflows, of future economic benefits in the form of increases in assets or reductions in liabilities of the entity, other than those relating to contributions by owners or that result in an increase in equity during the reporting period. Mostly, revenues arise from the sale of merchandise, the performance of services, the rental of property, and the proceeds of lending money. Any increase in revenues will eventually increase owner's equity.

Expenses are consumptions or losses of future economic benefits in the form of reductions in assets or increases in liabilities of the entity, other than those relating to distributions of owners or that result in a decrease in equity during the reporting period. Expenses include cost of goods sold, administrative expenses, selling expenses, and financial expenses, etc. Any increase in expenses will decrease owner's equity.

II Accounting Equation

Assets, liabilities, owner's equity and the relationship among them portray the financial position of a business. This equilibrium among them is called the accounting equation, expressed as follows:

$$\boxed{\text{Assets} = \text{Liabilities} + \text{Owner's equity}}$$

From the equation, we can see the sum of the assets of an entity will always be equal to the total sources from which those assets came—liabilities plus owner's equity. Transactions result in changes in assets, liabilities and owner's equity. Even though the elements of the accounting equation change as a result of transactions, the basic equality of the accounting equation remains unchanged.

There are two important facts about the accounting equation:

(1) Every transaction affected at least two components of the equation. This dual recording process, known as double-entry accounting, is the method followed in the vast majority of accounting systems.

(2) After the effects of each transaction were recorded, the equation remained in balance, with the sum of the assets equal to the sum of the liabilities plus owner's equity. Under double-entry accounting, this must always be the case.

III Accounting Cycle

In order to report on the periodic progress of the entity over time, its life is divided into arbitrary time periods of equal length called accounting periods. This division of the operating life of an entity into equal time intervals is referred to as the period assumption.

Accounting periods of equal length are established to enable the statement user to make meaningful comparisons of operating results of the current period with those of previous periods. During each period, steps and procedures are followed to ensure that all transactions are properly recorded, and records are kept to ensure that the financial statements can be prepared at the end of the accounting period. These steps and procedures, culminating in the preparation of financial statements, are referred to as the accounting cycle.

The accounting cycle (Figure 2-1) begins with the initial recording of business transactions and concludes with the preparation of formal financial statements summarizing the effects of these transactions on the assets, liabilities and owner's equity of the entity. In practice, there are a number of additional steps or procedures which will occur between the recording of transactions and the preparation of financial statements.

Steps in the accounting cycle　　　**Accounting records**

(1) Recognizing transactions　　　Source documents

(2) Making journals　　　General journals

(3) Posting to ledgers　　　General ledgers

(4) Preparing trial balance　　　Trial balance

(5) Preparing financial statements　　　Financial statements

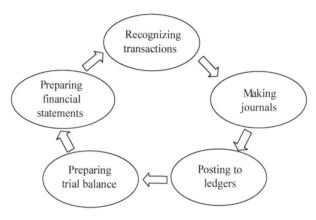

Figure 2-1　Accounting Cycle

Section 2　Ledger Accounting and Double-entry Bookkeeping

General Ledger and the T-account

A part of the accounting function is to classify the effects of transactions into six group of accounting elements and to summarize the results in the entity's financial statements. To facilitate the accumulation of financial statement data, transactions are recorded in ledger accounts. An account is a device used to provide a record of increases and decreases in each item that appears in an entity's financial statements. Thus, an entity will typically maintain an account for each kind of asset, liability, owner's equity, revenue and expense item. All the accounts maintained by an entity to enable preparation of the financial statements are collectively called the general ledger.

Each account has three basic parts: (1) a title, which should be descriptive of the nature of the items being recorded in the account; (2) a place for recording increases; and (3) a place for recording decreases. Also, accounts typically provide space for recording an account number, the date of the transaction and an explanation of the transaction. The basic format of an account is called a T-account because of its similarity to the letter T.

A T-account has a left-hand side and a right-hand side, called respectively the debit side and credit side. The words debit and credit have no other meaning in accounting except the left and the right side of an account respectively. An account is debited when an amount is entered on the left-hand side and credited when an amount is entered on the right-hand side. After the transactions are entered, the account balance can be calculated. If the sum of the debits exceeds the sum of the credits, the account has a debit balance. A credit balance results when the sum of the credits is greater than the sum of the debits. An account will have a zero balance if the sum of the debits equals the sum of the credits. For example, the T-account for Cash below has $70,000 on its debit side, $52,000 in total on its credit side, and a debit balance of $18,000 accordingly.

Cash

Dr.	Cr.
$70,000	$52,000
Bal. $18,000	

The T-account format is a convenient way to show the effects of transactions on individual accounts and is used primarily in accounting textbooks and in classroom illustrations. The rule of debit and credit will be clarified in detail in the double-entry system that comes soon.

Ⅱ Accounts Commonly Used

As mentioned previously, an account is established for each type of asset, liability, owner's equity, revenue and expense to be reported in the financial statements. The title or name given to a specific account should be descriptive of the item. Part of titles most commonly used for the preparation of the balance sheet and profit and loss statement are presented below.

Assets accounts

Cash at bank. The Cash at Bank account is used to record deposits into and withdrawals from a bank account. This account is the bank account of the entity. The account is referred to as a current account or check account.

Accounts receivable. Accounts receivable are amounts owed to an entity by customers to whom the entity has provided goods or services on credit. An account receivable may be based on an oral agreement to pay, but is more commonly recognized when an invoice for goods sold or services rendered is issued. The Accounts Receivable account is often called Trade Debtors account or simply Debtors.

Notes receivable. This account is used to record claims against another party that are evidenced by signed legal documents such as promissory notes. A note receivable, which is more formal than accounts receivable, contains an obligation by another party to pay to the entity holding the note for a definite sum of money at a future specified time.

Other receivables. At the end of the period, the entity may have receivables resulting from a variety of other transactions. For example, cash advances may have been made to employees, deposits may have been made with another entity for goods or services to be received in the future, interest revenue may have accumulated on an outstanding notes receivable, and a tenant may owe the entity rent. An entity will normally establish an individual account for each type of debtor.

Prepaid expenses. Prepaid expenses are goods or services that have been paid for but not yet received or used. Included in this category are advance payments of rent and insurance premiums. Each type of prepaid expense may be recorded in a separate account, e.g. Prepaid Rent and Prepaid Insurance.

Inventory. Inventory is used to designate all goods and property owned by a merchandising business and held for future sale to its customers in the ordinary course of business.

Land. The Land account is used to record land controlled by the entity. Land is recorded in an account separate from any buildings on the land.

Buildings. The Buildings account is used to record purchases or construction costs of buildings to be used during its normal operations.

Property, plant and equipment. Physical items used in the entity for a relatively long period of time are recorded in plant and equipment accounts. In general, these accounts include any item not permanently attached to the land or buildings. The accounts are used to record office furniture, factory equipment, machinery, store and office fixtures, and vehicles and delivery equipment. A separate account for each major type of equipment owned is usually established, e.g. Office Furniture and Machinery.

Accumulated depreciation. It reflects the portion of the cost that has been assigned to expense and accumulated since the fixed assets were purchased. The Accumulated Depreciation account is called a contra account which refers to an offset to or a deduction from a related account. Thus, in the balance sheet, the Accumulated Depreciation account is reported as a deduction from the original cost to reflect the asset's carrying amount.

Intangible assets. An intangible asset is one that usually does not have a physical substance but is expected to provide future benefits to the entity. Intangibles derive their value from the rights that possession and use confer on their owner. Like property, plant and equipment, intangibles are recorded initially at historical cost or other reliable measure, which is amortized to future periods over the asset's estimated useful life. Examples are patents, copyrights, franchises, brand names, trademarks and so on.

Liability accounts

Accounts payable. An account payable is an obligation to pay an amount to an outside party—a creditor—for the purchase of goods, supplies or services on credit. The account is also commonly called Trade Creditors or simply Creditors.

Notes payable. A note payable is a written promise to pay a specified amount to a creditor at a specified time. A note may be issued to a lending institution in exchange for cash, or the purchase of other assets may be made on credit by issuing a note payable.

Unearned revenue. Advances received from customers for goods yet to be delivered or services yet to be performed are not reported as revenue because the entity has a liability to the customer until the goods are delivered or the services are performed. When the goods are delivered or the services are performed, an amount is transferred from the unearned revenue account, a liability, to a revenue account. The revenue represents the reduction in the liability account. Examples are rent collected in advance from a tenant and a magazine subscription for 2 years received by a publisher.

Other current liabilities. At any given time, the entity may owe money to outside parties. For example, many entities are required to collect taxes on goods sold or services provided; a company may owe income tax; a telephone account may have been received for the quarter but not yet paid; interest may be due on a bank loan. It is not possible to list here all of the potential liabilities an entity may incur. The important fact is that an individual account can be used for each type of liability.

Long-term liabilities. Long-term liabilities are those obligations of the entity that do not require payment within the next year. In other words, liabilities not classified as current are long-term liabilities.

Owner's equity accounts

Paid-in capital. Paid-in capital is the amount of cash or other assets that owners put into a company for stock. Paid-in capital doesn't just happen when a company starts. In other words, whenever investors or current shareholders contribute money to a corporation, paid-in capital is created. In brief, it's the amount paid or contributed by owners in exchange for a corporation's stock.

Drawings or withdrawals. The drawings account is used to record the withdrawal of assets, usually cash, from the entity by the owner of a sole trader. Thus, drawings are recorded as reduction in both assets and owner's equity.

Retained earnings. Retained earnings are the cumulative net income of a corporation less its dividends paid to shareholders. In other words, it's the cumulative amount of money left over after all of the expenses and dividends are paid.

Reserves. Reserves represent those items of owner's equity other than retained profits and capital contributed by owners. Many reserves are created by transferring amounts out of the Retained Profits account for the setting aside of owner's equity for particular purpose.

Revenues accounts

Revenues are inflows, or savings in outflows, of economic benefits resulting in increases in owner's equity. They commonly arise from the performance of services or the sale of goods or other assets. Examples of revenue accounts are Service Revenue, Commission Revenue, Sales Revenue, and so on.

Expenses accounts

The costs of services and economic benefits consumed or lost during the reporting period, other than a withdrawal of capital by the owner, are called expenses. A number of expense accounts are normally needed to report the wide variety of expense items. For example, Salary Expense, Advertising Expense, Depreciation Expense, Interest Expense, etc.

Chart of Accounts

As previously defined, the collection of all the individual accounts for a particular business is referred to as a general ledger. Accounts contained in the general ledger are organized in the order they appear in the balance sheet and the profit and loss statement, thus making it easier to find them and prepare financial statements. A chart of accounts is a list of the complete ledger account titles and their related numbers, and is maintained in both manual and computerized systems.

A relatively simple chart of accounts used in this book to illustrate accounting procedures is shown as follows (Table 2-1):

Table 2-1 A Simple Chart of Accounts

Assets (100 – 199)		Owner's equity (300 – 399)	
100	Cash	300	Paid-in Capital
102	Accounts Receivable	310	Drawings
103	Notes Receivable	320	Reserves
110	Prepaid Insurance		
111	Office Supplies	**Revenue (400 – 499)**	
113	Inventory	401	Sales Revenue
150	Land	402	Service Revenue
160	Buildings	405	Commission Revenue
170	Equipment	407	Interest Revenue
171	Accumulated Depreciation		
180	Intangible Assets	**Expenses (500 – 599)**	
		501	Salary Expense
Liabilities (200 – 299)		502	Supplies Expense
200	Accounts Payable	505	Advertising Expense
210	Salaries Payable	506	Insurance Expense
214	Notes Payable	507	Rent Expense
215	Interest Payable	508	Electricity Expense
220	Unearned Revenue	509	Interest Expense
230	Mortgage Payable	512	Depreciation Expense

Ⅳ Double-entry Bookkeeping

As mentioned previously, each transaction affected at least two financial statement items, and that the accounting equation always remained in balance. Central to this process is the idea that every transaction has at least two effects, the dual effect. Hence the system, in which every transaction is recorded at least twice, is referred to as double-entry accounting.

The basic rule of double-entry bookkeeping is that every financial transaction gives rise to two accounting entries, one a debit and the other credit. The total value of debit entries is therefore always equal at any time to the total value of credit entries.

Whether a debit or a credit is an increase or a decrease to the account depends on whether the account is an asset, a liability, an owner's equity, a revenue or an expense account. Debit and credit rules for these accounts are shown below in T-account format (Figure 2-2):

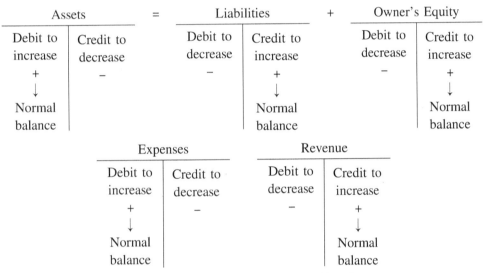

Figure 2-2 Rule of Double-Entry Bookkeeping

To put it another way (Table 2-2):

Table 2-2 Rule of Double-Entry Bookkeeping

Account type	Debit	Credit
Asset	Increase	Decrease
Expense	Increase	Decrease
Liability	Decrease	Increase
Owner's equity	Decrease	Increase
Revenue	Decrease	Increase

Notably, a debit may increase or decrease the account balance, depending on the type of account being adjusted. The same is true for a credit. Don't think of a debit or credit as an increase or decrease but simply as an entry on the left- or right-hand side of a T-account.

Lastly, an example will be shown how to make a record of transactions with the double-entry bookkeeping system. When you work on the transactions, you can follow these steps: (1) Analyze which accounts are affected; (2) Make judgments whether the accounts affected are increased or decreased; (3) Determine to debit or credit the accounts with corresponding amounts.

Example 2-1:

During the month of January, Ted Trump law firm had the following transactions:

(1) Ted invested $8,000 to open his practice.

(2) bought office supplies for cash $700.

(3) bought several pieces of office furniture from Frank Furniture Company on account, $2,000.

(4) received $3,500 in service fees earned during the month.

(5) paid office rent for January, $600.

(6) paid salary for part-time help, $800.

(7) paid $1,600 to Frank Furniture Company for the furniture purchased before.

(8) withdrew $470 for personal use.

These transactions might be analyzed and recorded in the accounts as follows.

Transaction (1)—Invested $8,000 to open his practice. The two accounts affected are Cash and Capital. Remember that an increase in an asset (cash) is debited, whereas an increase in owner's equity (capital) is credited.

Cash		Capital	
Dr.	Cr.	Dr.	Cr.
(1) 8,000			(1) 8,000

Transaction (2)—Bought office supplies for cash, $700. Here we are substituting one asset (cash) for another asset (supplies). We debit Supplies because we are receiving more supplies. We credit Cash because we are paying out cash.

Cash		Office Supplies	
Dr.	Cr.	Dr.	Cr.
	(2) 700	(2) 700	

Transaction (3)—Bought office furniture from Frank Furniture Company on account, $2,000. We are receiving an asset (furniture) and, therefore, debit Furniture to show the increase. We are not paying cash but creating a new liability, thereby increasing the liability account (Accounts Payable).

Furniture		Accounts Payable	
Dr.	Cr.	Dr.	Cr.
(3) 2,000			(3) 2,000

Transaction (4) —Received $3,500 in service fees earned during the month. In this case, we are increasing the asset account Cash, since we have received $3,500. Therefore, we debit it. We create a new account, Service Fee Revenue, and credit it.

Cash		Service Fee Revenue	
Dr.	Cr.	Dr.	Cr.
(4) 3,500			(4) 3,500

Transaction (5) —Paid office rent for January, $600. We must decrease the asset account Cash because we are paying out money. Therefore, we credit it for $600. Meanwhile, a new account for the expense, Rent Expense, is opened. The $600 is entered on the left side of Rent Expense.

Cash		Rent Expense	
Dr.	Cr.	Dr.	Cr.
	(5) 600	(5) 600	

Transaction (6) —Paid salary for part-time help, $800. Again, we must reduce our asset account Cash because we are paying out money. Therefore, we credit it. Trump's capital was reduced by an expense, and we open another account, Salaries Expense. A debit to this account shows an increase in expense.

Cash		Salaries Expense	
Dr.	Cr.	Dr.	Cr.
	(6) 800	(6) 800	

Transaction (7) —Paid $1,600 to Frank Furniture Company on account. This transaction reduced our asset account Cash since we are paying out money. We therefore credit Cash. We also reduce our liability account Accounts Payable by $1,600; we now owe that much less. Thus, we debit Accounts Payable.

Cash		Accounts Payable	
Dr.	Cr.	Dr.	Cr.
	(7) 1,600	(7) 1,600	

> Transaction (8) —Withdrew $470 for personal use. The withdrawal of cash means that there is a reduction in the asset account Cash. Therefore, it is credited. The amount in the owner's equity (capital) account is also $470 less. We must open the account Withdrawals, which is debited to show the decrease in capital.
>
> | Cash | | Withdrawals | |
> |---|---|---|---|
> | Dr. | Cr. | Dr. | Cr. |
> | | (8) 470 | (8) 470 | |

Cont.

Section 3 Journals, Ledgers and Trial Balance

① Recording Transactions in a Journal

In the accounting cycle, journalizing is the second step after analyzing the transactions and business documents. Journalizing is the process to record transactions in a journal and each transaction recorded is a separate journal entry.

The process for journalizing transactions is described below.

(1) The date of each transaction is entered in the date column.

(2) The name of the account to be debited and its amount are entered in the corresponding column.

(3) The name of the account to be credited and its amount are entered in the corresponding column.

(4) A brief explanation of the transaction is entered on the line immediately below the journal entry.

(5) At the time the journal entry is recorded, the posting reference column contains the number of the account as in the chart of accounts.

For illustration of the general journal, let's take the transaction data in Example 2-1 for instance (Table 2-3).

Table 2-3 General Journals for Example 2-1

Date		Account Titles and Explanation	P. R.	Debit/$	Credit/$
20×7					
Jan.	4	Cash	100	8,000	
		Ted Trump, Capital	300		8,000
		To record investment in cash in law practice			
	5	Office Supplies	111	700	
		Cash	100		700
		To record purchase of office supplies by cash			

Cont.

Date 20X7		Account Titles and Explanation	P. R.	Debit/$	Credit/$
	5	Furniture	130	2,000	
		Accounts Payable	200		2,000
		To record purchase of office furniture on credit			
	29	Cash	100	3,500	
		Service Fee Revenue	402		3,500
		To record receipt of service fee revenue			
	30	Rent Expense	507	600	
		Cash	100		600
		To record payment of rent for month			
	30	Salaries Expense	501	800	
		Cash	100		800
		To record payment of salaries of part-time employee			
	31	Accounts Payable	200	1,600	
		Cash	100		1,600
		To record payment of furniture purchased before			
	31	Ted Trump, Withdrawals	310	470	
		Cash	100		470
		To record personal withdrawal by the owner			

Posting from Journal to Ledger

After the transactions have been entered in the journal, they must be transferred to the ledger. The process of transferring amounts entered in the journal to the proper ledger accounts is called posting. The aim is to classify the effects of all transactions on each individual asset, liability, owner's equity, revenue and expense account.

In the posting procedure, each amount listed in the debit or credit column of the journal is posted by entering it to the debit or credit side of the corresponding account in the ledger respectively.

The steps involved in the posting process are:

(1) Locate in the ledger the account to be debited.

(2) Transfer the page number of the journal to the post reference column of the ledger.

(3) Post the debit amount from the journal as a debit figure in the ledger account, likewise the credit amount.

(4) Enter the account number in the posting reference column of the journal once the figure has been posted to the ledger.

The posting procedures from journal entries to ledger accounts are shown below still with the help of Example 2-1.

Cash	
Dr.	Cr.
Jan. 4 8,000	
5	700
29 3,500	
30	600
30	800
31	1,600
31	470
Bal. 7,330	

Furniture	
Dr.	Cr.
Jan. 5 2,000	
Bal. 2,000	

Office Supplies	
Dr.	Cr.
Jan. 5 700	
Bal. 700	

Accounts Payable	
Dr.	Cr.
Jan. 5	2,000
31 1,600	
	Bal. 400

Ted Trump, Capital	
Dr.	Cr.
Jan. 4	8,000
	Bal. 8,000

Ted Trump, Withdrawals	
Dr.	Cr.
Jan. 31 470	
Bal. 470	

Service Fee Revenue	
Dr.	Cr.
Jan. 29	3,500
	Bal. 3,500

Salaries Expense	
Dr.	Cr.
Jan. 30 800	
Bal. 800	

Rent Expense	
Dr.	Cr.
Jan. 30 600	
Bal. 600	

Trial Balance

The double-entry accounting system requires, for every transaction, equal dollar amounts of debits and credits to be recorded in the accounts. The equality of debits and credits posted to the ledger accounts is verified by preparing a trial balance—a list of all the accounts in the order in which they appear in the general ledger with their current balance. The dollar amounts of accounts with debit balances are listed in one column, and the dollar amounts of accounts with credit balances are listed in a second column. The sum of the two columns should be equal. When this occurs, the ledger is said to be "in balance".

Example 2-1 is continued to be illustrated for preparation of a trial balance (Table 2-4).

Table 2-4 Ted Trump Law Practice Trial Balance
as at January 31, 20X7

Account Title	Account No.	Debit/$	Credit/$
Cash	100	7,330	
Office Supplies	111	700	
Furniture	130	2,000	
Accounts Payable	200		400
Ted Trump, Capital	300		8,000
Ted Trump, Withdrawals	310	470	
Service Fee Revenue	402		3,500
Salaries Expense	501	800	
Rent Expense	507	600	
Balance		**11,900**	**11,900**

The trial balance simply verifies that equal debits and credits have been recorded in the accounts. It also verifies that the account balances were calculated correctly, based on the recorded data. A trial balance that does not balance is a clear indication of one or more errors in the accounts, or an error in preparing the trial balance. However, errors could be made that do not affect the equality of debits and credits. For example, a correct amount could have been posted to the wrong account, a journal entry might have been omitted, or an incorrect amount could have been posted to both of the correct accounts. The possibility of making such errors should serve to emphasize the need to exercise due care in entering and posting transactions.

Chapter Round-up

• Accounting elements means the basic classification for accounting objects. There are five groups of accounting elements.

• There is a close relationship between assets, capital and liabilities, which is presented in the form of what is called the "accounting equation".

• In the most basic form, an account has three parts: a title, the left-hand or the debit side and the right-hand or the credit side.

• In a double entry system, every transaction must be entered in the ledger accounts twice: once as a debit and once as an opposite credit.

• The rules of double-entry bookkeeping are:

Account type	Debit	Credit
Asset	Increase	Decrease
Expense	Increase	Decrease

Account type	Debit	Credit
Liability	Decrease	Increase
Owner's equity	Decrease	Increase
Revenue	Decrease	Increase

- A transaction is analyzed and recorded first in a book called a journal before the effects of the transaction are entered in the individual accounts in the ledger.
- The equality of debits and credits posted to the ledger accounts is verified by preparing a trial balance. A trial balance may be prepared at any time to test the equality of debits and credits in the ledger.

Glossary

accounting elements		会计要素
asset	n.	资产
liability	n.	负债
owner's equity		所有者权益
revenue	n.	收入
expense	n.	费用
consignment	n.	委托,托付
accounts receivable		应收账款
notes receivable		应收票据
inventory	n.	存货
discretion	n.	自由裁量权
accounts payable		应付账款
notes payable		应付票据
paid-in capital		实收资本
retained earnings/profit		留存收益
accounting equation		会计等式
double-entry bookkeeping		复式记账
journal	n.	日记账
ledger	n.	分类账
posting	n.	过账
trial balance		试算平衡表
financial statement		财务报表
source document		原始凭证
debit	n. & v.	借方;借记
credit	n. & v.	贷方;贷记
accumulated depreciation		累计折旧

intangible assets		无形资产
franchise	n.	特许经营
on credit		赊账
withdrawal	n.	提款,取款
reserves	n.	盈余公积,储备金
commission	n.	佣金

Review Questions

(1) What is the accounting equation? Why does it always balance?

(2) What are accounting elements?

(3) What are the main steps in an accounting cycle?

(4) List some frequently used accounts in each group of accounting elements.

(5) What is the normal balance of the following accounts?

    a. Equipment

    b. Rental Revenue

    c. Accounts Payable

    d. H. R. Wicks, Capital

    e. Salaries Expense

    f. Accumulated depreciation

(6) What is double-entry bookkeeping? What's the rule of it?

(7) Describe the procedures in making a journal.

(8) Why are journals required as part of the recording process?

(9) What's the purpose of posting?

(10) What are the function and the limitation of a trial balance?

Exercises

1. True or false

(1) The accounting equation states assets are the difference between the owner's equity and liabilities.

(2) The decrease of liabilities reduces owner's equity in the business.

(3) Accounts receivables are included in current assets.

(4) Withdrawals by the owner increase owner's equity.

(5) When expenses incur, they reduce the profit.

(6) Profit is the excess of cash receipts over cash payments.

(7) Service fee revenues increase assets.

(8) Owner's equity is the amount of cash a person has in the business.

(9) The accounting elements are further classified into different accounts because they reflect different components of the business.

(10) When liabilities, equity, and revenue accounts are credited, it stands for a decrease.

2. Identification of account categories

Listed below are the ledger accounts of Brown's Catering Services.

(1) Cash at Bank

(2) Land

(3) Bill Brown, Capital

(4) Building

(5) Interest Revenue

(6) Trade Debtors

(7) Loan Payable

(8) Insurance Expense

(9) Inventory

(10) Interest Receivable

(11) Prepaid Insurance

(12) Maintenance Equipment

(13) Unearned Revenue

(14) Interest Expense

(15) Rent Revenue

(16) Wages Expense

(17) Wages Payable

(18) Bill Brown, Drawings

Required:

Identify each of the above ledger accounts as either an asset, a liability, an owner's equity, a revenue or an expense.

3. Recording transactions in general journal

Sandy opens a Laundry in September, 20X9. During the first month of operation the following transactions occurred:

(1) Sept. 1   Invested $200,000 cash in business.

(2) Sept. 2   Paid $5,000 cash for rent for September.

(3) Sept. 3   Purchased washers and dryers for $10,000 with half paid in cash and the other half outstanding.

(4) Sept. 5   Paid $2,000 for advertising for the month.

(5) Sept. 10 Paid telephone bill for the month $100.

(6) Sept. 20 Withdrew $4,000 for personal use.

(7) Sept. 30 Determined that cash receipts for laundry fees for the month: $10,000.

◆ **Required:**

Open relevant accounts and journalize the above transactions.

4. Preparation of journal entries and trial balance

The following transactions occurred during the month of June 20X8 in a real estate business run by Megan Mooney.

(1) June 1 Megan Mooney deposited $60,000 cash in a check account opened for the real estate business.

(2) June 2 Purchased land and office building for $72,000. The terms of the agreement provided for a payment by check of $12,000, the remainder to be paid within 90 days. The purchase price is allocated $10,000 to land and $62,000 to the building.

(3) June 3 A payment by check of $960 was made for a 24-month insurance policy.

(4) June 5 Purchased office supplies for $620 on credit.

(5) June 5 Purchased office equipment for a total price of $9,600. Paid $5,000 by check with the balance due in 60 days.

(6) June 6 Paid $120 by check for advertisement in the local newspaper.

(7) June 15 Sold a residence that had been listed with the business. A commission of $4,200 was receivable on the sale, to be received when the agreement is closed.

(8) June 19 Sold a residence that had been listed with the business. A commission of $5,400 was receivable on the sale, to be received when the loan finance has been finalized.

(9) June 22 Paid salaries of $1,800 to the office assistant, part-time employees and sales staff for services rendered during the last two weeks.

(10) June 23 Conducted a real estate appraisal for a customer and received a fee of $250 in cash.

(11) June 23 Mooney withdrew $600 by check drawn on the business bank account for her personal use.

(12) June 27 Paid $620 by check to creditors for office supplies purchased on credit on June 5.

(13) June 29 Received a check for $280 for appraisals to be performed in July, and banked the check.

(14) June 30 Paid telephone bill of $72.

(15) June 30 A check for $4,200 was received for commissions receivable on the residence sold on June 15 and the check was deposited in the business bank account.

◆ **Required:**

① Prepare the general journal entries to record the above transactions.
② Post the entries from the general journal to the general ledger accounts.
③ Prepare a trial balance as at June 31, 20X8.

Group Activities

(1) The proprietor of a very small, part-time business was not interested in keeping detailed accounts for the business. Recently, an accountant advised that the business should have its accounts recorded under the double-entry system. The proprietor argued that the system was too costly and too detailed for the needs of the business. What arguments could the accountant use to support the double-entry system? Do you agree with the proprietor?

(2) Rebecca Weldon has been managing the office and reception centre for a partnership of medical practitioners for the last 3 years. She is in charge of hiring office staff, paying the bills, collecting unpaid accounts, banking the money, and reconciling the check book with bank statements.

In the current year, she has decided to further her studies and has enrolled in night classes at the nearby university for an accounting course as part of her commerce degree. Consider:

① How could an accounting course help Rebecca in her job?

② What assets are likely to be included in the chart of accounts for the medical practice?

③ What entries would Rebecca make (in general journal form) to record the following?

- billing a patient for services rendered
- collecting money from a patient who had previously been billed
- paying wages to other office staff
- withdrawal of $5,000 by one of the doctors for private use at home

Supplementary Reading

1 Types of Transactions

The initial source of assets for a business is an investment by the owner(s). Although the investment may take various forms (such as cash at bank, land or equipment), the initial investment is frequently cash. Individuals invest in a business in anticipation of eventually being able to withdraw assets in excess of those invested. They expect that the business will operate at a profit and that they will receive a return on their investment. However, the mere holding of cash invested by the owners will not provide a return. Cash is useful as a medium of exchange or as a measure of value, but it is essentially a non-productive asset. In order to generate revenues, the business acquires productive resources such as buildings, machinery and equipment. The non-cash resources are used to provide goods or services for customers in exchange for revenue in the form of cash or the customers' promise to pay cash in the future. Cash received from customers is then used to pay the operating expenses and obligations of the business. Any remaining cash may be held to pay future obligations, to finance future expansion, to invest, or to distribute to owners as a return on their investment. As for transactions of the entity, there are generally two types.

External transactions. An entity may engage in transactions with outside parties that affect its financial statements. Examples include the purchase of office supplies, the performance of a service for others, the performance by others of a service for the entity, borrowing money from a bank and the purchase of equipment. These transactions are recorded by the accountant and are called external transactions because there is an exchange of economic resources and/or obligations between the entity and one or more outside parties. In other words, in an external transaction the entity gives up something and receives something in return.

Internal transactions. Other economic events that do not involve external transactions are recorded because they affect the internal relationships between the entity's assets, liabilities and owner's equity. Use of office supplies by an employee and use of equipment to perform a service are examples of internal transactions. Other events, such as the destruction of an office building by fire, are also given accounting recognition because the entity's assets and owner's equity are decreased. The term transaction is often used to refer to all events that are given accounting recognition.

Non-transaction events. Some events of importance to the entity are not usually recorded because there has not been an exchange of goods or service. Examples include receiving an order from a customer, signing a contract to purchase an asset in the future, hiring an employee and changing interest rates. These situations are not recorded because a transaction is not considered to have taken place at this point. In other words, initially such events do not affect the entity's recorded assets, liabilities or owner's equity. These events will be given accounting recognition in the future if an exchange takes place.

Accounting Procedures Applicable to a Partnership or a Company

Although sole traders are the most numerous form of business organizations, the majority of business activity is conducted by the corporate form of business organization. A company is a business entity incorporated under the Corporations Law, while another common form of business organization is the partnership, which is a business owned by two or more people acting as partners. Accounting and reporting for partnerships and companies are similar in most respects to accounting and reporting for sole traders. The profit and loss statement and the balance sheet are essentially the same for all three forms of business organization except for transactions that directly affect the owners' equity accounts.

1. Accounting for a partnership

In accounting for a partnership, separate Capital and Drawings accounts are maintained for each partner as a minimum. Any investment by a partner is credited to his or her Capital account, and to his or her Drawings account. Any salary paid to a partner is normally regarded as drawings by that partner.

At the end of the accounting period, the Profit and Loss Summary account is closed by the balance, i.e. net profit, being allocated to each partner's Capital account in accordance with the partners' profit and loss sharing agreement. Each Drawings account is also closed to the appropriate Capital accounts so that the total of each partner's equity at the end of the period represents his or her capital contribution plus share of the profits as retained by him or her in the business.

2. Accounting for a company

The owners of a company are called shareholders because their ownership interests are represented by shares held in the company. In a company balance sheet, the total interest of the owners in the assets of the company is called shareholder's equity. The shareholders' equity section is separated into two main categories or sources of capital: (1) share capital, which represents the amount of assets invested in the company by the shareholders; and (2) retained profits, which reflect the accumulated profits (or losses) earned by the company and retained in the business.

The investment of assets in a company is recorded by debits to the appropriate asset accounts and a credit to an account called the Share Capital account. When an investment is made in the company, the investors are given shares in the company as evidence of their ownership. Just as the owner of a single proprietorship may periodically withdraw cash from the business in anticipation of profits, cash distributions called dividends may be made to the owners of a company. However, before dividend can be paid, it must be "declared". The Dividends Declared account is a temporary account but is not an expense account because dividends are considered a distribution or withdrawal of profits by the owners and are not a cost incurred for the purpose of producing revenue. At the end of the period, the Dividends Declared account is closed to the Retained Profits account.

One important difference between the three forms of business organization is the way income tax is determined. Although all three forms are recognized as separate business entity for accounting purposes, sole traders or partners must include their share of business profit or loss in their own personal tax returns. Thus, income tax expense will not appear in the profit and loss statement of a sole trader or a partnership. Companies, however, are separate taxable entities that must file tax returns and pay tax as assessed by the Taxation Office. Therefore, in its financial statements, a company must show the amount of income tax expense incurred for the period and any unpaid amount of the tax as a liability. The amount of income tax to be paid each period is determined in accordance with the Income Tax Assessment Act.

Critical Thinking Questions:

(1) Are transactions the same with events? If not, what's the difference?

(2) Give some examples of external transactions and internal transactions respectively.

(3) What's the most important difference between the three forms of business organization in terms of income tax issue?

Unit Three Financial Accounting

Unit Three

Financial Accounting

 Learning Objectives

When you have studied this chapter, you should be able to:
* define the term "cash" as it is used in accounting and how to account for it;
* define accounts receivable and identify different types of receivables;
* explain the nature of bad debts and how to account for them;
* clarify the difference between the perpetual and periodic inventory systems;
* understand the nature of property, plant and equipment;
* understand the nature of depreciation and identify different methods to determine the amount of depreciation expense;
* understand the nature of intangible assets and amortization;
* distinguish between current and non-current liabilities and explain how to account for them;
* clarify the nature of owner's equity and distinguish between paid-in capital and retained earnings;
* define the nature of revenues and expenses and explain how to recognize them.

 Warm-up: Dialogue

John: Accountants play a very important role in cash management, don't they?
Mary: Absolutely. They are primarily responsible for the daily cash management.
John: I think accountants should provide accurate accounting for cash receipts, cash disbursements and cash balances.
Mary: More than that. They should make sure that the business has sufficient cash for daily operations and create some income if possible.
John: By depositing the cash in the bank?
Mary: Not exactly. Generally, bank deposits don't generate much interest, so they should

John: make investment of the idle cash, for example, by purchasing some marketable securities.

John: So, accountants should have an all-round and feasible plan for the business to make good use of cash.

Mary: They should. Apart from that, the business should also have a good system of internal control over cash.

John: How to say? What specific procedures does the system include?

Mary: For example, cash handling should be separated from cash recording. That's to say, the cashier should not have access to the accounting records, and the accountant should not have access to cash.

John: It's segregation of duties, right? In this way, a good mechanism of controlling can be ensured.

Mary: Right. Also, accountants should reconcile bank statements with the accounting records and prepare a statement of bank reconciliation regularly. It's also a necessary procedure of internal control over cash.

John: It sounds cool.

Text

Section 1 Accounting for Assets

An asset is recognized on the balance sheet when it is probable that the future economic benefits will flow to the enterprise and the asset has a cost or value that can be reliably measured. Assets are normally divided into current assets and non-current assets.

Current assets are assets that are expected to be converted to cash or consumed within 12 months or within the business' normal operating cycle if longer than a year. Current assets normally include cash, accounts receivables, notes receivable, short-term investment, prepayments, inventory and so on. Non-current assets usually include fixed assets and intangible assets.

Cash

Cash is one of the most important and the most liquid item of the current assets. Generally, the Cash account includes cash and cash equivalents.

Cash includes coins, paper money, negotiable instruments like checks, money orders, and deposits held on call at financial institutions.

Cash equivalents are highly liquid investments with short periods to maturity, i.e. quickly convertible into cash, which are subject to an insignificant risk of changes in value. Examples of cash equivalents include bank bills, money market deposits close to maturity, and borrowings such as bank overdraft and money market funds repayable on demand. As a general rule, non-trading financial instruments with a term of 3 months or less would fall within the definition of cash equivalents provided that they were subject to an insignificant risk of changes in value.

In most businesses, transactions involving the receipt and payment of cash far outnumber any other types of transactions. Meanwhile, cash is the asset most subject to misappropriation, and it is therefore important to provide a good internal control system for handling cash and recording cash transactions. Such a system must contain procedures for protecting cash on hand as well as for handling both cash receipts and cash payments. Three particularly important elements of an internal control system for cash are: (1) the separation of responsibility for handling and custodianship of cash from responsibility for maintaining cash records; (2) the banking intact of each day's cash receipts; and (3) making all payments by check or electronic transfer to a bank account of another person or entity.

Example 3-1:
The following transactions occurred in Scooter Ltd in May. You're required to make the entry for each transaction.
(1) May 1. The owner invested $700,000 in the business.
(2) May 6. Purchased supplies and equipment for $120,000.
(3) May 17. Performed service for Moody Company and received $25,000.
Solution:
(1) Dr. Cash $700,000
      Cr. Paid-in Capital $700,000
(2) Dr. Supplies and Equipment $120,000
      Cr. Cash $120,000
(3) Dr. Cash $25,000
      Cr. Service Revenue $25,000

Accounts Receivable

Economy today is essentially a credit economy. Manufacturers, wholesalers and retailers regularly extend credit to buyers of their goods and services as a means of increasing sales, i.e. the buyer has a specified length of time, such as 30 or 60 days, before payment is due. The willingness of entities to extend credit has been an important factor in the significant growth of modern economy over time. This extension of credit has given rise to debtors or accounts receivable.

Accounts receivable stands for amounts due from customers for sales or services performed on credit. It is also commonly referred to as Trade Debtors. Sometimes credit is granted only on receipt of a formal legal instrument such as a promissory note, which means is a written promise made by a debtor to pay a certain amount of money on a predetermined date in the future. Receivables arising in such circumstances are called notes receivable, which is more formal than accounts receivable in that the debtor promises in written form to secure the payment on a predetermined date in the future. Apart from accounts receivable and notes receivable, there are also interest receivable, dividend receivable, etc.

A common feature of above receivables is that they are regarded as highly liquid assets which generally will be converted into cash in the short term, and hence are classified as current assets in the financial statements.

> **Example 3-2:**
>
> On June 1, Scooter Ltd sold products of $50,000 to Speed Company on credit. The credit term was 2/10, n/30, and the Speed made the payment on June 9.
>
> ***Solution:***
>
> | June 1 | Dr. Accounts Receivable—Speed | $50,000 |
> | June 9 | Cr. Sales Revenue | $50,000 |
> | | Dr. Cash | $49,000 |
> | | Sales Discount | $1,000 |
> | | Cr. Accounts Receivable—Speed | $50,000 |

Regardless of the diligence and care exercised in extending credit, there are always some customers who do not pay all or some of their accounts. Credit department personnel may have misjudged a customer's ability to pay, or sudden financial problems may have resulted in an inability to pay. When making the decision to sell goods and services on credit, business managers know that some of the resulting accounts receivable will eventually prove to be uncollectable. These uncollectable accounts are called bad debts and are considered an expense of doing business on a credit basis.

The common accounting practice of matching expenses to revenues has caused bad debts expense to be deducted commonly in the same accounting period in which the credit sales were recognized. Because the specific accounts that will eventually become bad are unknown, bad debts expense is estimated at the end of the accounting period by what is known as the allowance method of accounting for bad debts. To illustrate, assume that Scooter Ltd made credit sales for $400,000 during 20X8, and collected $300,000 of these accounts at the end of 20X8. After a careful review of the accounts receivable, the management estimated that $6,000 of the balance would be uncollectable. An adjusting entry is made on Dec 31, 20X8 as follows:

> Dr. Bad Debts Expense $6,000
> Cr. Allowance for Doubtful Debts $6,000

The estimate of the amount of doubtful debts is generally based on a combination of past experience and forecasts of future economic and business conditions, with considerable personal judgment involved. Two methods are widely used to estimate doubtful debts. One method determines the amount as a percentage of net credit sales for the period. Because this method uses net credit sales as a base, it is sometimes called the profit and loss statement approach. The other method analyses the age and probability of collection of the individual accounts receivable and is called ageing the accounts receivable. Since this method bases doubtful debts on an analysis of accounts receivable, it is often called the balance sheet approach.

Take the ageing method for example, the estimate of doubtful debts is derived from a schedule that analyses and classifies accounts receivable by age. The older an account receivable, the greater the probability that it will become bad. For instance, assume that an analysis of past accounting records shows the following percentages of accounts receivable that were written off as bad (Table 3-1):

Table 3-1 Percentage of Bad Debts

Age category	Percentage/%
Not yet due	1
1 – 30 days overdue	5
31 – 60 days overdue	10
61 – 90 days overdue	20
91 – 180 days overdue	30
Over 180 days overdue	60

The analysis of the accounts receivable of Scooter Ltd is demonstrated in Table 3-2:

Table 3-2 Ageing of Accounts Receivable

As at December 31, 20X8

unit: $

Customer	Balance	Not yet due	Number of days overdue				
			1 – 30	31 – 60	61 – 90	91 – 180	Over 180
A Ltd	680		680				
B Ltd	335	335					
C Ltd	590	240	350				
D Ltd	860			420	440		
E Ltd	470						470
F Ltd	215					215	
G Ltd	740	740					
H Ltd	930	830			100		
...	...	...	...	...	...	...	...
Total	83,400	55,800	10,600	6,600	4,200	3,800	2,400

With these data, the balance needed in the allowance for doubtful debts to reduce the accounts receivable to estimated net realizable value is calculated as follows (Table 3-3):

Table 3-3 Calculation of Estimated Bad Debts

Age category	Amount/$	Estimated bad debts amounts	
		Percentage/%	Amount/$
Not yet due	55,800	1	558
1 – 30 days overdue	10,600	5	530
31 – 60 days overdue	6,600	10	660
61 – 90 days overdue	4,200	20	840
91 – 180 days overdue	3,800	30	1,140
Over 180 days overdue	2,400	60	1,440
Total	83,400		5,168

As shown in Table 3-3, the total amount of $5,168 is the balance needed in the Allowance for Doubtful Debts account. When an account receivable is determined to be bad, it is written off by debiting the Allowance for Doubtful Debts account and crediting Accounts Receivable. In some cases, an account that has been written off is collected in part or in full at a later date. If this occurs, the account receivable should be re-established in the accounts in order to maintain a complete history of the customer's activity. This could be important for future credit rating purposes.

Ⅲ Short-term Investment

If the company has idle funds during its operation, the cash will be usually invested in short-term marketable securities such as bonds and stocks to earn capital gain, interest and dividend. Short-term investment account should be set up for marketable securities purchased or sold by the business. For trading securities, its debit side records the initial cost of securities and subsequent added amount of securities revalued at fair market value. Its credit side records the book value transferred at sale of securities and deducted amount due to the turndown of fair market value. Interest and dividend received or receivable from trading securities in current period and the difference between the proceeds obtained from sale of securities and their book value shall be accounted for as current profit and loss, that is, through Investment Income.

Ⅳ Inventory

The term "inventory" is used to designate goods or property owned and held for future sale to its customers, production or consumption in the ordinary course of business operations. Inventories usually include merchandise, finished goods, work in process and all kinds of raw materials, fuels, containers, low-value and perishable articles, etc. Being one of the most active assets in a business, inventories are continually being acquired, sold and replaced. Inventories also make up a significant part of a business' total assets.

Accounting for inventories involves recording the cost of purchased inventories and determining the cost of inventories to be allocated to cost of goods sold and to an asset representing ending inventories on hand. Two distinctly different inventory systems, perpetual and periodic, are used to determine the amounts reported for ending inventory and cost of goods sold. Among them, the perpetual inventory system is by far the most common system in use by businesses.

- Perpetual inventory system

It's a system of accounting for inventory that provides a continuous and detailed record of the goods on hand and the cost of goods sold. In a perpetual system, a new inventory balance is computed continuously whenever new transactions occur.

- Periodic inventory system

It's a system of accounting for inventory in which the goods on hand are determined by a physical count and the cost of goods sold is equal to the beginning inventory plus net purchases less ending inventory. In a periodic system, purchased items are kept in a continuous record and sales of inventories are not recorded.

Contrast:

The basic differences between the perpetual and periodic inventory systems are described as follows. First, under the perpetual inventory system the balance in the Inventory account provides a continuous and current record of inventory on hand. Second, a perpetual system provides for an accumulation of the cost of goods sold during the period. In contrast, a physical stock-take must be taken to determine the inventory on hand and the cost of goods sold when a periodic inventory system is used. A physical count of inventory is taken under the perpetual system only to verify the accuracy of the recorded ending inventory.

In the past, businesses which sell a large number of items with a low cost per unit sometimes find the maintenance of perpetual inventory records too costly and time-consuming to be practical. Such businesses often include chemists, fruit shops, newsagents, variety stores and hardware stores. However, with the introduction of computer-based inventory systems, more and more businesses have found it feasible to use a perpetual inventory system. For example, most retail businesses now use optical-scan cash registers to read product bar codes. They not only record the sales price of the item but also enter the item sold for inventory purposes. Cash registers are computer terminals entering transactions into the accounting and inventory records at the point of sale.

In order to measure the cost of goods sold expense, the allocation of total inventory cost between inventory and cost of goods sold must be based on some cost flow assumption. This is true whether a periodic or perpetual inventory system is being used. A number of methods based on different cost assumptions are used to assign costs: (1) specific identification; (2) first-in, first-out (FIFO); (3) last-in, first-out (LIFO); and (4) weighted average or moving average. The selection of a cost method to use for a particular type of inventory depends on many factors such as the effect that each method has on the entity's financial statements, income tax laws, information needs of management and statement users, the clerical cost of applying a costing method, and requirements of accounting standards. In practice, more than one of the methods may be considered appropriate in accounting for the same type of inventory. That is, accounting standards do not prescribe the use of a specific costing method as being "best" for a particular set of inventory conditions. It is up to management and the accountant to decide which method provides the most useful information to statement users.

Non-current assets refer to the items other than current assets of the assets part in the balance sheet. Basically, non-current assets contain long-term investments, property, plant and equipment (or fixed assets), intangible assets, and so on.

Ⅴ Property, Plant and Equipment/Fixed Assets

The terms property, plant and equipment are used to describe those non-current assets with physical substance acquired by an entity to last for more than one accounting cycle for the purpose of production of goods, rendering of services and management, rather than for resale to customers. Examples include land, buildings, equipment, machinery, and motor vehicles. Management's intention to use these assets for the future production of goods or services over several accounting periods is the main factor that distinguishes them from other assets.

1. Acquisition of fixed assets

The increase of fixed assets is mainly achieved by purchase, construction and investment by owners. Whenever an entity acquires a fixed asset from an outside party, their acquisition cost is recorded at their historical cost to get them in place and ready to use, including purchase price, freight and transportation fees, insurance, installation fees, test fees, legal fees, taxes, commissions and so on.

Example 3-3:

Scooter Ltd purchased a piece of equipment on July 5 that needs to be installed. The list price of the equipment is $25,000 with a trade discount of 10%. Freight charge amounts to $800 and the installation expenditures totals $675. The company paid $10,000 in cash, with the balance to be paid in 30 days. Calculation and entry is illustrated as follows:

List price of the equipment	$25,000
Less: Trade discount	$2,500
Net price	$22,500
Plus: Freight charge	$800
Installation fees	$675
Purchase consideration	$23,975

The related entry is:

July 5	Dr. Equipment		$23,975
	Cr. Cash		$10,000
		Accounts payable	$13,975

When an entity constructs an asset for its own use, the purchase consideration includes all expenditures incurred directly for construction, such as labor, materials and insurance premiums paid during construction. The cost of buildings also includes architectural fees, engineering fees, building permits and excavation for the foundations. In addition, a reasonable amount of general overhead for such things as power, management supervision during construction, and depreciation on machinery used for construction should be included.

For those fixed assets invested by the owners, they should be accounted for at agreed value in the investment contract or fair value.

Example 3-4:
Scooter Ltd received a machine which was invested by the owner on July 10. The agreed value is $50,000, the same as fair market value. The entry for the transaction is:

July 10　Dr. Machine　　　　　　　　　　$50,000
　　　　　　　Cr. Paid-in Capital　　　　　　$50,000

Whenever land is purchased, the cost of land includes the price paid to the seller plus estate agent's commission and other necessary expenditures such as title-search and survey fees, taxes, etc. Land is generally not depreciable because it has an unlimited life.

2. Depreciation for fixes assets

Accounting for depreciation represents the process that the decline in future economic benefits of an asset through wear, tear and obsolescence is progressively brought to account as a periodic charge against revenue. Factors needed to determine the amount of periodic depreciation for a depreciable asset are cost, estimated useful life and estimated residual value.

Useful life is the estimated period of time over which the future economic benefits embodied in a depreciable asset are expected to be consumed by the entity. The useful life of an asset is most commonly assessed and expressed on a time basis. In assessing useful life, the accountant needs to consider not only the physical wear and tear on the asset but also its technical and commercial life as well as its legal life.

Residual value, also called salvage value or scrap value, of a depreciable asset is an estimate of the net amount recoverable on ultimate disposal of the asset at the end of its useful life to the entity. The cost of an asset less its residual value is the amount that should be charged to depreciation expense over the asset's useful life. If the residual value is expected to be an insignificant amount in relation to the asset's cost, it is often ignored in calculating depreciation.

As for depreciation methods, several methods can be used to allocate the cost of an asset over its useful life. The four most frequently used are the straight-line, reducing-balance, sum-of-years'-digits, and units-of-production or usage methods. It is not necessary that an entity use a single depreciation method for all of its depreciable assets. The methods chosen must reflect the pattern in which the asset's future economic benefits are consumed or lost by the entity, with regard to the underlying physical, technical, commercial and legal facts. Let's take the straight-line method for example.

The straight-line depreciation method allocates an equal amount of depreciation to each accounting period in the asset's useful life. The amount of depreciation for each period is determined by dividing the cost of the asset minus its residual value, i. e. its depreciable amount, by the number of periods in the asset's useful life.

> **Example 3-5:**
> Assume a machine has a cost of $22,000, a residual value of $2,000, and a useful life of 4 years. Depreciation for each year is calculated as follows:
> Annual depreciation = (22,000 − 2,000)/4 = $5,000
> The entry for the depreciation in the current year is:
> Dr. Depreciation Expense—Machine $5,000
>   Cr. Accumulated Depreciation—Machine $5,000

The different methods allocate different amounts to depreciation expense over the life of an asset even though the cost of acquisition, residual value and useful life are the same. The straight-line method produces uniform charges to depreciation over the life of the asset. Meanwhile the benefits received from the use of the asset are assumed to be received evenly throughout the asset's life.

Ⅵ Intangible Assets

Intangible assets refer to non-current assets that are non-monetary and have no physical substance and are used in the operations of an entity. Their value is derived from the future economic benefits that will probably eventuate for the entity which controls them. Intangible assets may be further classified as identifiable or unidentifiable. Identifiable assets are those which are capable of being both individually identified and specifically brought to account. Some intangibles, such as patents, trademarks, brand names, franchises, and copyrights are often called identifiable intangibles. These intangibles which are purchased by an entity are recorded at their initial purchase price. Unidentifiable assets are referred to as "goodwill", which is often thought of as the favorable reputation of an entity among its customers. Goodwill arises from many factors, including customer confidence, superior management, favorable location, manufacturing efficiency, good employee relations and market penetration. A successful entity continually develops these factors, but the expenditures made in doing so cannot be specifically identified with each of these factors.

The allocation of the cost of intangibles to the periods benefiting from their use is called amortization. Amortization is therefore similar to depreciation of property, plant and equipment. Any identifiable intangible assets that have been brought to account should be amortized over the period of time during which the benefits embodied in the assets are expected to arise. The amortization would then be charged to expense. The amortization process in practice generally is carried out using the straight-line method.

> **Example 3-6:**
> Scooter Ltd purchased a patent of $20,000 by cash on January 2, 20X8. And the patent is expected to have a useful life of 10 years. The related entries are:
> Jan. 2　　Dr. Patents　　　　　　　　　　　　　　$20,000
> 　　　　　　　Cr. Cash　　　　　　　　　　　　　　$20,000
> Dec. 31　Dr. Amortization Expense—Patents　　$2,000
> 　　　　　　　Cr. Accumulated Amortization—Patents　　$2,000

Section 2　Accounting for Liabilities and Owner's Equity

Liabilities are defined as future sacrifices of economic benefits that the entity is presently obliged to make to other entities as a result of past transactions or other past events. In practice, classifying liabilities is based on the timing of the expected outlays of economic resources to discharge the liabilities. Consequently, liabilities that are expected to be paid within 1 year of the reporting date are classified as current liabilities, such as accounts payable, notes payable, wages and salaries payable, unearned revenue, interest payable, tax payable, etc. Current liabilities are normally paid out of current assets, or from funds generated by the creation of new current abilities. Non-current liabilities can be defined as liabilities that are expected to be paid beyond 1 year of the reporting date, such as a long-term loans, mortgage payable, bonds payable, etc.

Owner's equity is the claim of the entity's owners to the assets shown in the balance sheet. For single proprietorships and partnerships, the term "capital" is frequently used instead of "owner's equity". For a corporation, the components of owner's equity are basically paid-in capital (investment by the stockholders) and retained earnings (earnings from profitable operation of the business).

Accounts Payable & Notes Payable

Accounts payable designate amounts owed to creditors for the purchase of merchandise, supplies and services as part of the business operating cycle. Because they are not evidenced by a formal debt instrument such as a formal contract or note, they often are referred to as open accounts. Each time merchandise, supplies or services are purchased on credit, the appropriate asset or expense account is debited and the Accounts Payable account is credited.

Notes payable are often used instead of accounts payable because they give the lender written documentation of the obligation. A note payable can become a negotiable instrument, enabling the holder of the note to transfer it to someone else. Notes payable usually required the borrower to pay an interest charge. When the liability happens, asset is debited and Notes

Payable is credited. When the notes are repaid, Notes Payable are debited and Cash is credited.

Example 3-7:

Scooter Ltd purchased a batch of raw materials of $5,000 on October 10 with a term of 2/10, n/30. The company made the payment 9 days later. The related entries are:

Oct.10	Dr. Raw Materials	$5,000	
	Cr. Accounts Payable		$5,000
Oct.19	Dr. Accounts Payable	$5,000	
	Cr. Cash		$4,900
	Purchase Discount		$100

Example 3-8:

Scooter Ltd purchased inventory of $5,000 on October 12, and signed a 6%, 30-day note. The related entries are:

Oct.12	Dr. Inventory	$5,000	
	Cr. Notes Payable		$5,000
Nov.10	Dr. Notes Payable	$5,000	
	Interest Expense		$25
	Cr. Cash		$5,025

Ⅱ Bonds Payable

Bond is a certificate of liability providing information of the issuing company, face value, maturity date and the contracted interest rate. When a corporation needs to raise a large amount of long-term capital, it generally issues additional shares of capital or issues bonds, which are sold to the public, thus allowing many different investors to participate in the loan.

Issuance of bonds at an amount different from face value is quite common. According to the difference between issuing price and face value of bonds, there are three forms of issuing bonds: issuing at face value, issuing at premium and issuing at discount. When the bond is issued at face value, the bond rate conforms to the market interest rate. When issuing price is higher than face value, it is called issuing at premium. And usually, when the contracted interest rate of bond is higher than market interest rate, bonds can be issued at premium. When issuing price is lower than face value, it is called issuing at discount. Bonds can be issued at discount when the contracted interest rate of bond is lower than market interest rate.

Example 3-9:

Scooter Ltd plans to issue $1,000,000 face value of 10%, 10-year bonds. At the issuance date of November 1, the market interest rate is slightly above 10% and the bonds sell at a market price of only $950,000. The issuance of the bonds will be recorded by the following entry:

Nov.1	Dr. Cash	$950,000
	Discount on Bonds Payable	$50,000
	Cr. Bonds Payable	$1,000,000

Ⅲ Long-term Loans

Companies sometimes may desire a longer term for their loans, like for construction, research and development, and reform of a fixed asset. These loans borrowed by the business are actually "term loans" with the repayment period exceeds one year. The calculation for long-term loans involves the repayment of the principal together with the interest.

Example 3-10:

Scooter Ltd borrowed a 3 year long-term loan of $1,500,000 with an annual rate of 6% on December 15. The borrowing has been deposited into the bank and the interest is computed yearly. At the end of the third year, the principal and interest were paid off. Entries should be:

Dec.15	Dr. Cash	$1,500,000
	Cr. Long-term Loan	$1,500,000

At the end of the first year when the interest was accrued:

	Dr. Interest Expense	$90,000
	Cr. Interest Payable	$90,000

At the end of the third year when the principal and the interest were paid off:

	Dr. Long-term Loan	$1,500,000
	Interest Payable	$270,000
	Cr. Cash	$1,770,000

Owner's equity is the claim of the entity's owners to the assets shown in the balance sheet. For single proprietorships and partnerships, the term "capital" is frequently used instead of "owner's equity". For a corporation, the components of owner's equity are basically paid-in capital (investment by the stockholders) and retained earnings (earnings from profitable operation of the business). The followings are accounts pertaining to owner's equity.

Ⅳ Paid-in Capital

Paid-in capital of a corporation usually includes common stock, preferred stock and additional paid-in capital. Common stock represents the residual ownership of the corporation and common stockholders are ultimate owners of the corporation. They have claims to all assets that remain in the entity after all liabilities and preferred stock claims have been satisfied. In the case of bankruptcy or liquidation, this residual claim may not have any value because the liabilities and preferred stock claims may exceed the amount realized from the assets in liquidation. In most cases, common stockholders prosper because the profits of the business usually exceed the claims of creditors (interest) and preferred stockholders (preferred dividends). Notably, there is no upper limit to the value of their ownership. Besides, common stockholders have the right and obligation to elect members to the corporation's board of directors.

Preferred stock is a class of paid-in capital that is different from common stock in that preferred stock has some debt-like features. Also, in most cases, preferred stock does not have a voting privilege. The preference of preferred stock lies in dividends and the priority of claims on assets in the event of liquidation.

To summarize and emphasize, the paid-in capital of a corporation represents the amount invested by the owners and indicates the source of owner's equity.

Ⅴ Retained Earnings

The retained earnings account reflects the cumulative earnings of the corporation that have been retained for use in the business rather than distributed to the stockholders as dividends. Most important of all, the existence of retained earnings means that net assets generated by profitable operations have been remained in the company to help it grow or to meet other business needs. A credit balance means that net assets as a whole have been increased. A debit balance arises when a company's losses and distributions to stockholders are greater than its profits from operations. In such a case, the company is said to have a deficit in retained earnings.

Dividends are a distribution of earnings of the corporation to its stockholders and are treated as a direct reduction of retained earnings. The only requirement in the Corporations Law in relation to dividends is that dividends may be paid only out of the profits of the company. If a balance sheet is dated between the date the dividend is declared and the date it is paid, the dividends payable account will be included in the current liability section of the balance sheet. Dividends can take the form of cash dividend and stock dividend. In order to pay a cash dividend, it should meet several requirements: the firm must have retained earnings, the board of directors must declare the dividend, and the firm must have enough cash to pay the dividend. A stock dividend is the issuance of additional shares of common stock to the existing stockholders in proportion to the number of shares they currently possess. Expressed as a percentage, a 5% stock dividend means the issuance of 5% of the previously issued shares.

> **Example 3-11:**
>
> Scooter Ltd issued 100,000 shares of $1 par value common stock for $10 per share on January 1, 20X8. The entry would be:
>
> Jan. 1 Dr. Cash $1,000,000
>   Cr. Share Capital $100,000
>   Share Premium $900,000

> **Example 3-12:**
>
> On December 30, 20X8, the directors of Scooter Ltd declare a 40 cents per share cash dividend on 100,000 shares of $10 par value common stock. The dividend is $40,000 (100,000 × 0.4), and the entry to record the declaration is as follows:
>
> Dec. 30 Dr. Dividends Declared $40,000
>   Cr. Dividends Payable $40,000
>
> At the end of the year, the dividends account is closed to retained earnings by the following entry:
>
> Dec. 31 Dr. Retained Earnings $40,000
>   Cr. Dividends Declared $40,000
>
> The payment of dividends is made by the company on January 10, 20X9. The entry should be:
>
> Jan. 10 Dr. Dividends Payable $40,000
>   Cr. Cash $40,000

Section 3 Accounting for Revenues and Expenses

The definition of revenues is wide in its scope, in that revenues in the form of inflows of future economic benefits can arise from the provision of goods or services, the investment in or lending to another entity, the disposing of assets, and the receipt of contributions such as grants and donations. To qualify as revenues, the gross inflows of economic benefits must have the effect of increasing the equity, excluding capital contributions by owners. Another important aspect of the definition is that, if revenue arises as a result of an increase in future economic benefit, it is necessary that the entity control that increase in economic benefits. A revenue should be recognized in the operating statement when and only when: (a) it is probable that the inflow or other enhancement or saving in outflows of future economic benefits has occurred; and (b) the inflow or other enhancement or saving in outflows of future economic benefits can be measured reliably.

Likely, to qualify as an expense, it should have the effect of decreasing the entity's equity.

For example, the purchase of an asset would not decrease equity and therefore would not create an expense. Similar to the recognition of a revenue, an expense should be recognized in the operating statement when and only when: (a) it is probable that the consumption or loss of future economic benefits resulting in a reduction in assets and/or an increase in liabilities has occurred; and (b) the consumption or loss of future economic benefits can be measured reliably.

Expenses can be classified into three categories: selling expenses, administrative expenses and financial expenses. Selling expenses generally arise from transportation, insurance, rent, advertising, sales services, and so on. Administrative expenses refer to expenses incurred by enterprise's administrative sections for organizing and managing production and operation, generally including board of directors expenses, consulting expenses and other expenses. Financial expenses refer to expenses incurred in financial management activities for raising funds, such as interest expenses. All of the above are also named as period expenses.

Example 3-13:

Scooter Ltd sold the products to Spider Company for $150,000 on credit on August 17, 20X8. The entry should be:

Aug. 17　Dr. Accounts Receivable　　　　$150,000
　　　　　　Cr. Sales Revenue　　　　　　　　$150,000

Example 3-14:

Scooter Ltd paid in cash $10,000 for advertisement in a local newspaper on August 20, 20X8. The entry should be:

Aug. 20　Dr. Advertising Expenses　　　　$10,000
　　　　　　Cr. Cash　　　　　　　　　　　　$10,000

Example 3-15:

Scooter Ltd paid accrued interest for $6,000 on September 30, 20X8. The entry should be:

Sep. 30　Dr. Interest Expenses　　　　　$6,000
　　　　　　Cr. Cash　　　　　　　　　　　　$6,000

Chapter Round-up

- Assets can be classified into two groups: current assets and non-current assets. The former includes cash, accounts receivables, notes receivables, prepayments, short-term investment and inventory. The latter includes fixed assets and intangibles.

- Sales on credit give rise to accounts receivable, which in turn give rise to bad debts. Two methods are widely used to estimate doubtful debts. One is net credit sales method. The other is ageing method.
- Two different inventory systems, perpetual and periodic, are used to determine the amounts reported for ending inventory and cost of goods sold.
- Property, plant and equipment are primarily composed of land, buildings, equipments, machinery, storage facilities and motor vehicles.
- Due to wear, tear and obsolescence, the value of fixed assets (excluding land) will decline gradually. Therefore, depreciation is taken into account.
- Intangible assets may be classified as identifiable or unidentifiable. Like fixed assets, intangibles also involve amortization.
- Liabilities can be split into two categories: current liabilities and non-current liabilities.
- Owner's equity is the claim of the entity's owners to the assets. For a corporation, the components of owner's equity are basically paid-in capital and retained earnings.
- Revenues and expenses are income statement items. Recognition of them should meet some criteria.

Glossary

internal control		内部控制
segregation of duties		职责分离
cash equivalents		现金等价物
overdraft	n.	透支
misappropriation	n.	侵吞,挪用,滥用
custodianship	n.	保管
uncollectable	adj.	无法收回的
bad debts/doubtful debts		坏账
allowance for doubtful debts		坏账准备
write off		冲销
security	n.	证券
consumption	n.	消耗,消费
merchandise	n.	商品,货物
perpetual inventory system		永续盘存制
periodic inventory system		实地盘存制
costs of goods sold		销售成本
stock-take	n.	盘点
time-consuming	adj.	耗时的

optical scan		光学扫描
bar codes		条形码
FIFO		先进先出法
LIFO		后进先出法
acquisition	n.	获得,获取
insurance premiums		保险费
residual value		残值
intangible assets		无形资产
amortization	n.	摊销
franchise	n.	特许经营权
license	n.	许可,许可证
goodwill	n.	商誉
bond	n.	债券
paid-in capital		实收资本
common stock		普通股
preferred stock		优先股
period expenses		期间费用

Review Questions

(1) How many categories are assets divided into? What are they?

(2) What are two basic methods to estimate the amount of bad debts?

(3) After the accounts are adjusted at the end of the financial year, Accounts Receivable has a balance of $135,000 and Allowance for Doubtful Debts has a balance of $7,000. Consider:

① What is the net realizable value of accounts receivable?

② If a $1,000 account receivable is written off as a bad debt, what effect will the write-off have on the net realizable value of accounts receivable?

(4) What's the difference between perpetual inventory system and period inventory system?

(5) What factors will determine depreciation expenses of fixed assets?

(6) What should be included in the cost of fixed assets?

(7) What are intangible assets? Give some examples of intangible assets.

(8) Describe the essential characteristics of a liability.

(9) What are the purposes of long-term loans made?

(10) Outline the criteria which should be fulfilled before the revenue can be recognized.

Exercises

1. True or false

(1) The ageing method estimates the uncollectible accounts from the credit sale of a given period.

(2) To protect cash a company should set strict regulations and controls.

(3) Current assets are important to a business in that they represent a large amount on the balance sheet.

(4) Short-term investments mean that the investment in bonds and stocks shall not exceed a year.

(5) Under the declining balance method, for the first year of use for equipment costing $10,000, with an estimated residual value of $1,000 and an estimated life of 3 years, the amount of depreciation is $3,000.

(6) Examples of intangible asset include patents, franchise, copyrights.

(7) Intangible assets with definite life are amortized evenly throughout the useful life.

(8) When a bond is issued at a price higher than the face value, the bond will be issued at a premium.

(9) Prepayment to suppliers and accounts payable are both typical current liabilities.

(10) Business expenses should be recognized in the same period as the revenues they helped to produce. This concept is known as matching principle.

2. Making journals

The following are transactions which happened in Frankston Ltd in October 20X8:

(1) Oct. 1　The owner invested $20,000 to open a real estate agency along with $3,000 in office equipment.

(2) Oct. 2　Rented office and paid rent for the month $700.

(3) Oct. 3　Purchased a company automobile and wrote a check $18,000.

(4) Oct. 10　Purchased office supplies $600.

(5) Oct. 15　Sold a house and collected a $5,000 commission.

(6) Oct. 20　Paid gas bill for car $50.

(7) Oct. 30　Paid salary to the office secretaries $900.

(8) Oct. 31　Took a short-term bank loan of $1,000.

◆ **Required:**

Open appropriate accounts and journalize the above transactions.

3. Calculation

The following is a summary of Surfing Outdoors Company's revenues and expenses for a certain accounting period. Calculate the profit and transfer the balance in revenues and expenses to income summary.

Revenues:	
Sales	$86,000
Costs and Expenses:	
Cost of Goods Sold	$18,000
Salaries	$10,800
Advertisement	$20,200
Rent	$15,000

4. Making journals with ageing method

At the end of its financial year, December 31, Hammer Ltd completed an age analysis of its accounts receivable and determined that an allowance for doubtful debts of $6,490 was needed in order to report accounts receivable at their net realizable value in the balance sheet.

◆ **Required:**

① Prepare the entry to record bad debts expense assuming that the Allowance for Doubtful Debts account currently has a $1,100 credit balance.

② Prepare the entry to record bad debts expense assuming that the Allowance for Doubtful Debts account currently has a $465 debit balance.

③ Prepare the entry to write off an account receivable from M. Bush for $410.

Group Activities

The accountant of Lolita's Variety Store explained to Lolita that it is good practice to prepare cash budgets covering a 3-month period to ensure that any excess cash that builds up in the business is invested to produce returns, and to arrange financing in advance if cash funds are going to be inadequate. Lolita's response was that she could not plan that far ahead and any budgeted figures would be pure guesswork. In addition, she contended that she and other staff would be taken away from normal tasks and any potential benefits from a budget would not be worthwhile.

◆ **Required:**

In groups of three or four, prepare a draft letter to Lolita Variety Store which could be given to the accountant to help him convince Lolita to change her attitude.

Supplementary Reading

Cash Management

The development of a good system of internal control over cash receipts and cash payments, and the preparation of cash budgets are essential ingredients in effective control over the asset cash. These activities are only elements in any total cash management strategy. Cash management strategies are, of course, determined to a large extent by the nature and size of the activities of a business entity. However, there are basic principles that can be followed to ensure adequate management of cash. Most of these principles can be derived from an appreciation of the role of cash flows in the operating cycle. It is apparent that there is a need to collect cash from accounts receivable as quickly as possible, in order to be able to pay accounts payable for the purchase of inventory and services. It therefore follows that tying up cash in receivables and inventory is to be avoided as much as possible. In addition to demands for cash generated by the operating cycle, cash surpluses must be built up to help finance non-current assets, and any cash surplus to requirements from time to time should be invested to produce revenue and hence increase overall cash inflows. The broad principles of good cash management are set out below.

Reduce collection time for accounts receivable. Money owed by accounts receivable represents money that cannot be used by the business. The business needs to develop a collections policy to speed up the collection of monies owing, i.e. reduce the average collection time for receivables. The policy must ensure, however, that customers are not subjected to actions that may lead to the loss of their custom.

Postpone payments to accounts payable. There are due dates for all payables and payment should be delayed until those due dates. This allows the business to have use of funds which would otherwise be unavailable if, for instance, payments are made before they have to be. This policy should, however, include a requirement to take advantage of any discounts on offer, and must ensure that the business' credit rating is not threatened by tardy payment of accounts.

Keep inventory levels to a minimum. Although there is a need to keep adequate levels of inventory to meet the demands of customers, remember that inventories tie up cash and incur costs of storage and insurance. It is therefore sound cash management policy to keep inventory levels to a minimum, thereby freeing up cash for other uses.

Invest surplus cash. As we have already noted, cash is intrinsically a non-productive asset. Good cash management will ensure that any cash surplus to immediate requirements is invested in appropriate ways to produce a return in the form of additional cash, or savings in cash outlays. There are many forms of investment which enable quick return of the cash if the need arises.

Plan for capital expenditures. The acquisition of non-current assets is an important and ongoing decision all business entities have to make. These capital investments involve large outlays of cash, obtained either from internal sources or from external borrowings. These decisions require careful long-term planning to ensure that cash surplus to requirements can be used to help finance these large expenditures whenever possible, thus reducing reliance on external financing and its associated costs.

Management of Accounts Receivable

Accounts receivable originate in the extension of credit to customers. A number of important managerial decisions need to be made in this process—the entity has to decide how it will determine which customers will be offered credit, what the terms of the credit will be, and how to communicate these terms to existing and potential customers. The entity must also determine policies to ensure satisfactory collection of amounts owing, methods to encourage accounts receivable to pay on time, and the methods to use to follow up slow-paying customers or clients.

A business entity also needs to constantly review the composition of its accounts receivable in terms of amounts presently owing and amounts past due. The success or otherwise of the entity's credit and collection policies can be gauged by a number of techniques, including ratios. An appropriate system of internal control needs to be in place. Management must also be mindful of the costs of carrying a large volume of accounts receivable, and be aware of opportunities and methods that can be used to reduce these costs.

It is important that all matters relating to the control of credit policies and accounts receivable be properly organized and administered, and most organizations of any size establish a credit department, under the control of a credit manager. Some of the more important functions of a credit department are discussed below under the headings of (1) credit policies; (2) monitoring credit policies; (3) internal control of accounts receivable; and (4) disposal of accounts receivable.

Credit policies. No business entity wants to extend credit to a customer or client who is unlikely to pay the account when due. The credit department has responsibility for investigating the credit history and determining the debt-paying ability of customers who apply for credit. If the customer is a business entity, the credit department normally requests a set of its audited financial statements for use in judging its ability to pay. If the customer is an individual, the credit department will ask for information about current earnings, current expenses, outstanding debts, general financial position and past experiences in handling obligations. In addition, the credit department may obtain a credit report from a local or national credit-rating agency that accumulates data on the credit history of individuals and business entities. This decision is an important one since, if the entity is too generous in extending credit to risky customers, losses will be incurred. But if credit policies are too tight, existing customers will be lost and potential customers may go elsewhere. If approved credit customers do not prove worthy of credit, then credit could be withdrawn, and future sales made only on a cash basis.

The credit department, having established the credit worthiness of a potential customer, must then communicate the established terms to the customer. Terms will normally state the period after the date of the invoice by which the amount due should be paid, e. g. 30 days, and any cash discounts for prompt payment to which the customer is entitled. Cash discounts will be stated as a percentage of the invoice amount if paid within a certain period of time, e. g. 2/10, n/30 days. Credit terms may need to be reviewed from time to time both for receivables as a whole and for individual customers.

Monitoring credit policies. The best measure of success or otherwise of the credit policies of a business entity is receipt of cash collections within normal credit terms. Poor credit policies will usually see a gradual rise in the number of accounts receivable exceeding the normal period for payment, and an increase in the number of accounts that have to be written off as bad. It is essential that overdue accounts be detected early, and steps taken to encourage payment. This may entail reminder notices, polite and subsequent not-so-polite letters, phone calls to discuss payment problems, and handing the debt over to a collection agency. If all these methods fail, a decision must then be taken to write the account off as a bad debt.

Internal control of accounts receivable. As in the case of cash, adequate safeguards must be established for accounts receivable. It is important that people who maintain the accounts receivable records should not have access to cash receipts. Recording of sales returns and allowances, discounts allowed, and bad debts write-offs should be authorized by a responsible officer and should be separated from the cash receipts and cash payments functions. Monthly statements of account should be verified and forwarded to customers by someone other than the person in charge of the accounts receivable records. Another independent check should be made to ensure that the statements sent to customers are in agreement with the accounts receivable records. Slow-paying accounts should be reviewed periodically by a senior official of the business. Adequate control over receivables begins with the receipt of an approved purchase order and continues through all the remaining stages in the credit sales process: approval of credit terms, shipment of goods, customer invoicing, recording of the account receivable and its ultimate collection.

Disposal of accounts receivable. As many business transactions are conducted on credit, the size of accounts receivable has risen to the point that it constitutes a very large asset for many businesses, representing sales that have not been collected in cash. Entities are not only foregoing cash but also incurring considerable costs in credit control, preparing and sending accounts, and collecting debts, and consequently incurring losses through bad debts. It is therefore becoming common practice for businesses to sell their accounts receivable.

Businesses sell their accounts receivable in order to realize cash to finance trading operations, to provide a source of cash for other reasons, and to minimize the costs of credit control, collection expenses and bad debt losses. Disposal of accounts receivable is referred to as the factoring of accounts receivable. The business entity or financial institution which buys the receivables for a fee and then collects the amounts receivable is known as a factor. There are now businesses which specialize in factoring. Credit card companies such as American Express and Diners Club and financial institutions which issue MasterCard, Visa card and similar credit cards are, in effect, specializing in collection of accounts receivable. Factoring arrangements differ from factor to factor, but normally a commission of 2% - 3% is charged.

Critical Thinking Questions:

(1) What are main principles of cash management?
(2) Why to keep inventory levels to a minimum?
(3) What is factoring? What's the purpose of factoring?
(4) How to implement an efficient credit policy?
(5) As for accounts receivable, how to separate the related duties to achieve a good control over the accounts?

Unit Four
Financial Reporting and Financial Analysis

 Learning Objectives

When you have studied this chapter, you should be able to:
* identify the basic financial statements used in a business;
* outline the structure and function of balance sheet, income statement and cash flow statement;
* understand horizontal, vertical and trend analyses of an entity's financial statements;
* identify the various financial ratios and their inference to assess an entity's performance and financial position;
* interpret the ratio analysis and appreciate some important relationships among ratios.

 Warm-up: Dialogue

Lily: Could you tell me the main components of financial statements?
Mike: Sure. There are three basic parts which compose the financial statements of a company. They are the balance sheet, the income statement and the cash flow statement. Oh, one more thing, there are notes to the financial statements.
Lily: Notes? Why should the financial statements include notes?
Mike: Well, notes are very important and necessary because they provide supplementary information which cannot be contained in the tables.
Lily: Could you explain it in detail?
Mike: OK. Notes will provide the information of specific accounting policy, accounting estimates, detailed calculation and so on. Such information is very helpful for users to have a good understanding of data provided in the financial statements.
Lily: I got it. Then what's the main function of financial statements?
Mike: To put it easy, the financial statements provide information about the financial situation, financial performance and cash-in and cash-out of the company for the users to make the

economic decision, like investment decision, lending decision, etc.

Lily: Oh, the information should be very important and helpful.

Mike: That's right.

Lily: Are the financial statements the same with the financial report?

Mike: No, not exactly. The financial report contains much more than the financial statements.

Lily: How to say?

Mike: For example, a financial report should contain an audit report, the director's report, the director's declaration, etc. All in all, there is much more information in the financial report than in the financial statements.

Text

Section 1 Financial Statements

For the purpose of providing information useful for people who make economic decisions, and for the purpose of company managements to discharge their accountability to shareholders, a company is required to prepare an annual financial report for presentation to users. The annual financial report must include the following items: a set of financial statements, notes to those financial statements, and a directors' declaration. Also attached to the annual financial report would be operation review, the annual directors' report, an annual auditor's report and so on.

The financial statements to be included in the annual financial report of a company would basically contain:

- a profit and loss statement for the year;
- a balance sheet as at the end of the year;
- a statement of cash flows for the year.

This unit will discuss the format and function of a company's profit and loss statement and balance sheet at an introductory level.

① Balance Sheet

The balance sheet reflects the financial position of an entity at a specific point in time by representing its assets, liabilities and owner's equity. It is like a snapshot photograph, since it captures a still image at a given moment. The heading of the balance sheet indicates the name of the entity, the name of the report and the date. Besides, the basic balance sheet is divided into three main sections: assets, liabilities and owner's equity. The basic accounting model underlying the balance sheet is just the accounting equation: Assets = Liabilities + Owner's equity.

Basically, the balance sheet can provide information to evaluate and predict solvency and capital structure of an entity. Solvency means the financial ability of a company to pay debts when they become due. For one thing, accounting information in the balance sheet about current assets and current liabilities helps to understand the short-term solvency. For another, long-term solvency is determined both by the profitability and capital structure which means the structural percentage of liabilities to owner's equity. Generally, the larger the percentage of liabilities, the bigger the risks burdened by creditors and the weaker the long-term solvency, and vice versa (Table 4-1).

Table 4-1 Scooter Ltd Company Balance Sheet
as at December 31, 20X7

ASSETS	
Cash at bank	$16,700
Accounts receivable	5,930
Office supplies	4,900
Equipment	36,950
Building	20,000
Land	75,000
TOTAL ASSETS	159,480
LIABILITIES	
Accounts payable	6,900
Long-term loan	67,000
TOTAL LIABILITIES	73,900
NET ASSETS	85,580
OWNER'S EQUITY	
Scooter, Capital	85,580
TOTAL OWNER'S EQUITY	85,580

Income Statement (Profit and Loss Statement)

The income statement reports the results of operation over a given period such as a month, half-year or a year. Net profit for the period is the excess of revenues over expenses for that time. If expenses for the period exceed revenues, a net loss is incurred. The heading identifies the entity being reported upon, the name of the statement and the time period covered by the statement. Identification of the time period covered is particularly important because it indicates the length of time it takes to earn the reported net profit.

Obviously, the income statement provides the information about revenues generated and expenses incurred. Most important of all, the accounting information can help users to evaluate the profitability of the entity. By comparing and analyzing the operating results of the same business in different periods or different businesses in the same period, we can know whether the business has better profitability in a given period of time (Table 4-2). Thus, the management performance could be assessed, which will in turn help the users to make decisions of investment or lending accordingly.

Table 4-2 Scooter Ltd Company Income Statement

For the year ended December 31, 20X8

REVENUES	
Sales revenue	$800,000
Service revenue	200,000
Interest revenue	20,000
TOTAL REVENUES	1,020,000
COSTS AND EXPENSES	
Cost of goods sold	500,000
Wages expense	180,000
Rent expense	100,000
Gas expense	5,000
Other expense	50,000
TOTAL COSTS AND EXPENSES	835,000
EARNINGS BEFORE TAX	185,000
Income tax	55,500
EARNINGS AFTER TAX (NET INCOME)	129,500

The Cash Flow Statement

Another important financial statement prepared by an entity is a statement of cash flows. As a matter of fact, an entity's income statement does not report on the cash flows of the entity, but on its revenues and expenses. However, revenues and expenses do not necessarily represent cash flows. Consequently, a statement of cash flows is prepared to report on the cash flows in and out of the entity. It is particularly useful in helping the users to assess the sources and uses of an entity's cash, and the ability of the entity to remain solvent, so that the users can make informed decisions.

The statement reports on the entity's performance in generating cash flows from operating activities, investing activities and financing activities. By comparing the entity's statement of cash flows with the entity's profit and loss statement, we can see how well the reported profits from operations are represented by cash inflows from operations (Table 4-3). It is also useful in checking the accuracy of past assessments of future cash flows and in examining the relationship between profitability and net cash flow, and the impact of changing prices.

Table 4-3 Scooter Ltd Company Cash Flow Statement

For the year ended December 31, 20X9

CASH FLOWS FROM OPERATING ACTIVITIES	
Receipts from customers	$141,600
Payments to suppliers and employees	(113,000)
Net cash from operating activities	28,600
CASH FLOWS FROM INVESTING ACTIVITIES	
Purchase of land and buildings	(104,000)
Purchase of equipment	(36,900)
Net cash used in investing activities	(140,900)
CASH FLOWS FROM FINANCING ACTIVITIES	
Amount borrowed under mortgage	68,000
Investment by owner	78,100
Drawings by owner	(15,000)
Net cash from financing activities	131,100
Net increase (decrease) in cash held	18,800
Cash at beginning of year	—
Cash at end of year	18,800

Last but not the least, a company which is classified as a "disclosing entity" is also required to prepare a set of interim financial statements. Interim financial statements represent a set of half-year statements, and are to include an income statement, a balance sheet, a statement of cash flows and selected explanatory notes.

Section 2 Interpretation of Financial Statements

Interpretation of financial statements is a process of reclassification and summarization of financial data through the establishment of percentage, ratios and trends to interpret the company's operation and to understand the company's financial situation.

Percentage analysis and ratio analysis have been developed to provide an efficient means by which a decision-maker can identify important relationships between items in the same statements and trends in financial data. Percentages and ratios are calculated in order to reduce the financial data to a more concise and more understandable basis for the evaluation of past operation of the entity and prediction of the entity's performance in the near future.

Percentage Analysis

1. Horizontal analysis

Most reporting entities include in their annual report financial statements for the two most recent years. An analysis of the change from year to year in individual statement items is called horizontal analysis. In horizontal analysis, the individual items or groups of items on comparative financial reports are generally placed side by side. Subsequently, the difference between the figures for two separate years is calculated in dollar amounts and percentage change. In calculating the increase or decrease in dollar amounts, the earlier statement is used as the base year. In calculating the percentage, the change is calculated by dividing the increase or decrease from the base year in dollars by the base-year amount. A percentage change can be calculated only when a positive amount is reported in the base year. If the item in the base year is reported as a negative or a zero amount, the amount of change cannot be stated as a percentage.

A review of the percentage increases or decreases reveals those items that show the most significant change between the periods under study, and important and unusual changes will be investigated further by the analyst. The objectives of the investigation are to determine the cause of the change, to determine whether the change is favorable or unfavorable, and to assess whether any trends are expected to continue. An illustrative example is given as follows (Table 4-4 and Table 4-5):

Table 4-4　Scooter Ltd Company Comparative Balance Sheets (Horizontal Change, Extracted) as at December 31, 20X9 and 20X8

	Year ended December 31		Horizontal change during year	
	20X9	20X8	$	%
ASSETS				
Current assets				
Cash at bank	390	300	90	30.0
Marketable securities	380	440	(60)	(13.6)
Accounts receivable	1,460	1,290	170	13.2
Inventory	2,010	1,770	240	13.6
Prepaid expenses	100	100	—	—
Total current assets	4,340	3,900	440	11.3
...	...	...	...	...

Table 4-5　Scooter Ltd Company Comparative Income Statements (Horizontal Change, Extracted) for the years ended December 31, 20X9 and 20X8

	Year ended December 31		Horizontal change during year	
	20X9	20X8	$	%
Sales revenue (net)	10,320	9,582	738	7.7
Less: Cost of Goods Sold	7,719	6,975	744	10.7
GROSS PROFIT	2,601	2,607	(6)	(0.2)
Selling expenses	1,030	800	230	28.8
Administrative expenses	567	620	(53)	(8.5)
Financial expenses	252	230	22	9.6
...	...	...	...	...

2. Vertical analysis

While horizontal analysis compares the proportional changes in a specific item from one period to the next, vertical analysis involves restating the dollar amount of each item reported on an individual financial statement as a percentage of a specific item on the same statement, referred to as the base amount. For example, on the balance sheet, individual components are stated as a percentage of total assets or total liabilities and shareholders' equity. On the income statement, net sales revenue or operating revenue are usually set equal to a base of 100%, with each income statement item expressed as a percentage of the base amount, as in Table 4-6 and Table 4-7:

Table 4-6 Scooter Ltd Company Comparative Balance Sheets (Vertical Change, Extracted)
as at December 31, 20X9 and 20X8

	Year ended December 31		Percent of Total Assets	
	20X9	20X8	20X9	20X8
ASSETS				
Current assets				
Cash at bank	390	300	5.2	4.7
Marketable securities	380	440	5.1	7.0
Accounts receivable	1,460	1,290	19.6	20.5
Inventory	2,010	1,770	27.1	28.1
Prepaid expenses	100	100	1.3	1.6
Total current assets	4,340	3,900	58.3	61.9
...	...	...	...	...
TOTAL ASSETS	7,440	6,300	100.0	100.0

Table 4-7 Scooter Ltd Company Comparative Income Statements (Vertical Change, Extracted)
for the years ended December 31, 20X9 and 20X8

	Year ended December 31		Percent of net sales	
	20X9	20X8	20X9	20X8
Sales revenue (net)	10,320	9,582	100.0	100.0
Less: Cost of Goods Sold	7,719	6,975	74.8	72.8
GROSS PROFIT	2,601	2,607	25.2	27.2
Selling expenses	1,030	800	10.0	8.4
Administrative expenses	567	620	5.5	6.5
Financial expenses	252	230	2.4	2.4
...	...	...	...	...

3. Trend analysis

When financial data are available for three or more years, trend analysis is a technique commonly used to assess the entity's growth prospects. In this analysis, the earliest period is the base period, with all subsequent periods compared with the base. It is assumed that the base year selected is fairly typical of the entity's operations. For example, assume that sales revenue ($) and operating profit after income tax ($) were reported for the last 5 years as in Table 4-8 (000 omitted):

Table 4-8 Sales Revenue and Operating Profit After Income Tax for the Successive Five Years

Year	20X5	20X6	20X7	20X8	20X9
Sales revenue	1,000	1,050	1,120	1,150	1,220
Operating profit after income tax	200	206	218	220	232

It is clear that the dollar amounts of both sales revenue and operating profit after income tax are increasing. However, the relationship between the change in sales and operating profit can be more explicitly interpreted if the changes are expressed in percentages (with the base year being 100%) by dividing the amount reported for each subsequent year by the base year (20X5) amount, thus producing Table 4-9:

Table 4-9 Percentage of the Changes

Year	20X5	20X6	20X7	20X8	20X9
Sales revenue	100%	105%	112%	115%	122%
Operating profit after tax	100%	103%	109%	111%	116%

Now it can be seen that operating profit after tax is growing more slowly than sales revenue. Obviously, the trend in other items should be investigated. The level of profit is affected not only by sales, but also by expenses. It is possible that the entity's cost of goods sold is increasing faster than selling prices. The point is that other related operating data must also be reviewed before drawing conclusions about the significance of one particular item. The overall objective is to evaluate various related trends and try to assess whether the trend can be expected to continue.

Ratio Analysis

Ratio analysis is a most useful means of comparing one figure with another because it expresses the relationship between lots of amounts explicitly and simply. Relevant relationships can exist between items in the same financial statement or between items reported in two different financial statements, so there are a number of ratios that could be calculated. The analyst must give careful thought initially to choosing those ratios that express relationships relevant to the area of immediate concern. The analyst must also keep in mind that a ratio, when used by itself, may have little significance. Consequently, to evaluate the adequacy of a certain relationship, the ratio should be compared with other standards, e.g. industry standards.

As a decision-making tool, ratio analysis reduces reliance on intuitive factors but establishes a basis for rational and reasonable judgment. By comparing ratios with the average of businesses similar to the entity and comparing the entity's own ratios for several successive years, we can find competitive advantages and weaknesses of the company. Ratios could be classified and presented in several different ways. In this unit, three general groups of ratios are discussed, which are commonly used to evaluate profitability, liquidity and financial stability of a company.

1. Profitability ratios

Profitability analysis consists of tests used to evaluate an entity's profit performance during the year. The results are combined with other data to forecast potential profitability. Profit potential is important to long-term creditors and shareholders because, in the long run, the entity must operate at a satisfactory profit to survive. Profit potential is also important to statement users such as suppliers and trade unions who are interested in maintaining a continuing relationship with a financially sound entity. Financial soundness obviously depends on current and future profitability.

(1) Rate of return on total assets

$$\text{Rate of return on total assets} = \frac{PBIT}{Total\ assets}$$

Rate of return on total assets is an attempt to measure the rate of return earned by management through operations. PBIT refers to profit before interest and tax. Interest is added back to profit before tax in the numerator to reflect that efficient use of the resources is not affected by the method of financing the acquisition of the assets. In all, it's a formula to measure the profitability of total assets.

(2) Profit margin

$$\text{Profit margin} = \frac{Net\ income}{Net\ sales}$$

Profit margin, also called rate of return on sales, is a measure of the percentage of each dollar of sales that results in net income. It's computed by dividing the net income by net sales for the period.

(3) Earnings per share (EPS)

$$\text{Earnings per share} = \frac{Operating\ profit\ after\ income\ tax - Preference\ dividends}{Number\ of\ ordinary\ shares\ issued}$$

Earnings per share is a measure of the net income earned on each share of common stock. It's a measure often quoted by the financial press, because the shareholders are particularly interested in knowing how much has been earned during the financial year for each of the shares held by them.

(4) Price-earnings ratio (P/E)

$$\text{Price-earnings ratio} = \frac{Market\ price\ per\ ordinary\ share}{Earnings\ per\ ordinary\ share}$$

This ratio indicates how much an investor would have to pay in the market for each dollar of earnings. It enhances a user's ability to compare the market value of one ordinary share relative to profits with that of other entities.

(5) Dividend yield ratio

$$\text{Dividend yield ratio} = \frac{\text{Annual dividend per ordinary share}}{\text{Market price per ordinary share}}$$

This ratio is normally calculated by an investor who is acquiring ordinary shares mainly for dividends rather than for appreciation in the market price of the shares. The percentage yield indicates a rate of return on the dollars invested and permits easier comparison with returns from alternative investment opportunities. Dividend yield is also often quoted in daily newspapers as part of stock exchange price reports.

2. Liquidity ratios

Liquidity is an important factor in financial statement analysis since an entity that cannot meet its short-term obligations may be forced into liquidation. The focus of this aspect of analysis is on working capital, or some component of working capital.

(1) Current ratio

$$\text{Current ratio} = \frac{\text{Current assets}}{\text{Current liabilities}}$$

The current ratio is a measure of the entity's ability to satisfy its obligations in the short term. It indicates how much current assets exceed current liabilities. A low ratio may indicate inability to meet short-term debts in an emergency. A high ratio is considered favorable to creditors, but may indicate excessive investment in working-capital items that may not be producing profits. Analysts often contend as a rule of thumb that the current ratio should be at least 2:1; in other words, an entity should maintain $2 of current assets for every dollar of current liabilities.

(2) Quick ratio

$$\text{Quick ratio} = \frac{\text{Current assets} - \text{Inventories}}{\text{Current liabilities}}$$

One of the limitations of the current ratio is that it includes inventory in the numerator. However, inventories are not as liquid as cash, marketable securities, notes receivable and accounts receivable. In the normal course of business, inventories must be sold and cash collected before cash is available. Therefore, quick ratio is used to supplement the current ratio that provides a more rigorous measure of liquidity.

(3) Receivables turnover ratio

$$\text{Receivables turnover ratio} = \frac{\text{Net sales revenue}}{\text{Average receivables balance}}$$

It is a measure of how many times the average receivables balance is converted into cash during the year. It is also considered a measure of the efficiency of the credit-granting and collection policies. The higher the receivables turnover ratio is, the shorter the period of time between recording a credit sale and collecting the cash is. To be competitive, the credit policies established by an entity are influenced by industry practices. Comparison of this ratio with industry norms can reveal deviations from competitors' operating results.

(4) Average collection period

$$\text{Average collection period} = \frac{365 \text{ days}}{\text{Receivables turnover ratio}}$$

Frequently, 365 days could be divided by the receivables turnover ratio to derive the average number of days it takes to collect receivables from credit sales.

(5) Inventory turnover ratio

$$\text{Inventory turnover ratio} = \frac{\text{Cost of goods sold}}{\text{Average inventory balance}}$$

The inventory turnover ratio is a measure of the adequacy of inventory and how efficiently it is being managed. The control of the amount invested in inventory is an important aspect of managing a business. The size of the investment in inventory and inventory turnover depend on such factors as the type of business and time of year. A supermarket has a higher turnover than a motor vehicle dealer, and the inventory level of a seasonal business is higher at certain times in the operating cycle than at others.

3. Financial stability ratios

We will now focus on several tests used to analyze the ability of an entity to continue operations in the long term, to satisfy its long-term commitments, and still have sufficient working capital left over to operate successfully.

(1) Debt ratio

$$\text{Debt ratio} = \frac{\text{Total liabilities}}{\text{Total assets}}$$

The proportion of total assets financed by creditors is important to long-term investors since the creditors have a prior claim to assets in the event of liquidation—the creditors must be paid before assets are distributed to shareholders. The greater the percentage of assets contributed by shareholders, the greater the protection to the creditors.

(2) Equity ratio

$$\text{Equity ratio} = \frac{\text{Total shareholders' equity}}{\text{Total assets}}$$

The equity ratio, which attempts to assess long-term stability, examines the relationship between shareholders' equity and total assets.

(3) Interest coverage ratio (Times interest earned)

$$\text{Interest coverage ratio} = \frac{\text{PBIT}}{\text{Interest expense}}$$

This ratio is an indication of the entity's ability to satisfy periodic interest payments from current profits. Interest expense and income taxes are added back to profit in the numerator because the ratio is a measure of profits available to pay the interest charges.

A summary of the financial ratios are shown in Table 4-10.

Table 4-10 A Summary of Financial Ratios

Ratio	Method of calculation	Significance of ratio
Profitability ratios		
Rate of return on total assets	$\dfrac{PBIT}{Total\ assets}$	Measures rate of return earned through operating total assets provided by both creditors and owners.
Profit margin	$\dfrac{Net\ income}{Net\ sales}$	Measures net profitability of each dollar of sales.
Earnings per share	$\dfrac{Operating\ profit\ after\ income\ tax - Preference\ dividends}{Number\ of\ ordinary\ shares\ issued}$	Measures profit earned on each ordinary share.
Price-earnings ratio	$\dfrac{Market\ price\ per\ ordinary\ share}{Earnings\ per\ ordinary\ share}$	Measures the amount investors are paying for a dollar of earnings.
Dividend yield ratio	$\dfrac{Annual\ dividend\ per\ ordinary\ share}{Market\ price\ per\ ordinary\ share}$	Measures the rate of return to shareholders based on current market price.
Liquidity ratios		
Current ratio	$\dfrac{Current\ assets}{Current\ liabilities}$	A measure of short-term liquidity. Indicates the ability of an entity to meet its short-term debts from its current assets.
Quick ratio	$\dfrac{Current\ assets\ -\ Inventories}{Current\ liabilities}$	A more rigorous measure of short-term liquidity. Indicates the ability of the entity to meet unexpected demands from liquid current assets.
Receivables turnover ratio	$\dfrac{Net\ sales\ revenue}{Average\ receivables\ balance}$	Measures the effectiveness of collections; used to evaluate whether receivables balance is excessive.
Average collection period	$\dfrac{365\ days}{Receivables\ turnover\ ratio}$	Measures the average number of days taken by an entity to collect the receivables.
Inventory turnover ratio	$\dfrac{Cost\ of\ goods\ sold}{Average\ inventory\ balance}$	Indicates the liquidity of inventory. Measures the number of times inventory was sold on the average during the period.

Cont.

Ratio	Method of calculation	Significance of ratio
Financial stability ratios		
Debt ratio	$\dfrac{Total\ liabilities}{Total\ assets}$	Measures percentage of assets provided by creditors and extent of using gearing.
Equity ratio	$\dfrac{Total\ shareholders'\ equity}{Total\ assets}$	Measures percentage of assets provided by shareholders and the extent of using gearing.
Interest coverage ratio	$\dfrac{PBIT}{Interest\ expense}$	Measures the ability of the entity to meet its interest payments out of current profits.

Chapter Round-up

- Financial statements basically comprise:
(1) Balance sheet
(2) Income statement
(3) Cash flow statement

- An annual financial report will also contain notes to the financial statements, operation review, directors' declaration, directors' report, auditor's report, and so on.

- The balance sheet shows the business' financial position as at the balance sheet date whereas the income statement shows its trading results, overheads, interest, tax and dividends for the year. The cash flow statement reconciles the trading profit to operational cash flows and shows other movements in cash for capital transactions etc.

- The dollar amounts reported in financial statements are often converted into percentages of some base item and, in other cases, expressed as ratios.

- The purpose of percentage analysis and ratio analysis is to identify significant changes of and relationships among statement figures.

- Percentage analyses contain horizontal analysis, vertical analysis and trend analysis.

- The ratios you are supposed to be able to calculate and comment on can be divided into three groups: profitability, liquidity and financial stability. They are:
(1) Rate of return on total assets
(2) Profit margin
(3) Earnings per share
(4) Price-earnings ratio
(5) Dividend yield ratio
(6) Current ratio
(7) Quick ratio

(8) Receivables turnover ratio
(9) Average collection period
(10) Inventory turnover ratio
(11) Debt ratio
(12) Equity ratio
(13) Interest coverage ratio

Glossary

horizontal	adj. & n.	水平的;水平,水平线
vertical	adj. & n.	垂直的;垂直,垂直线
notes	n.	财务报表附注
due	adj.	到期的
solvency	n.	偿债能力
assessment	n.	评估,评定
interpretation	n.	解释,翻译
ratio	n.	比率,比例
favorable	adj.	有利的,良好的,赞成的
illustrative	adj.	说明的,作例证的,解说的
proportional	adj.	成比例的,相称的
gross profit		毛利
prospect	n.	前途,预期
intuitive	adj.	直觉的,凭直觉获知的
appreciation	n.	增值,感谢,欣赏
stock exchange		证交所
working capital		营运资本
a rule of thumb		经验法则
contend	vt.	主张,争论
marketable securities		有价证券
PBIT/EBIT		息税前利润
rate of return on total assets		资产回报率
profit margin		利润率
earnings per share		每股收益
price-earnings ratio		市盈率
dividend yield ratio		股息收益率
current ratio		流动比
quick ratio		速动比

receivables turnover ratio	应收账款周转率
average collection period	平均收账期
inventory turnover ratio	库存周转率
debt ratio	资产负债比
equity ratio	资产权益比
interest coverage ratio	利息保障倍数

Review Questions

(1) What's the general purpose of a balance sheet?

(2) What information is shown by a statement of cash flows? Why is knowledge of cash flows important to a decision maker?

(3) What's the function of an income statement from the perspective of a statement user?

(4) What's the difference between the financial statements and the financial report?

(5) What's the difference between horizontal analysis, vertical analysis and trend analysis?

(6) What's the purpose of ratio analysis?

(7) How are the current ratio and the quick ratio similar? How do they differ?

(8) What ratio will help to answer each of the following questions?

① How effective are the credit policies of the entity?

② How much confidence do investors have in the entity?

③ Are the assets being used efficiently?

④ How is the entity being financed?

(9) What risk does an entity assume as the inventory increases?

(10) How could earnings per share decrease even though profit has increased from the previous year?

Exercises

1. True or false

(1) Balance sheet is the backbone of the whole accounting system and it reflects the profitability of a business.

(2) Income statements are prepared at the end of each year and provide a picture of the operating results of a business.

(3) Both income statement and balance sheet can show solvency of a business.

(4) Income statement helps evaluating the management efficiency of a company because it lists how much assets overweight liabilities in a certain period of time.

(5) Vertical analysis is also called trend analysis because it compares the same item in serial years.

(6) Horizontal analysis sets a base year to carry the weight of 100 and compares the same item from different years with it.

(7) One of the most widely used liquidity measures is the current ratio which compares current assets and current liabilities.

(8) The annual cash dividend per share divided by the current market price of stock is the EPS.

(9) Inventory turnover ratio and receivables turnover ratio are examples of liquidity ratios.

(10) Profitability ratios measure the ability of a business to meet current debts and obligations as they come due.

2. Preparation of profit and loss statement and balance sheet

Asset, liability, owner's equity, revenue and expense amounts for Darwin Decorating at December 31, 20X8 are presented below:

unit: $

Cash at bank	20,500	Advertising expense	25,000
Accounts receivable	98,000	Insurance expense	5,000
Supplies	22,000	Rent expense	27,000
Equipment	96,000	Supplies expense	10,500
Accounts payable	19,000	Telephone expense	8,000
Darwin, Capital	217,500	Electricity expense	15,000
Design revenue	295,000	Wages expense	88,000

Required:

① Prepare a balance sheet for the business as at December 31, 20X8.

② Prepare an income statement for the year ended December 31, 20X8.

3. Analysis of financial statement elements

Financial data for James Crane, a sole trader business, as of December 31, 20X9 are:

unit: $

Accounts receivable	48,000	Wages expense	56,000
Revenue earned	136,000	Advertising expense	24,000
Accounts payable	32,000	Land	60,000
J. Crane, Capital	?	Equipment	144,000
Cash at bank	36,000	Notes payable	40,000
Mortgage payable	104,000	Electricity expense	16,000
Building	68,000	Telephone expense	4,000

Required:

Without preparing formal financial reports, calculate the following:

① Total assets at the end of the year

② Total liabilities at the end of the year

③ James Crane's capital balance at the end of the year (given current profit and loss)

④ Profit/Loss for the year

4. Trend analysis

Kangaroo Ltd reported the following financial data over a 5-year period.

unit: $

	20X5	20X6	20X7	20X8	20X9
Sales revenue	720,200	770,400	777,650	799,200	820,880
Gross profit	288,000	296,650	305,280	313,920	319,600
Operating expenses	205,200	217,500	225,300	231,650	235,700

Required:

① Prepare a trend analysis of the data.

② Do the trends signify a favorable or unfavorable situation? Explain.

5. Profitability and financial stability analysis

The following information is available for Platypus Ltd.

unit: $

	20X8	20X9
Sales revenue	800,000	735,000
Interest expense	32,000	34,000
Income tax expense	62,000	68,000
Operating profit after income tax	73,000	72,000
Preference dividends	4,000	4,000
Total assets	750,000	715,000
Total liabilities	420,000	431,000
Preference share capital	85,000	85,000
Ordinary share capital	150,000	140,000
Retained profits	95,000	59,000

Required:

Calculate the following ratios for 20X8 and 20X9.

① Rate of return on total assets

② Profit margin

③ Debt ratio
④ Times interest earned

Group Activities

(1) In analyzing the financial statements of an entity, the following ratios were calculated:

	20X8	20X9
Current ratio	2 : 1	1.3 : 1
Quick ratio	1 : 1	0.7 : 1
Receivables turnover ratio	30 days	45 days
Inventory turnover ratio	3 times	4 times
Profit margin	10%	7%

Discuss any potential weaknesses that these ratios may reveal in the overall performance of the entity, and comment on possible causes for these results.

(2) The 20X9 annual report of Jumbuck Ltd contains the following information: Balance Sheet and Income Statement.

JUMBUCK LTD

Balance Sheet

As at December 31, 20X9

($ 000 omitted)

	20X9	20X8
Current Assets		
Cash at bank	612	880
Marketable securities	150	125
Accounts receivable	1,900	1,750
Inventory	3,250	3,300
	5,912	6,055
Non-current Assets		
Plant and equipment (net)	7,960	7,300
TOTAL ASSETS	13,872	13,355
Current Liabilities		
Accounts payable	2,600	2,730
Wages expenses	75	125
	2,675	2,855
Non-current Liabilities		

Loan payable	400	300
Debentures	4,200	4,200
	4,600	4,500
TOTAL LIABILITIES	7,275	7,355
NET ASSETS	6,597	6,000
Shareholders' Equity		
Preference share capital (issued at $2)	250	250
Ordinary share capital (issued at $1)	3,600	3,600
Retained profits	2,747	2,150
	6,597	6,000

JUMBUCK LTD

Income Statement

for the year ended December 31, 20X9

($ 000 omitted)

	20X9	20X8
Sales revenue	25,000	22,000
Less: Cost of goods sold	16,250	14,330
GROSS PROFIT	8,750	7,670
Less: Selling expenses	3,250	2,500
Administrative expenses	2,300	2,650
Interest expenses	720	700
OPERATING PROFIT BEFORE INCOME TAX	2,480	1,820
Income tax expense	868	637
OPERATING PROFIT AFTER INCOME TAX	1,612	1,183

Additional information:

Preference dividends declared and paid during 20X9: $85,000

Ordinary dividends declared and paid during 20X9: $900,000

Market price per preference share on December 31, 20X9: $4.60

Market price per ordinary share on December 31, 20X9: $10.00

◆ Required:

① Calculate the following ratios for both year 20X8 and 20X9.

a. Rate of return on total assets

b. Profit margin

c. Current ratio

d. Quick ratio

e. Average collection period

f. Inventory turnover ratio

g. Debt ratio

h. Interest coverage ratio

i. EPS

j. P/E ratio

k. Dividend yield ratio

② Given the changes of financial ratios from year 20X8 to 20X9, as well as the following industry averages, write a report on the performance of Jumbuck Ltd in year 20X9, with regard to its profitability, liquidity and financial stability. Supporting reasons should be given.

	Industry Average
Profit margin	4.1%
Earnings per share	45c
P/E ratio	11.0
Dividend yield ratio	4.8%
Current ratio	2.5
Quick ratio	1.3
Average collection period	30 days
Inventory turnover ratio	5 times
Debt ratio	40.0%
Interest coverage ratio	6.0

Supplementary Reading

Limitations of Financial Analysis

The analytical techniques are useful for providing insights into the financial position and results of operations for a particular entity. There are, nevertheless, certain limitations that should be kept in mind:

• Financial analysis is performed on historical data mainly for the purpose of forecasting changes in the general state of the economy, the business environment in which the entity must operate, or internal factors such as change in management or changes in the policies established by management.

• The measurement base used in calculating the analytical measures is historical cost. Failure to adjust for inflation or changes in fair values may result in some ratios providing misleading information on a trend basis and in any comparison between entities. The return on total assets includes operating profit in the numerator, which is affected by the current year's sales and current operating expenses measured in current dollars. Non-current assets and other non-monetary items however, are measured in historical dollars, which are not adjusted to reflect current price levels. Thus, the ratio divides items measured mainly in current dollar amounts by a total measured mainly in terms of historical dollars. This limitation is partly overcome where entities report inflation-adjusted data or current value data as supplementary information to the historical cost statements.

- Year-end data may not be typical of the entity's position during the year. Knowing that certain ratios are calculated at year-end, management may attempt to improve a ratio by entering into certain types of transactions near the end of the year. For example, the current ratio can be improved by using cash to pay off short-term debt. Also, if the financial year-end coincides with a low point of activity in the operating cycle, account balances such as receivables, payables and inventory may not be representative of the balances carried in these accounts during the year.

- Lack of disclosure in general-purpose financial reports may inhibit the extent of the analysis. For example, some entities may not disclose cost of goods sold as, at the time of writing, there is no requirement to do so. Any trends in such figures and any ratios using such information therefore cannot be determined.

- The existence of extraordinary items within a profit and loss statement, e. g. losses through floods, may inhibit the determination of trends to assess business efficiency. Hence, many analysts may exclude extraordinary items from all ratios. Nevertheless, in determining profitability the extraordinary items must inevitably be considered in calculating the rate of return to ordinary shareholders.

- Sometimes the information contained in the general-purpose reports may be subject to modifications, supplementations and/or qualifications expressed in accompanying documents such as directors' reports and auditors' reports. Any analysis and interpretation should take into consideration such matters.

- Entities may not be comparable. Throughout this chapter it has been emphasized that one important comparison is between competing entities. However, because of factors such as the use of different accounting methods, size, and the diversification of product lines, data may not provide meaningful comparisons.

A further, not inconsiderable, difficulty with financial analysis is that the analysis assumes share markets are inefficient. In other words, it is assumed that an analyst can study all of the published information in relation to an entity in order to determine whether the entity's shares are under- or overvalued. As consequence, the fundamental analysis assumes that people, merely by careful analysis of public information, can make abnormal profits by investing in shares which are undervalued, and by selling shares which are overvalued.

Considerable research into the efficiency of share markets has questioned the reality of the assumptions of this fundamental analysis. Research into the behavior of share prices has assumed that share markets are efficient in terms of incorporating all publicly available information into the share price of an entity. Thus, the share price is seen to reflect the entity's value at a point in time, and it is impossible for any analyst to generate abnormal profits by studying publicly available information. Instead, the investor encouraged to invest in shares in accordance with the extent of the risk that he or she is prepared to take. Investors are encouraged, by this research, to diversify their portfolio of investments, in order to spread the risk in the event that any investment should fail.

Even though capital markets research has pushed the view that the fundamental analysis of an entity's shares has been misguided, there are, nevertheless, many analysts who still engage in the practice of fundamental analysis. Why? There are a number of reasons. Firstly, some may not be educated sufficiently as to the "futility" of their task. Secondly, many people are still of the belief that they can make a "killing" in the stock market, and are prepared to consult analysts to help them in their quest. Thirdly, if the share market is efficient, this may have come about because of the existence of many analysts who are prepared to study publicly available information very closely. If these analysts ceased to do this work, the share market may become less efficient. And finally, the evidence from capital markets research is not conclusive, as some researchers appear to have developed strategies which suggest that abnormal profits can still be made by analyzing publicly available information.

To conclude, the findings of capital markets research are not beyond question in spite of considerable research efforts. Hence, it is premature and perilous to discard fundamental analysis for analyzing and interpreting the performance of an entity in the market. Although there are other limitations of the techniques illustrated, those above should provide sufficient evidence that a user of general-purpose financial reports must exercise caution in interpreting trends and ratios calculated.

Critical Thinking Questions:

(1) What are the limitations of financial analysis?

(2) Since a lot of limitations exist, why do people still engage in the financial analysis of the annual report?

Unit Five

Managing Financial Resources

 Learning Objectives

When you have studied this chapter, you should be able to:
* define finance and identify different sources of finance;
* explain the characteristics of each type of financing;
* understand the costs occurring to different sources of finance;
* understand the importance of the time value of money and the implication of discounted cash flows;
* use different methods to evaluate investment projects, e.g. a ROI method, a PBP method, a NPV method and an IRR method.

 Warm-up: Dialogue

Michael: Hi, Michelle, could you tell me the meaning of finance?
Michelle: Well, to be simple, finance just means money, but it's used in a bigger sense than just "money". Actually, it is any arrangement that you can make in exchange for the ability to do all the different things you want to do.
Michael: You mean any arrangements I make to exchange for other things?
Michelle: That's right. For example, if you want to buy an ice-cream, you can finance it with the cash in your pocket. If you want to buy a car but cannot pay for it, you can get a five-year loan from the bank to finance yourself.
Michael: Oh, I see. But what you mentioned seems to be personal finance. And I'm also interested in business finance. Could you explain it?
Michelle: Sure. A business, whether it is a local café or a listed company, has exactly the same need for money, just like you and I. There are a lot of sources of finance.
Michael: Really? What are they?
Michelle: Yes, there are. For instance, if you want to set up a business of your own, you have

Michael: to use the money in your own pocket at first. Then founders of a start-up business may also look to private financing sources such as parents or friends. If you are lucky enough, you can even receive money from venture capitalists or angel investors.

Michael: Wow, it sounds cool!

Michelle: Well, if it is a listed company, like Amazon, it can raise money through issuing shares.

Michael: And in this way, a large amount of funds could be obtained for the company, is it right?

Michelle: Exactly. But apart from that, a business can also finance its operation through borrowing. For example, it's a common case for a company to borrow from the banks or other commercial lenders. In some other cases, a business can issue a bond to raise money.

Michael: Oh, I'm a little confused. Anyway, there are various sources of finance for a business, isn't it?

Michelle: Right. I'll explain the difference between them in detail later.

Text

Section 1 Sources of Finance

Business Finance

Finance could be simply defined as the obtaining of funds or capital. Financing activities are those which relate to the raising of funds for an entity to carry out its operating and investing activities. Examples of financing activities include the raising of capital by issuing shares, the receipt of a government grant, the borrowing of money from a bank or other financial institution, the repayment of these borrowed funds, and a buyback of an entity's shares from the shareholders.

Finance can be obtained from many different sources (Figure 5-1). Basically, debt (borrowed capital) and equity (ownership capital) are the two major sources of financing. Equity financing, which, to a large extent, means exchanging a portion of the ownership of the business for a financial investment, mostly includes share capital and retained earnings. There are some other forms, like venture capital, government grants, franchise, etc. Debt financing, which involves borrowing funds from creditors with the stipulation of repaying the borrowed funds plus interest at a specified future time, mainly contains bank borrowings, bonds, factoring and so on.

Unit Five　Managing Financial Resources

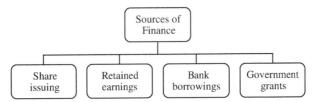

Figure 5-1　Different Sources of Finance

As a matter of fact, the financial needs of a business will vary according to the type and size of the business. Therefore, choosing the right source and right mix of finance is a key challenge for every finance manager. The process of selecting the right source of finance involves in-depth analysis of each source of finance. For analyzing and comparing the sources of finance, it needs understanding of all the characteristics of the financing sources.

1. Share issuing

Share capital is the fund raised by a company by issuance of shares. It may take two forms: ordinary shares capital and preference shares capital.

As the owners of the business, ordinary shareholders enjoy the rewards and bear the risks of the ownership. Usually a potential investor can become the owner of a company by paying for a new issue of shares. In most cases, a new issue can raise large amounts of cash without the risk of a future takeover, owing to the introduction of new shareholders. However, a new issue could incur considerable expenses and often trigger the dilution of the control of existing shareholders.

Accordingly, a listed company usually chooses to issue further shares through a rights issue. A rights issue involves the offer of new shares, at a discount below market value, to current shareholders in proportion to their current shareholding. The shareholders may take up the rights and buy the shares offered at the specified price. Alternatively, he may sell his rights in the markets.

Preference shareholders are entitled to a fixed rate of dividend which is paid before ordinary shareholders are paid. Like ordinary dividends, preference dividends can only be paid if there are profits available for distribution. However, preference shares do not carry voting rights. In other words, preference shareholders don't have a say in the business' operations.

2. Retained earnings

Retained earnings represent the earnings not distributed to shareholders. A firm may retain a portion or whole of its profits and utilize it for financing its projects. The major reasons for using retained earnings to finance new investments, rather than to pay higher dividends, are as follows:

(1) The management of many companies believes that the use of retained earnings as a source of finance does not lead to a payment of cash.

(2) The dividend policy of the company is actually determined by the directors. From their

viewpoint, retained earnings are an attractive source of finance because investment projects can be undertaken without involving either the shareholders or any outsiders.

(3) The use of retained earnings avoids issue costs and banks fees.

(4) The use of retained earnings avoids the possibility of a change in control resulting from an issue of new shares.

A company must restrict its self-financing through retained profits because shareholders should be paid a reasonable dividend, in line with realistic expectations, even if the directors would rather keep the funds for re-investing.

3. Venture capital

Venture capital, which comes from companies or individuals, refers to the capital provided by means of equity investment for the long term. Venture capitalists provide capital to young businesses in exchange for an ownership share of the business. There is a serious risk of losing the entire investment, and it might take a long time before any profits and returns realize. But there is also the prospect of very high profits and a substantial return on the investment. A venture capitalist will require a high expected rate of return on investments, to compensate for the high risk. Generally, venture capital firms prefer to invest in companies that have received significant equity investments from the founders and are already profitable.

When a company's directors look for help from a venture capital firm, they must recognize that:

(1) The venture capitalists will want an equity stake in the company.

(2) They will need a convincing statement that the company can be successful.

(3) The venture firm may want to have a representative appointed to the company's board, to look after its interests.

4. Franchise

Franchising is a method of expanding business on less capital than would otherwise be needed. Under a franchising arrangement, a franchisee pays a franchisor for the right to operate a local business, under the franchisor's trade name. The franchisor must bear certain costs (possibly for architect's work, establishment costs, legal costs, marketing costs and the cost of other support services) and will charge the franchisee an initial franchise fee to cover set-up costs, relying on the subsequent regular payments by the franchisee for an operating profit.

Although the franchisor will probably pay a large part of the initial investment cost of a franchisee's outlet, the franchisee will be expected to contribute a share of the investment himself. The advantages to the franchisor are as follows:

(1) The capital outlay needed to expand the business is reduced substantially.

(2) The image of the business is improved because the franchisees will be motivated to achieve good results and will have the authority to take whatever action they think fit to improve the results.

(3) The franchisor is freed from the administrative burden of maintaining a branch network

and employ staffs.

The advantage to a franchisee is that he obtains ownership of a business for an agreed number of years together with the backing of a large organization's marketing effort and experience. The franchisee is able to avoid some of the mistakes of many small businesses, because the franchisor has already trained him and developed a scheme that works.

5. Bank loans

The first thing that most people think about when trying to obtain finance is their own bank. Banks borrowings are actually most popular sources of business financing. Mostly, there are two methods of lending. One is an overdraft and the other is a formal loan. An overdraft is a very flexible form of finance which, with a healthy income in your business, can be paid off more quickly than a formal loan. A company should keep an overdraft within the limit set by the bank and interest is charged on the amount by which the company is overdrawn from day to day.

Many businesses prefer a fixed term loan. They have the comforting knowledge that the regular payments to be made on the loan make cash flow forecasting and budgeting more certain. They also feel that, with a term loan, the bank is more committed to their business for the whole term of the loan. Many smaller loans will not require any security but, if substantial amounts of money are required, the bank will ask for some form of security. It is common for business owners to offer their own homes as security although more risk-averse borrowers may prefer not to do this.

6. Bonds

Bonds may be used to raise financing for a specific activity. They are a special type of debt financing because the debt instrument is issued by the company. Bonds are different from other debt financing instruments in that the company specifies the interest rate and when the company will pay back the principal (maturity date). Also, the company does not have to make any payments on the principal (and may not make any interest payments) until the specified maturity date. The price paid for the bond at the time it is issued is called its face value.

7. Factoring

Factoring is a financial transaction in which a business sells its invoices, or receivables, to a third-party financial company known as a "factor". The factor then collects payment on those invoices from the business' customers. The main reason that companies choose to factor is that they want to receive cash quickly on their receivables, rather than waiting the 30 to 60 days which it often takes a customer to pay.

Typically, the company can receive 80% – 95% of the value of the invoice or receivables immediately. For example, if a business makes credit sales of $100,000, the factor might be willing to advance 85% of the invoice value ($85,000) usually in 24 hours in return for a commission charge, and the interest will be charged on the amount of funds advanced. The balance of the money will be paid to the company when the customers have paid the factor or after an agreed period.

Factoring allows companies to quickly and flexibly build up their cash flow, which makes it easier for them to pay employees, handle customer orders or finance daily operations.

Ⅱ Costs of Different Sources of Finance

The costs of some basic sources of finance are as follows.

1. Share capital

- Dividends

A dividend is a distribution of part of the earnings of the company to its equity shareholders. If the company is profitable in the current year, the investors would mostly expect the company to reward them in terms of dividends, which would usually take the form of cash dividend and scrip dividend.

The dividend policy, which means the policy a company uses to decide how much it will pay out to shareholders, is determined by the company's board of directors, within certain legal constraints. Because dividends represent a form of income for investors, a company's dividend policy is an important consideration for some investors. As such, it is an important consideration for company leadership, especially because company leaders are often the largest shareholders. Essentially, management must decide on the dividend amount, timing and various other factors that influence dividend payments. Dividends also have some quite complicated tax implications, both for investors and for companies.

- Cost of information provision

The cost of providing shareholders with information about the performance of the company is quite considerable. It usually includes the cost of preparation of financial reports, annual general meetings at a glamorous location, audit fees and the administrative costs of complying with legal and Stock Exchange requirements for disclosure of information to shareholders.

- Cost of issuing new shares

Issuance of new common stock incurs a variety of direct costs both at the initial offering and throughout the process of managing this funding source, which includes those related to legal, accounting, marketing, management, and taxation. For example, there are legal fees for the distribution of business shares to the general public, marketing costs for recruiting investors, the time and effort of management and so on. Actually, the issuance of new shares is quite expensive, complex and time consuming.

Issuing new common stock also incurs a variety of indirect costs revolving around dilution of ownership, legal requirements of financial statement releases, and unreliability of demand for shares.

2. Borrowed funds

- Interest expense is the main cost. The rate of interest may either be fixed or variable. A variable rate is usually the bank "base rate" (effectively dictated by the governments' economic policy) plus an extra amount (a premium) so that the bank makes a profit. On the whole, businesses prefer fixed rate loans because they then know for certain how much their future cost is going to be. Naturally, the interest cost for a business tends to go up when prevailing market interest rates are rising during times of economic expansion and increased inflation.

- There will often be an initial management fee to cover the lender's administrative costs on setting up the loan.
- Factors charge commission for advancing funds as well as interest for the period during which a debt remains unpaid.

Section 2 Investment and Project Appraisal

The expenditures made to generate operating capacity are referred to as capital expenditures because they involve investments with long lives. Examples of capital expenditures are replacing equipment, expanding production facilities, opening new offices or stores, improving product quality, introducing new product lines and improving cost efficiency, etc.

Capital budgeting is the process used to evaluate capital expenditures in a rational and systematic way. The main objective of capital budgeting is to add to the value of a business by selecting capital expenditures that are compatible with the goals of the organization and which provide the highest rates of return. As such, capital budgeting decisions are critical to the long-term profitability of an entity. Once these decisions are implemented, the related operating capacity will be available and management must make sure it is used efficiently and effectively.

Capital budgeting decisions must be carefully considered by top management for several reasons:

(1) They involve large sums of money and the success or failure of an entity may depend on a single decision.

(2) The resources invested are committed for a long period of time.

(3) They cannot be reversed easily since the investment becomes a sunk cost that can be recovered only by the productive use of the relevant assets.

(4) Since they are long-term oriented, substantial risk is involved because of such uncertainties as economic conditions, technological developments, consumer preferences and social responsibilities.

In theory and in practice, a number of methods are available to management for the evaluation of capital expenditures or the appraisal of a capital project.

① Return on Investment Method (ROI)

A capital investment project may be assessed by calculating the return on investment (ROI) or accounting rate of return (ARR) and comparing it with a pre-determined target level or with the returns of alternative investments. Being a rough approximation of an investment's profitability, it is calculated by dividing the average annual net profit after tax from an investment by the average investment. A formula for the ROI is (straight-line depreciation is used):

$$ROI = \frac{Average\ profits}{Average\ investment} \times 100\%$$

$$= \frac{Average\ profits}{Initial\ cost + Residual\ value} \times 100\%$$

The method is widely used because it is easy to use and understand and the relevant data is available through accounting information. Unlike the Payback Period method, the Return on Investment method does consider the profitability of an investment over its useful life. However, it has a serious weakness—it does not consider the time value of money.

Payback Period Method (PBP)

The payback period is the length of time required to recover the cost of an investment from the net cash flows it generates. In other words, it is the length of time the investment takes to pay itself back. The formula is:

$$PBP = \frac{Initial\ cost\ of\ investment}{Annual\ net\ cash\ flows}$$

The method is also widely used in practice because it is simple to calculate and easy to understand. Apparently, a quick payback period may help liquidity and reduce the risk of the investment since uncertainty usually increases with the passage of time. Disadvantages of the method are that it ignores the time value of money and the total profitability of the investment. Nevertheless, many businesses use the method to make a final choice among alternatives when other methods of evaluation indicate they are equally attractive.

Net Present Value Method (NPV)

Both NPV method and IRR method are actually two approaches of Discounted Cash Flow method (DCF) which is used to compare the cost of an investment with the present value of the net cash flows from it in the future. Actually, DCF is an evaluation technique which takes into account the time value of money.

The time value of money can be expressed in terms of its future value or its present value. Given that the annual interest rate is 12%, the $1,120 is the future value of the $1,000, because of the interest earned for year. In contrast, the $1,000 is the present value of the $1,120 if we discount the future value back to today's dollars. The process of converting a future value into a present value is called discounting, and we use the term discount rate to indicate that a present value is being calculated. However, the interest rate and the discount rate are both the same in a given future value-present value relationship. The formulas are:

Present value = Future value $\times (1 + r)^{-n}$

Future value = Present value $\times (1 + r)^{n}$

r: interest rate (or discount rate)

n: time periods

In project appraisal, we focus on discounted cash flows so we can compare the present cost of an investment with the present value of the net cash flows expected from it in the future. The expected future net cash flows from an investment can be compared with the investment only when both are measured in equivalent dollars. We make it by discounting the future dollars to their present value, which is the equivalent dollar value today of a known future amount.

With regard to the NPV method, it is used to discount future net cash flows into present value and to compare it with the cost of capital. Actually, the difference between the present value of future benefits and the cost of capital is treated as the net present value. If the NPV is positive, or the present value of benefits exceeds the present value of costs, the project could be accepted. If the NPV is negative, the project would mostly not be worth investing in.

The primary strength of the NPV method is that the decision will maximize the wealth of shareholders. Besides, it takes into consideration time value of money.

Example 5-1:

Scooter Ltd is wondering whether to invest $18,000 in a project which would make profits of $10,000 in the first year, $8,000 in the second year and $6,000 in the third year. Its cost of capital is 10% (in other words, it would require a return of at least 10% on its investment). You are required to evaluate the project with the NPV method.

Solution:

Year	Cash flow/$	Present value/$
0	(18,000)	(18,000)
1	10,000	9,090
2	8,000	6,608
3	6,000	4,506
		NPV: 2,204

The NPV is positive, which means that the project will earn more than 10%. So the project is acceptable.

Ⅳ Internal Rate of Return Method (IRR)

The Internal Rate of Return (IRR) is defined as the discount rate that will produce a net present value of zero for an investment. In other words, the discounted cash inflows will be equal to the discounted cash outflows when the IRR is used as the discount rate. An investment with an IRR that exceeds the cost of capital will be attractive to a business.

A formula for the IRR is:

$$IRR = A + \left[\frac{a}{a+b} \times (B - A)\right]$$

Where A is the discount rate which provides the positive NPV,

a is the amount of the positive NPV,

B is the discount rate which provides the negative NPV,

b is the amount of the negative NPV.

The strengths of the IRR method are that it summarizes the project information into one number and that it takes time value of money into account. However, there are some inevitable problems with the IRR method. For example, it may give conflicting recommendations with mutually exclusive projects, because the result is given in percentages and not in absolute dollar amount. Also, the manual calculation of IRR is not so easy since it involves some guesswork and approximation. In practice, financial calculators and spreadsheet programs can calculate the IRR quickly and accurately.

Chapter Round-up

- Finance is a monetary arrangement made in exchange for the ability to do something.
- Finance can be obtained from many different sources. Basically, borrowed capital and ownership capital are the two major sources of financing.
- Finance cannot be obtained without incurring costs. Besides interest and dividends, there are arrangement fees, commissions, the cost of information provision and non-financial costs such as loss of control.
- The return on investment method calculates the estimated profits as a percentage of the estimated average investment.
- The payback period is the time taken for the initial investment to be recovered in the cash inflows from the project. The PBP method is particularly relevant if there are liquidity problems.
- Discounted cash flow techniques take account of the time value of money.
- The net present value method calculates the present value of all cash inflows and outflows, and sums them to give the net present value. If it is positive, then the project is acceptable.
- The internal rate of return technique uses a trial and error method to discover the discount rate which produces the NPV of zero. This discount rate will be the return forecast for the project.

Glossary

buyback	n.	回购
venture capital		风险资本,风险投资
franchise	n.	特许经营权
factoring	n.	(应收账款)保理
grant	n.	拨款
	v.	授予

shareholder	n.	股东
rights issue		优先认股权,配股
discount	n. & v.	折扣,贴现
revolve	v.	围绕,旋转
inflation	n.	通货膨胀
appraisal	n.	评估,估价
capital budgeting		资本预算
yield	n.	收益,产出
liquidity	n.	流动性
evaluation	n.	评价,评估
present value		现值
future value		终值
equivalent	n.	等价物
exclusive	adj.	独有的,排他的
ROI (Return On Investment)		投资回报率
PBP (Payback Period)		投资回收期
DCF (Discounted Cash Flow)		贴现现金流
NPV (Net Present Value)		净现值
IRR (Internal Rate of Return)		内部收益率

Review Questions

(1) Differentiate borrowed capital and ownership capital. Give examples for each respectively.

(2) What's the advantage of using retained earnings by the company?

(3) What's the main cost associated to share issuing?

(4) What are the strengths and the risks of borrowing from outsiders?

(5) What are the advantages for the franchisor and the franchisee respectively under a franchising arrangement?

(6) What is capital budgeting? Why is it important for decision making by the management?

(7) What's the implication of the time value of money?

(8) What is the payback period? What is the main limitation of the use of the payback period?

(9) What are the main advantage and disadvantage of using the IRR method?

(10) What is the NPV method? What are the strengths of using it?

Exercises

1. True or false

(1) All forms of economic resources that a business owns have a specific source. They don't just appear.

(2) There are normally two sources from which a business can obtain funds: one is loans from creditors and the other is the owners' investments.

(3) Preference shareholders usually have the dividend paid before the ordinary shareholders have and they also have the same voting rights like ordinary shareholders do.

(4) The only cost occurring to borrowed funds is interest.

(5) Money raised from venture capitalists and factors are both borrowed funds.

(6) Banks borrowing is actually the most popular source of business financing because it is very cheap and less risky.

(7) Capital budgeting is the process of evaluating capital expenditures with the objective of selecting the one which provides the highest rates of return to the company.

(8) Calculation of present value and determining discounted cash flows are two techniques which are the same.

(9) Both the NPV method and the IRR method take account of the time value of money. So, they are preferred choices rather than the PBP method in any case.

(10) Unlike the PBP method, the ROI method does consider the profitability of an investment over its useful life and the time value of money as well.

2. Calculation with the ROI method

Queen Limited is contemplating the purchase of a new machine and has two alternatives. Suppose the annual profit is just the difference between the annual cash flows and the deprecation.

	Machine A	Machine B
Cost	$10,000	$10,000
Estimated scrap value	$2,000	$3,000
Estimated life	4 years	4 years
Estimated future cash flows		
Year 1	$5,000	$2,000
Year 2	$5,000	$3,000
Year 3	$3,000	$5,000
Year 4	$1,000	$5,000

◆ Required:

Use the ROI method to determine which of the two machines would be purchased.

3. Calculation with the PBP and the NPV methods

Queen Limited is evaluating three comparable investments. Summary data for the three investments, each of which would be paid for in current dollars, is listed below. The company's cost of capital is 12%.

Investment	Expected annual net cash flows	Estimated life	Initial cost
X	$20,000	8 years	$99,352
Y	$16,000	14 years	$87,480
Z	$15,000	18 years	$72,183

◆ Required:

Rank the three investments using:

① The PBP method

② The NPV method

Group Activities

The manager of a medium-sized service organization has just been briefed on the desirability of adopting the discounted cash flows approach to capital budgeting decisions. During the briefing, the manager expressed his preference for the payback period approach, a method he had used in the past. He had also heard details about rate of return on average investment, and he believed that using this approach would be better than payback period since he could relate the method back to accounting records.

◆ Required:

In groups of four or five, draft a letter to the manager outlining the pros and cons of the three methods mentioned, at the same time arguing the case that the discounted cash flows approach is superior.

Supplementary Reading

Venture Capital Investment Continues to Grow

By Wang Zhenghua (*China Daily*)

Venture capital investment on the Chinese mainland registered continued growth in 2006, with significant activity in healthcare, retail companies and clean technologies, industry reports show. According to the China Quarterly Venture Capital Report released last month by Dow Jones VentureOne and Ernst & Young, venture capital investment in mainland-headquartered companies reached the highest point in three years, with 214 deals and $1.89 billion invested last year, a 37 percent growth in the number of transactions and a 55 percent jump in capital investment over 2005.

"In 2006, venture capital investment in China was characterized by development in the environment and diversification in the industries attracting investors," says Bob Partridge, China leader of Ernst & Young's Venture Capital Advisory Group. "While investment was up in the fourth quarter of 2006 compared to the fourth quarter of 2005, we saw a slowdown in the fourth quarter compared to the third quarter, which might be due to the introduction of new mergers and acquisitions rules in that took effect in September 2006, or part of a similar seasonal trend in developed markets," he says. The fourth quarter showed gains over the same period a year ago, with some 50 deals and $417.5 million invested, increases of 11 percent and 3 percent, respectively. It was the second-slowest quarter of the year, similar to activity in the United States and Europe, the report says. VentureOne is the publisher of the VentureSource database and compiles investment figures based on the findings of its proprietary Chinese research. The data was collected by surveying professional venture capital firms using in-depth interviews with company CEOs and chief financial officers, and from secondary sources.

Another report says that new rules on overseas investors undertaking mergers or acquisitions with Chinese companies have yet to influence the industry in the quarter that started from October. The annual report, compiled by the Zero2IPO Group, which provides services in China's venture capital and private equity industry, says that money continued to flow into the information technology sector in the second half of 2006 despite a decrease in overall investment during the period. The report, based on research on 300 venture capital institutions with active performance in China, put the growth of investment at a "stunning" 51.5 percent last year, with some $1.778 billion at play. "While information technology remains the dominant industry for investment, there was significant growth in areas such as healthcare, consumer and retail companies and clean technologies," Partridge says. "The continuing growth of the Chinese economy and the middle class as well as increasing focus on innovation are the primary reasons for significant investment growth in these sectors," he added.

By industry, 131 information technology companies were financed in 2006, receiving $920.7 million, a surge of 34 percent in capital from 2005, the China Quarterly Venture Capital Report shows. The most popular segment within the IT industry was the Internet-dominated information services segment, which attracted $464.6 million and 73 of the deals. The business, consumer and retail industry category, which is made up of non-technology companies, posted 57 deals and $613.3 million in investment in 2006, a rise of 20 percent more deals and 40 percent more capital than in 2005. While healthcare is a relatively small investment sector in China, particularly in comparison to the US and Europe, it did see 10 deals in 2006 and $47.5 million invested, up from six deals and $5.8 million in 2005.

"Another sign of the strength of the market is that investors are helping their companies to ramp up quickly in the global marketplace by funding them with increasingly larger sums a trend that was also apparent in other major venture capital regions over the past year," says Stephen Harmston, Director of Global Research for VentureOne. "The median deal size in China is now $5.9 million, up from $3.7 million in 2005, the highest median in at least seven years," he says.

As well, the level of second-round investment activity illustrates the growing maturity of the venture capital market in China. Investors are helping companies to move past the start-up stage into the next phase of development. As expected, considering the relative youth of the Chinese venture capital market, new and first-round deals continue to make up the majority in China, some 62 percent, but that is down from 68 percent in 2005. Deal flow to second and later rounds is also increasing. Second-round investment contributed 22 percent, up from 15 percent in 2005. In addition, 156 percent more capital was invested in second-round development in 2006 compared to 2005. Deal sizes also grew. The median size of a first-round deal was $4 million in 2006, up from $3.1 million in 2005. For second-round investment, the median was $10 million, up from $7.5 million a year ago illustrating that investors in China are willing to provide substantial amounts to companies that are maturing into their concept. In fact, it was larger than second-round deals in the US in 2006, where the median was $8.5 million.

(http://www.chinadaily.com.cn/business/2007-03/12/content_825342.htm)

Venture Capital—Lifeblood of Innovation

By Hao Nan (*China Daily*)

Today Chinese consumers are using smartphones to pay for purchases and check on their e-bank as the country's digital financial services become a way of life for the young and sophisticated. Helping drive the trend is Zhongguancun Science Park, an icon of innovation in Beijing, which now has a range of e-finance companies. One of the star performers is 91JinRong.com Inc. The company's founder Xu Zewei was born to a banking family. Even when young, he hoped to design a way of improving the efficiency of bank employees so his parents would have more time to spend with him. When he finished college his dream was still alive. After discussions with angel investors, the idea of changing service patterns from traditional banking was confirmed. He saw that the Internet could enhance efficiency and lower costs.

In 2011, he set up 91JinRong.com Inc with an investment of 5 million yuan ($817,000) from an angel investor. The company had fewer than 10 staff members at the time. But the money was far from enough to support the company's development. Xu was luckier than many other startup entrepreneurs. They often fail due to financing problems, but he got another round of investment from a venture capital fund jointly established by the China Broadband Capital and Zhongguancun Venture Capital Funds. Backed by the investment and CBC's rich management experience, 91JinRong.com Inc got through the worst days and now has its business covers 87 cities across the country. The company has established cooperative partnerships with more than 300 banks and financial institutions nationwide including Sunshine Insurance Group and Industrial and Commercial Bank of China.

Guo Hong, director of the Zhongguancun Science Park Administrative Committee, said there is now a consensus that the level of investment in fresh entrepreneurship will determine the development level of the overall high-tech industry. The Silicon Valley, for example, attracts about 40 percent of the total venture capital funds in the United States. Recognizing such investment is the catalyst for high-tech, the administrative committee established China's first government-guided entrepreneurship fund at the end of 2001. In 2006, Zhongguancun selected four venture capital partners and established the joint funds in 2007. After years of development, Zhongguancun is now the top choice for people to start a business and most active area for venture capital. Its venture capital accounts for nearly 33 percent of the nation's total. Zhongguancun is also improving the fund management system and enhancing cooperation with top venture capital partners over a wider range. Currently it has participated in the establishment of more than 30 venture capital funds worth a total of 17.8 billion yuan covering such strategic emerging industries as mobile Internet, new energies and biomedicine. As of May, those funds injected more than 4.2 billion yuan in 181 high-tech companies, including 128 based in Zhongguancun.

(http://www.chinadaily.com.cn/beijing/2014-11/13/content_18896465.htm)

Critical Thinking Questions:

(1) In which sector did venture capital investment have the most rapid development in China?

(2) What are the primary reasons for significant investment growth in these sectors?

Unit Six

Management Accounting

Learning Objectives

When you have studied this chapter, you should be able to:
* explain the difference between management accounting and financial accounting;
* explain the difference between product and period costs;
* define and identify the three manufacturing cost elements—direct materials, direct labor and manufacturing overhead;
* distinguish between variable and fixed costs;
* define budget and budgeting;
* identify the procedures of preparing a master budget;
* explain how CVP analysis can be used by management for decision making;
* explain break-even point and identify the method to determine the break-even point.

Warm-up: Dialogue

Flora: Morning Frank. I heard that you selected the course of management accounting yesterday.

Frank: Yes, I did. But actually, I'm still a little confused about the course. I know you are a postgraduate of MPAcc. Could you tell me what management accounting is concerned about?

Flora: Well, I will put it in an easy way. Management accounting focuses on internal reporting to managers who'd like to make business decisions with the help of such information.

Frank: As far as I know, the information needs of managers are rather different from those of external parties.

Flora: Quite right. That's why management accounting is also vital and necessary to the management of an entity. In fact, management accounting covers many activities, such as the determination of manufacturing costs, budgeting, cost control, cost behavior and cost-volume-profit analysis and so on.

Frank: I think management accounting is, to a large extent, distinctive from financial accounting.
Flora: Exactly. They are different in a number of ways.
Frank: Could you explain it to me in more detail?
Flora: Sure. First of all, they have different users. Users of financial accounting information are mainly external users, such as shareholders, creditors, stock exchanges, tax authorities and the public. In contrast, users of management information are mainly internal users like managers.
Frank: Then what about reports?
Flora: OK. Financial accounting mostly records and reports past economic transactions while management accounting provides information for internal decision-making and forecasting. What's more, the former should follow GAAP, but the latter could go beyond GAAP and meet internal needs only.
Frank: Sounds interesting.
Flora: Yes, you will find more difference when you pursue your selected course.

Text

Section 1 What Is Management Accounting?

Definition of Management Accounting

Management accounting (also termed as managerial accounting) is a branch of accounting which is concerned with the provision of financial and other information to all levels of management in an organization, to enable them to carry out their planning, controlling and decision-making responsibilities. Management accounting is used in all forms of organizations—profit-seeking businesses, not-for-profit organizations and the government.

Management Accounting versus Financial Accounting

There exist similarities between management accounting and financial accounting. Both of them deal with the economic events of a business and many areas are overlapping, e. g. inventory valuation, cost calculation, etc. However, management accounting can be distinguished from financial accounting in a number of ways: (1) primary users of the information; (2) types of reports; (3) frequency of reports; and (4) external verification.

1. **Primary users of the information**

The users of financial accounting information are external to the entity, e. g. shareholders, creditors, potential investors, customers and government agencies. The users of management accounting information are internal to the entity—mostly management.

2. **Types of reports**

Financial accounting meets the information needs of external users who are provided with general-purpose financial reports. These traditionally include the income statement, balance sheet and statement of cash flows. Such general-purpose financial reports are required, in most cases, by regulatory authorities and must comply with relevant accounting standards, such as GAAP. Reports generated from management accounting systems are special-purpose reports for internal users who demand specific financial and non-financial data on which to base their operating decisions. These reports, that do not have to comply with accounting standards, include financial budgets, sales forecasts, performance reports, cost reports, incremental analysis reports and so on. Besides, management can also have access to the details which underlie the preparation of the general-purpose financial reports.

3. Frequency of reports

In financial accounting system, reports are prepared at the end of each reporting period, usually at the end of the accounting year. Less detailed half-year reports are also prepared. Reports are required to be produced at regular intervals in compliance with income tax legislation and the demands of accounting standards. In contrast, reports derived from management accounting are prepared on demand as requested by management—daily, weekly, monthly, or at irregular intervals, as desired. Management must rely on the most up-to-date information available for its decision making.

4. External verification

General-purpose financial reports produced by an entity generally are required to be audited by external auditors, who verify that the reports provide a true and fair view of the financial position and performance of the entity. Management accounting's special-purpose reports are not required to be audited, although internal verification may be sought by management.

Section 2　Different Cost Classifications

A cost is an economic sacrifice of resources made in exchange for a product or service. Costs can be classified in different ways depending on the specific purpose of cost analysis. In other words, different costs will be used for different purposes. Moreover, these alternative classifications are not mutually exclusive, but are complementary to each other.

Cost Classifications for Income Measurement: Product and Period Costs

The terms product cost and period cost are fairly important in the development of an entity's income statement. Product costs can be thought of as attaching to the products since they are necessary for the physical existence of a saleable product. Product costs contain three groups of manufacturing elements which are direct materials, direct labor and manufacturing overhead.

1. Direct materials

All manufactured products require raw material ingredients. The flour used for bread, the steel used for a motor vehicle, the wood used for a furniture and the plastic used for a mobile phone are all examples of direct materials. Since direct materials physically become part of a finished product, they can be traced to the product. The cost of raw materials directly traceable as an integral part of a finished product is called direct materials cost. Direct materials do not include such miscellaneous items as lubricants, glue, screws or nails, which are treated as indirect materials and included in manufacturing overhead.

2. Direct labor

Direct labor costs comprise all labor costs for specific work performed that are conveniently and economically traceable to finished products. Examples are the wages paid to carpenters in the construction of a house or wages paid to assembly line workers in the workshop. Some other labor will be required to support the production process but cannot be directly traceable to finished products. For example, the salaries paid to maintenance personnel and production supervisors will be classified as indirect labor costs and included in manufacturing overhead.

3. Manufacturing overhead (Factory overhead)

All manufacturing costs except direct materials and direct labor are included in manufacturing overhead cost. Indirect materials, indirect labor, light and power, maintenance, insurance, rent and depreciation are all examples of manufacturing overhead items. Manufacturing overhead costs are not practically or conveniently traceable to finished products. Therefore, an overhead application rate is developed by dividing the total expected factory overhead cost by the basis used to measure normal productive capacity (e. g. direct labor hours).

Period costs (also called period expenses) are identified with a specific time interval since they are not directly required to produce a saleable product. Accordingly, they are charged as expenses on the income statement mostly in the period in which they are incurred. The period costs are generally classified into three categories: selling, administrative and financial expenses according to their functional nature. For example, advertising expense and the general manager's salary would be treated as period costs. So does interest expense.

Cost Classifications for Planning and Control: Variable and Fixed Costs

Management commonly must evaluate the effect of changes in sales or production volume on the profits of the entity. One of the most widely used ways to classify costs is by their cost behavior, which means the measure of how a cost will react to changes in the level of business activity, e. g. units produced, machine hours or labor hours. In this sense, costs mainly fall into two broad types: variable costs and fixed costs.

1. Variable costs

Variable costs are defined as costs which vary in direct proportion to the volume of production. Direct materials, direct labor and certain manufacturing overhead items such as the electricity cost for machinery operation are variable costs.

2. Fixed costs

Fixed costs are defined as those costs which remain relatively constant, within normal operating ranges, irrespective of variations in the volume of production. In a manufacturing operation, a fixed cost is the same regardless of the units of production completed during the period. Many of the manufacturing overhead items are fixed costs. Examples are depreciation of equipments, factory rent and supervisors' salaries. A fixed cost may be termed as "fixed" only in a given period of time and a given range of capacity. In other words, costs which are fixed in the short run may become variable in the longer run when capacity is increased.

Section 3 Management Accounting and Decision-making

Decision making involves a choice between alternative courses of action, and the alternative chosen is usually selected on the basis of some measure of profitability or cost savings. Business decisions range from the routine and repetitive to the complex and non-recurring. What products to produce, how to produce them, what price to charge, how to sell them, how to allocate resources, what equipment to buy, and whether or not to expand the operating capacity are all examples of business decisions.

Although there is no universal way managers make decisions, the decision-making process generally is composed of these steps: establish goals and define the problems, gather information on alternative courses of action, evaluate consequences of alternatives, and make a decision. Normally, the quality of decision-making is highly dependent on the information available to the decision maker. In a business, management accounting provides most of the quantitative information (revenues, costs, investing and operating statistics) required to make a choice among alternatives. At the same time, qualitative factors such as management intuition and experience, public image, social responsibility, competition, etc. often play an important role in a decision.

In most cases, management accounting tools are adopted by managers to make business decisions. Such tools contain budgeting, cost-volume-profit analysis, cost behavior analysis and so on.

① Budgeting

A budget is a detailed written plan that shows how resources are expected to be acquired and used during a specified time period to achieve organizational objectives. A budget period is commonly the accounting year. Usually, the budget for the year would be subdivided into shorter periods such as months or quarters so that timely comparisons of actual and budgeted results can be made. The process of preparing a budget is an essential phase of managing a business in an efficient and effective manner. A budget, as a management tool, serves management by providing a formal plan of an entity's future course of action according to well-defined goals.

Initially, budgeting identifies certain financial and operating targets which provide the direction for the entity's activities and transactions. Then, as actual performance occurs, it is monitored and verified against the related budgets for control purposes. When significant differences (variances) between actual and planned performances are identified, they are investigated and corrected whenever possible. Therefore, budgeting mainly has the following benefits:

- It can force management to make plans on a systematic basis.
- It can provide management with a framework for responsibility.
- It can coordinate the activities of different departments of the organization to ensure maximum integration of effort towards common goals.
- It can serve as a communication device with which the various managers could exchange information concerning goals, ideas and achievements.
- It can furnish management as well as employees with motivation in the form of the goals to be achieved.

A master budget is a set of interrelated budgets representing a comprehensive plan of action for a specified time period. In the preparation of the master budget, a business will normally prepare the following budgets one after another:

(1) Sales budget
(2) Production budget
(3) Direct material budget
(4) Direct labor budget
(5) Manufacturing overhead budget
(6) Cost of goods sold budget
(7) Selling expense budget
(8) Administrative expense budget
(9) Financial expense budget
(10) Master budget

Example 6-1: Production budget

Scooter Ltd manufactures two products, A and B, and is preparing its budget for 20X8. Both products are made by the same grade of labor, grade Q. The company currently holds 800 units of A and 1,200 units of B in stock, but 250 of these units of B have just been discovered to have deteriorated in quality, and must therefore be scrapped. Budgeted sales of A are 3,000 units and of B are 4,000 units, provided that the company maintains finished goods stocks at a level equal to 3 months' sales.

Grade Q labor was originally expected to produce 1 unit of A in two hours and 1 unit of B in three hours, at an hourly rate of $5.50 per hour. In discussions with trade union negotiators, however, it has been agreed that the hourly wage rate should be raised by $0.5 per hour, provided that the times to produce A and B are reduced by 20%.

◆ **Required:**

Prepare the production budget and direct labor budget for 20X8.

> ***Solution:***
> Closing stocks of A should be 3/12 × 3,000 = 750 units
> Closing stocks of B should be 3/12 × 4,000 = 1,000 units
> The expected time to produce a unit of A will now be 80% × 2 hours = 1.6 hours, and the time for a unit of B will be 2.4 hours. The hourly wage rate will be $6.
>
> (1) Production budget
>
> | | Product A/units | Product B/units |
> | --- | --- | --- |
> | Budget sales | 3,000 | 4,000 |
> | Closing stocks | 750 | 1,000 |
> | Opening stocks | (800) | (1,200) |
> | Stocks scrapped | | 250 |
> | Production | 2,950 | 4,050 |
>
> (2) Direct labor budget
>
> | | Grade Q/hours | Hourly wage/ $ | Costs/ $ |
> | --- | --- | --- | --- |
> | 2,950 units of Product A | 4,720 | 6 | 28,320 |
> | 4,050 units of Product B | 9,720 | 6 | 58,320 |
> | Total | 14,440 | | 86,640 |

II CVP Analysis

Cost-volume-profit (CVP) analysis is mostly used by management to evaluate the inter-relationships of selling price, sales volume and costs so that acceptable profits can be planned. CVP analysis is particularly important to management during the budgeting process, when various alternative strategies regarding the future financial performance must be evaluated. Cost-volume-profit analysis can assist in answering following questions:

(1) What is the business' break-even point?

(2) What level of sales must be achieved to earn a desired amount of net profit?

(3) If selling prices are increased or decreased, what will be the effect on sales volume and the break-even point?

(4) What will be the impact on sales volume and profit if advertising costs are increased?

(5) What additional sales volume is required to offset an increase in purchasing cost?

(6) What is the most profitable sales mix?

In all, CVP analysis is used by management to identify the levels of operating activity needed to avoid loss, achieve target profit and supervise performance.

Break-even analysis is actually the starting point for CVP analysis. The break-even point is the sales volume at which revenues and total costs are equal, with no net profit or loss. Net profit is earned above the break-even point and a net loss is incurred below it. Although a break-even point is not a desired performance target because of the lack of profit, it does indicate the level of activity necessary to avoid a loss. As such, the break-even point represents a target of the minimum sales volume that must be achieved by business.

The formulas for calculating the break-even point in units of product and in dollar of sales are:

$$\text{Units of products to break even} = \frac{\text{Total fixed expenses}}{\text{Contribution margin per unit}}$$

$$\text{Break-even sales} = \text{Break-even units} \times \text{Sales price per unit}$$

In the above formula, contribution margin per unit is the difference between the selling price per unit and its variable costs.

Graphically, the break-even point can be illustrated as follows (Figure 6-1):

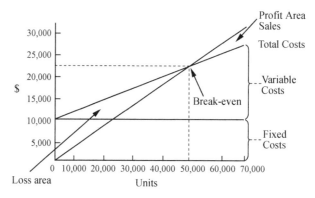

Figure 6-1 CVP Analysis Graph

Chapter Round-up

- Management accounting differs from financial accounting in a couple of ways despite that both of them provide information of business transactions and events.
- Costs can be categorized in different ways depending on different purposes of cost analysis.
- Generally, costs can be divided into product costs and period costs, which is particular decisive in establishing an income statement.
- According to different cost behavior, costs can be classified into two types: variable costs and fixed costs.
- There are a number of management accounting tools including budgeting, cost-volume-profit analysis, cost behavior analysis and so on. They play a vital and critical role in decision-making by the management.
- A budget is a quantified plan of action for a forthcoming accounting period.
- CVP analysis concerns on the relationship among cost, volume and profit.
- The break-even point is the sales volume at which revenues and total costs are equal, with zero profit.

Glossary

verification	n.	确认,核实,查证
incremental	adj.	增加的,增值的
legislation	n.	立法,法律
audit	v. & n.	审计
product costs		生产成本
period costs		期间费用
manufacturing overhead		制造费用
miscellaneous	adj.	混杂的,各种各样的
assembly line		流水线
traceable	adj.	可追溯的,可查出的
maintenance	n.	维护,维修
cost behavior		成本性态
variable costs		变动成本
fixed costs		固定成本
quantitative	adj.	定量的
qualitative	adj.	定性的
cost-volume-profit	n.	本量利
variance	n.	差异
integration	n.	集成,综合
motivation	n.	动机,推动
strategy	n.	战略,策略
break-even	adj.	保本的,不盈不亏的
contribution margin		边际贡献

Review Questions

(1) What are the basic differences between financial accounting and management accounting?

(2) Distinguish between product and period costs. Identify which of the following is a product cost and which is a period cost:

a. containers used to package finished goods;

b. depreciation—manufacturing equipment;

c. financial manager's salary;

d. salaries of workers handling inventory during production;

e. insurance—factory;

f. production supervisor's salary.

(3) Explain the basic difference between a fixed cost and a variable cost. Give some examples of a fixed cost and a variable cost respectively.

(4) Why is cost-volume-profit analysis such an important management topic?

(5) What is the contribution margin? Why is it an important management accounting measure?

(6) How can break-even analysis be extended to determine the sales volume required to earn a desired net profit?

(7) What are the benefits of budgeting?

(8) Which budget is mostly the starting point for the preparation of a master budget?

(9) Explain a budget period.

(10) What are the components of a master budget?

Exercises

1. True or false

(1) Management accounting information is prepared primarily for external parties such as stockholders and creditors.

(2) Management accounting pertains to both past and future items; financial accounting focuses primarily on past transactions and events.

(3) Financial accounting reports could go beyond accounting standards while management accounting should comply with GAAP.

(4) Management accounting is directed to facilitate the management function of planning and controlling.

(5) Decision making can be viewed as an integral part of planning and controlling rather than as a separate independent management function.

(6) Costing is an integral part of management accounting.

(7) Fixed costs refer to the costs that never change.

(8) CVP analysis portrays the relationship among cost, volume and price.

(9) The business can make a profit at the break-even point.

(10) Contribution margin per unit is the difference between the selling price per unit and its fixed costs.

2. Fill in the parentheses

Management uses different costs for different purposes in decision-making. Included in the different costs are: product costs, period costs, variable costs and fixed costs.

◆ **Required:**

Choose the concept of cost mentioned above that best describes the cost involved in each of the following situations.

① The paper used to produce this textbook is a (   ) cost on the profit and loss statement. It is also a (   ) cost in terms of cost behavior.

② Depreciation for printing equipment used for this book is a (   ) cost on the profit and loss statement. It is a (   ) cost in terms of cost behavior.

③ A commission paid to the sales representative who sold this book is a (   ) cost on the profit and loss statement.

④ Depreciation for the delivery vehicle used by the sales representative is a (   ) cost on the profit and loss statement. In terms of cost behavior, it is a (   ) cost.

3. Case: CVP analysis

Rich-up Ltd sells a new product, an electric hedge trimmer. The trimmer sells for $160 per unit with a contribution margin rate of 40%. Annual fixed costs are $1,600,000.

◆ **Required:**

① What are the variable costs per unit?

② How many units must the company sell to break even?

③ What is the break-even point in sales dollars?

④ If the company wants to earn a before-tax net profit of $96,000, how many units must be sold? What sales dollar level is required?

4. Case: Production budgets

JK Limited has recently completed its sales forecasts for the year to December 31, 20X8. It expects to sell two products J and K at prices of $135 and $145 each respectively. Sales demand is expected to be as follows: J 10,000 units and K 6,000 units.

Both products use the same skilled labor but in different hours. J requires 6 hours per unit and K requires 4 hours per unit. The skilled labor rate is expected to be $6.00 per hour.

Stocks of finished goods on January 1, 20X8 are expected to be as follows: J 600 units at $70 each and K 800 units at $60 each. All stocks are to be reduced by 15% from their opening levels by the end of 20X8 and are valued using the FIFO method.

◆ **Required:**

Prepare production budget and direct labor budget for the year to December 31, 20X8.

Group Activities

Managers who are responsible for the planning, organizing, controlling and evaluation of the area under their control are also accountable for their performance to their superiors. Managers' performance can be evaluated by their superiors using a number of criteria appropriate to the activities under the control of the managers. For example, the manager in charge of production in a manufacturing business could be evaluated by means of the physical units of output, the average cost of the product produced, the level of units wasted, the number of reworks necessary on faulty units produced, labor turnover and machine breakdowns.

◆ **Required:**

Break the class into three groups. Each group should be assigned one of the following types of management units: a sales department of a manufacturing enterprise; a local police station; the lending department of a financial institution; a local suburban library. Each group should then consider and identify which criteria (financial and non-financial) could be used to evaluate the performance of the manager in charge of the organizational unit.

 Supplementary Reading

Activity-Based Costing (ABC)

Cost accounting systems are concerned with assigning costs of manufacturing to products using a job order cost system or process cost system. Costs are assigned to cost objects (the job or process) directly in the case of direct materials and direct labor, and by an overhead application rate in the case of indirect costs categorized as manufacturing overhead. Traditionally, overhead costs have been applied to products on the bases of direct labor hours or costs. Recent years there is a decrease in the role played by labor in modern manufacturing processes, with labor costs continually falling to a small proportion of total costs in computerized and automated production systems. This fact, together with situations where a manufacturing entity produces a large number of products which vary in both volume and complexity of production, has led to the conclusion that applying overheads on a single basis of labor hours or costs can produce distorted and inaccurate unit costs. Activity-based costing (ABC) has been developed as a means of overcoming these problems and increasing the accuracy of overhead allocation and hence unit cost of products.

Activity-based costing is a system in which the production processes have been analyzed and broken down into activities. An activity is any event or act which causes the incurrence of costs. Costs associated with these activities are assigned to products on the basis of cost drivers appropriate to these activities. Under ABC, the final cost of a product is the sum of the costs of all the activities which have contributed to the manufacturing of the product. Examples of these activities include machine set-ups, materials purchasing, processing production orders, receipt of materials, machine time and computer hours logged. Cost drivers have to be determined as a means of assigning costs to products depending on how they consume these activities. Examples of activities and possible cost drivers which would be used to assign costs to products are set out below:

Activities	**Cost drivers**
Machine set-ups	Set-up hours
Materials purchasing	Number of orders
Production orders	Number of orders
Materials receipts	Number of receipts
Machine usage	Number of hours used
Computer usage	Computer hours logged

To appreciate how ABC can reduce the degree of distortion that can result from inappropriate overhead application, consider a company which produces two products, A and B. Product A is a high-volume item requiring little machine set-up time, few purchase and production orders, and little computer time. Product B, on the other hand, is a low-volume item, which requires numerous machine set-ups, many purchase and production orders to be processed, and relatively high usage of computer time. If the direct labor hours worked for both products are the same, overheads costs associated with the activities highlighted would lead to an equal amount of overhead being allocated to A and B. Assigning the costs of the activities on the basis of the cost driver for each activity would invariably lead to a different overhead cost amount being allocated in line with the product's demand on those activities. ABC is sometimes referred to as transaction costing since it improves the accuracy with which costs are traced or assigned to units of production.

Activity-based costing provides many benefits such as accurate pricing, better allocation of resources, elimination of non-value adding activities, and the like. The method however has many disadvantages or limitations as well.

Once implemented, an activity-based costing system is costly to maintain. Data concerning numerous activity measures must be collected, checked and entered into the system. Besides, ABC produces numbers such as product margins, that are odds with the numbers produced by traditional costing systems. But managers are accustomed to using traditional costing systems to run their operations and traditional costing systems are often used in performance evaluation. In all, a major limitation is that activity-based costing places too much attention to detail and control on processes. This causes a severe problem in that it obscures the bigger picture by causing the organization to lose sight of strategic long-term objectives in a quest for small or short term savings.

Critical Thinking Questions:

(1) What is the activity-based costing system? Give some examples of cost drivers.

(2) What are the advantages and disadvantages of activity-based costing?

Unit Seven

Auditing

 Learning Objectives

When you have studied this chapter, you should be able to:
* identify the basic definition of auditing and its objective as well;
* understand the professional standards and professional ethics;
* differentiate the different types of audits;
* define audit risk, identify the components of audit risk and know the relationship among them;
* illustrate the audit process model and define materiality;
* describe the meaning of "sufficient and appropriate audit evidence" and understand the frequently used procedures for obtaining audit evidence;
* define test of control and substantive procedures respectively;
* understand the contents and form of the auditor's report;
* distinguish between the different types of audit opinions;
* state the two circumstances that require an auditor's report containing an opinion other than an unqualified one.

 Warm-up: Dialogue

Richard: Good morning, Rebecca.
Rebecca: Good morning, Richard. Welcome to our company. How are you getting along with the work here?
Richard: Rather busy. What we have done is just overall understanding of business operation and review of part of the accounting records, source documents and financial statements.
Rebecca: That's great. You know our primary concern is whether you could complete your audit work by the end of this month. If so, we could complete the report to the

	board of directors, including the audit report.
Richard:	Don't worry, please. I think we would finish the work before the deadline.
Rebecca:	Sounds good. Would you please tell me something about the report?
Richard:	Definitely. The most important thing in the report is to express an opinion whether the financial statements are true and fair and in compliance with related laws and regulations.
Rebecca:	Well, what about the development with your opinion of our company?
Richard:	To be frank, your financial records and statements which we have reviewed are mostly presented fairly and they are in accordance with generally accepted accounting principles.
Rebecca:	Great! That's to say, our accounting practice and records are consistent with that of the previous years.
Richard:	Exactly.
Rebecca:	Thank you very much. We are looking forward to the formal report.

Text

Section 1 Definition and Objective

Definition of Auditing

In financial accounting, we have learned that one reason that an entity issues financial statements is to convey information about the financial condition and operation results of the entity to interested parties. These parties or users of financial statements may be present and prospective shareholders, creditors, government, customers and suppliers. Because these users do not have access to inside information about a company, they must rely on the integrity of management to ensure that the financial information disclosed is not materially misstated. Therefore, one reason for auditing is to reduce the information risk that the financial statements are false or misleading. Additionally, companies regulated by Securities and Exchange Commission are required to have annual independent audits. For example, the major stock exchanges (including NYSE, NASDAQ, London Stock Exchange, Tokyo NIKKEI, and so on) have statuary rules that require all listed companies to have their annual report audited.

An audit is defined as an evidence-based engagement in which the auditor provides reasonable assurance that financial information is free of material misstatement when compared to an identified financial reporting framework.

The objective of an audit is to enable auditors to express an opinion whether the financial statements give a true and fair view of the entity's affairs, and have been properly prepared in accordance with the applicable reporting framework (e.g. relevant legislation and accounting standards).

Professional Standards and Professional Ethics

1. Professional standards

Issued by the International Auditing and Assurance Standards Board of the International Federation of Accountants (IFAC), International Standards on Auditing (ISA) are professional standards for the performance of financial audit of financial information. ISA covers a number of areas of auditing, such as audit objectives, responsibilities, audit planning, audit evidence, internal control and audit report.

Many countries have issued their own auditing standards, many of which predated the international standards. The professional or regulatory bodies in those countries usually provide a detailed comparison between their standards or guidelines and the International Standards on Auditing. It should be noted that ISA does not override local or national standards or regulations.

2. Professional ethics

Many national professional accounting and auditing organizations have their own codes of ethics and rules of professional conduct. The general ethical principles which govern an auditor's duties and responsibilities include:

- Independence

Being a major attribute of the professional accountant in public practice and a special condition of objectivity, independence applies in several ways during an audit. For example, when auditors provide audit services for client company, referral fees are not acceptable in order to keep independent. Therefore, auditors should have a position to take an unbiased viewpoint in the performance of audit tests, analysis of results and attestation in the audit report. Remarkably, auditors are required to be independent in fact and appearance.

- Integrity and objectivity

It requires a professional accountant should be straightforward and honest in all professional and business relationships. The principle of objectivity imposes the obligation on all professional accountants to be fair, intellectually honest, and free of conflicts of interest. For instance, professionals should neither accept nor offer gifts that might appear to have a significant improper influence on their professional judgment.

- Professional competence and due care

A professional accountant has a continuing duty to maintain professional knowledge and skill at the level required to ensure that a client receives competent professional service based on current developments in practice, legislation and techniques.

- Confidentiality

A professional accountant should respect the confidentiality of information acquired as a result of professional and business relationships and should not disclose any such information to third parties without proper and specific authority unless there is a legal or professional right or duty to disclose.

- Professional behavior

An accountant should act in a manner consistent with the good reputation of the profession and should refrain from any conduct that might bring discredit to the profession regarding responsibilities to clients, third parties, other members of the accountancy profession, employers and the general public.

- Technical standards

Professional services should always be carried out in accordance with the relevant technical and professional standards. These services should follow the technical standards such as International Standards on Auditing, rules of the accountant's professional body and relevant legislation.

Limitations of Audit

Auditing can provide reasonable but not absolute assurance as to the "truth and fairness" of financial statements. There are a number of reasons why this is so:

(1) Auditing is not a purely objective exercise. Auditors have to make professional judgments which involve subjective assessment.

(2) Auditing must be justified on a cost-benefit basis. The high volume of transactions and the potentially enormous cost of carrying out 100% verification results in auditors selecting samples, testing transactions and balances, and drawing conclusions from the samples selected. As a result, some sampling risk is inevitable.

(3) There are inherent limitations in accounting and internal control systems. The potential of management override of controls and the possibility of collusive circumvention of controls mean that there is always the possibility of material fraud or error occurring. Auditing procedures are not designed to identify 100% of such frauds or errors.

(4) Audit evidence is persuasive; it can seldom be conclusive. In other words, audit evidence indicates what is probable rather than what is certain. The underlying fact is that some figures in the accounts are estimates and some require judgment.

Hence, auditors can only express an opinion; they cannot certify whether accounts are completely correct.

Section 2   Types of Audits

Audits are typically classified into three types: audits of financial statements, operational audits, and compliance audits.

Audits of Financial Statements (External Auditing)

Audits of financial statements examine financial statements to determine if they give a true and fair view or fairly present the financial situation and performance in conformity with specified criteria.

Operational Audits (Internal Auditing)

An operational audit is a study of a specific unit of an organization for the purpose of measuring its performance. Operational audits review all or part of the organization's operating procedures to evaluate effectiveness and efficiency of the operation. They may include the review of internal control system, financial and operating information, compliance with laws or whatever area the organization feels evaluation is needed. Recommendations are normally made to management for improvements.

Compliance Audits

A compliance audit is a review of an organization's operating process to determine whether the organization is following specific procedures, rules or regulations set out by some higher authority. An example of a compliance audit is an audit of a bank to determine if they comply with capital reserve requirements. Another example would be an audit of taxpayers to see if they comply with national tax law. Compliance audits are quite common in not-for-profit organizations funded at least in part by government. Many government entities and non-profit organizations that receive financial assistance from the federal government must arrange for compliance audits.

As a consequence, there are two basic types of auditors: independent external auditors and internal auditors. The independent external auditor is primarily concerned with financial statement audits, while the internal auditor concentrates on operational audits. The governmental auditor, who is most likely to determine compliance, takes both the functions of internal and external auditor.

Co-ordination between the external and internal auditors of an organization will minimize duplication of work and encourage a wide coverage of audit issues and areas. This co-ordination will involve: periodic meetings to plan overall audit and to discuss matters of mutual interest, mutual access to audit programs and working papers, exchange of audit reports and management letters, and common development of audit techniques.

Section 3 Audit Risk

Definition of Audit Risk

In recent years there has been a shift towards risk-based auditing. This refers to the development of auditing techniques which are responsive to risk factors in an audit. Auditors apply judgment to determine what level of risk pertains to different areas of a client's system and devise appropriate audit tests. This approach should ensure that the greatest audit effort is directed at the riskiest areas, so that the chance of detecting errors is improved and excessive time is not spent on "safe" areas. The increased use of risk-based auditing reflects two factors.

(1) The growing complexity of the business environment increases the danger of fraud or misstatement. (2) Pressures are increasingly exerted by audit clients for the auditors to keep fee levels down while providing an improved level of service.

In essence, audit risk is the risk that the auditor gives an inappropriate audit opinion when the financial statements are materially misstated. Audit risk can never be completely eliminated. The higher the audit risk, the more evidence must be gathered in order for the auditor to obtain sufficient assurance as a basis for expressing an opinion on the financial statements. Audit risk has three components: inherent risk, control risk and detection risk (Figure 7-1).

Inherent risk is the susceptibility of an account balance or class of transactions to misstatement that could be material, individually or when aggregated with misstatements in other balances of classes, irrespective of related internal controls.

Control risk is the risk that a material misstatement is not prevented, or detected and corrected on a timely basis by the accounting and internal control systems of the client.

Detection risk is the risk that an auditor's substantive procedures will not detect a misstatement that exists in an account balance or class of transactions and that could be material.

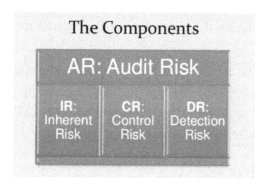

Figure 7-1 Components of Audit Risk

Audit Risk Model

The relationship among the components can be expressed mathematically in the audit risk model:

$$AR = IR \times CR \times DR$$

Among them, IR and CR exist independently of the audit and auditors have no control over IR and CR. In contrast, DR relates to the nature, extent and timing of the auditor's procedures, which means auditors can control the level of DR. In practice, the auditor determines an acceptable value for AR (based on the assessment of the auditor's business risk for the particular audit), inserts the values assessed for IR and CR (neither of which the auditor can change), and computes DR, which determines the amount of testing to be done.

Section 4 Audit Process Model, Audit Evidence and Audit Procedures

Audit Process Model

The audit process model is to provide detailed audit steps to be performed during the audit fieldwork that will achieve the specific audit objectives. It is illustrated in the as follows (Table 7-1):

Table 7-1 Audit Process Model

	Phase I: Client Acceptance
Objective	Determine both acceptance of a client and acceptance by a client. Decide on acquiring a new client or continuation of relationship with an existing one and the type and amount of staff required.
Procedures	(1) Evaluate the client's background and reasons for the audit. (2) Determine whether the auditor is able to meet the ethical requirements regarding the client. (3) Determine need for other professionals. (4) Communicate with predecessor auditor. (5) Prepare client proposal. (6) Select staff to perform the audit. (7) Obtain an engagement letter.
	Phase II: Audit Plan (Audit Program)
Objective	Determine the amount and type of evidence and review required to give the auditor assurance that there is no material misstatement of the financial statements.
Procedures	(1) Perform audit procedures to understand the entity and its environment including the entity's internal control. (2) Assess the risks of material misstatements of the financial statements. (3) Determine materiality. (4) Prepare the planning memorandum and audit program containing the auditor's response to the identified risks.
	Phase III: Testing and Evidence
Objective	Test for evidence supporting internal controls and the fairness of the financial statements.
Procedures	(1) Tests of controls. (2) Substantive tests of transactions. (3) Analytical procedures. (4) Tests of details of balances. (5) Search for unrecorded liabilities.
	Phase IV: Evaluation and Reporting
Objective	Complete the audit procedures and issue an opinion.
Procedures	(1) Evaluate governance evidence. (2) Perform procedures to identify subsequent events. (3) Review financial statements and other report material. (4) Perform wrap-up procedures. (5) Prepare Matters for Attention of Partners. (6) Report to the board of directors. (7) Prepare Audit report.

II Planning Materiality

Information is material if its omission or misstatement could influence the economic decisions of users of the financial statements. Thus, materiality provides a threshold or cutoff point rather than being a primary qualitative characteristic which information must have. Materiality is the degree of inaccuracy or imprecision that is still considered acceptable given the purpose of the financial statements.

Planning materiality is a concept that is used to design the audit such that the auditor can obtain reasonable assurance that any error of a relevant (material) size or nature will be identified. The lower the materiality, the more costly the audit. If any error of whatever small size needs to be found in the audit, the auditor would spend significantly more time than when a certain level of imprecision (higher materiality level) is considered acceptable.

What is material is often difficult to determine in practice. However, four factors are generally considered: size of item, nature of item, the circumstances, and the cost and benefit of auditing the item. Considering all these materiality factors, then, at what amount should materiality be set? The international standards give no guidelines. In practice, however, every accounting firm has its own set of guidelines or "rules of thumb" related to a financial statement base such as net income, total revenues, etc. Rules of thumb commonly used in practice include: 5 to 10 percent of net income before taxes, 5 to 10 percent of current assets, 5 to 10 percent of current liabilities, 0.5 to 2 percent of total assets, and so on.

Take the following case for example. A few days before the end of 20X9, $50,000 expenditure for the repair of equipment was incorrectly charged to the equipment account rather than to operating expenses. As a result (ignoring depreciation), total assets should be stated at $1,490,000 rather than $1,540,000 and income before taxes should be stated at $58,000 rather than $108,000. Are the financial statements fairly presented and not materially misleading?

Analysis: The financial statements are materially misstated, primarily because net income, an important basis of materiality, is overstated by 86%. This overstatement of net income is something that could definitely change the decisions of a financial statement user, i.e. it is material.

III Audit Evidence and Audit Procedures for Obtaining Audit Evidence

1. Audit evidence

Management is responsible for the true and fair presentation of financial statements so that they reflect the nature and operations of the company based on the applicable financial reporting framework. Management prepares the financial statements based upon the accounting records and other information that the auditor may use as audit evidence such as minutes of meetings, confirmations from third parties, analysts' reports, comparable data about competitors, and controls manuals.

Audit evidence is all of the information used by the auditor in arriving at the conclusions on which the audit opinion is based. It includes the accounting records and other information underlying the financial statements. It is the auditor's job to obtain "sufficient and appropriate audit evidence" to be able to draw reasonable conclusions. Among them, sufficiency is the measure of the quantity of audit evidence while appropriateness is the measure of the quality of audit evidence. The sufficiency and appropriateness of audit evidence to support the auditor's conclusions are a matter of professional judgment.

2. Audit procedures for obtaining audit evidence

An auditor obtains audit evidence by one or more of the following evidence gathering techniques:

Inquiry. Been the most frequently used techniques for evidence gathering, inquiry consists of seeking information of knowledgeable persons inside or outside the entity. Examples are written or oral information from the client in response to specific questions during the audit.

Observation. Observation consists of looking at a process or procedure being performed by others, for example, the observation by the auditor of the accounting of inventories by the entity's personnel or observation of internal control procedures that leave no audit trail. Observation provides audit evidence about the performance of a process or procedure.

Inspection. Inspection is the auditor's examination of the client's documents and records to substantiate the information that is or should be included in the financial statements. Examples of evidence gathering by inspection techniques is the review of sales orders, sales invoices, shipping documents, bank statements, etc.

Re-calculation. Re-calculation consists of checking the arithmetical accuracy of source documents and accounting records or performing independent calculations.

Re-performance. Re-performance is the auditor's independent execution of procedures or controls that were originally performed as part of the entity's internal control, either manually or through the use of CAATs (Computer Assisted Audit Techniques), for example, reperforming the ageing of accounts receivable.

Confirmation. Confirmation consists of the response to an inquiry of a third party to corroborate information contained in the accounting records. For example, the auditor ordinarily seeks direct confirmation of receivables by communication with debtors. Confirmation is the auditor's receipt of a written or oral response from an independent third party verifying the accuracy of information requested.

Analytical procedures. It consists of the analysis of significant ratios and trends including the resulting investigation of fluctuations and relationships that are inconsistent with other relevant information.

Test of Control and Substantive Procedures

The auditor's assessment of the identified risks provides a basis for determining which is the appropriate audit approach for designing and performing audit procedures. Risk assessment procedures by themselves do not provide sufficient appropriate audit evidence on which to base the audit opinion, however. Risk assessment must be supplemented by further audit procedures in the form of tests of control and substantive procedures. In some cases, the auditor may determine that only tests of controls are appropriate, whereas in other cases, the auditor may determine that only substantive procedures are appropriate. Generally, some combination of the two is used.

1. Tests of control

Tests of control are audit procedures to test the effectiveness of control policies and procedures in support of a reduced control risk. Key internal controls must be supported by assessed control risk. The lower the assessed control risk, the more extensive the tests should be in order to support the high degree of reliance upon internal control. How much and what evidence is sufficient to support a specific assessed level of control risk is a matter of professional judgment.

The nature of tests of control is that the tests generally consist of one (or a combination) of four types of evidence-gathering techniques: inquiry of client personnel, observation, inspection (examination of documents), and reperformance (or recalculation). For example, the auditor may determine that unauthorized personnel are not allowed access to the computer files by asking the computer librarian or a user of the computer system. For another example, one might be assured about the effectiveness of inventory counting control procedures by seeing that those performing the count follow management's written instructions.

The assessed level of control risk has a direct effect on the design of substantive tests. The lower the assessed level of control risk, the less evidence the auditor needs from substantive tests. The auditor's control risk assessment influences the nature, timing and extent of substantive procedures to be performed. Even if the auditor tests controls, there are inherent limitations to internal control including the risk of management override, the possibility of human error, and the effect of systems changes. Therefore, substantive procedures for material classes of transactions, account balances, and disclosures are always required to obtain sufficient appropriate audit evidence.

2. Substantive procedures

Substantive procedures are tests performed to obtain audit evidence to detect material misstatements in the financial statements. Substantive procedures are responses to the audit's assessment of the risk of material misstatement. The higher the assessed risk, the more likely the extent of the substantive procedures will increase and the timing of procedures will be performed close to the period. Actually, substantive procedures in the audit are designed to reduce detection risk relating to specific financial statement assertions (existence, completeness, rights and obligations, valuation, etc).

The nature of the test is of two types: tests of details of transactions and balances, and analytical procedures. Tests of transactions are audit procedures related to examining the processing of particular classes of transactions through the accounting system and are usually performed for accounts such as property and equipment, long-term debt and equity accounts. An example of a test of transactions is the search for unrecorded liabilities.

Tests of balances are substantive tests that provide either reasonable assurance of the validity of a general ledger balance or identify a misstatement in the account. When testing balances the auditor is concerned with overstatement or understatement of the item in the financial statement. These tests are used to examine the actual details making up high turnover accounts such as cash, accounts receivable, accounts payable, etc. Tests of balances are important because the auditor's ultimate objective is to express an opinion on financial statements that are made up of account balances. In audits of small businesses, auditors may rely exclusively on tests of balances.

Analytical procedures refer to the analysis of significant ratios and trends including the resulting investigation of fluctuations and relationships that are inconsistent with other relevant information or deviate from predictable amounts. One of the advantages of performing analytical procedures is that it can indicate whether account balances or other data appear reasonable with the use of comparisons and relationships analysis. When analytical procedures identify significant fluctuations or relationships that are inconsistent with other relevant information or that deviate from predicted amounts, the auditor should perform other procedures like investigating and obtaining adequate explanations and appropriate corroborative evidence.

Section 5 Audit Report and Audit Opinion

Audit Report

The audit report is the means by which the external auditors express their opinion on the truth and fairness of a company's financial statements. Hence, the audit report should contain a clear written expression of opinion on the financial statements taken as a whole.

A formal and complete audit report should include the following basic elements:
- Title
- Addressee
- Introductory paragraph
- Scope paragraph
- Opinion paragraph
- The date of the report
- The auditor's address
- Auditor's signature

The following one is a standard unqualified opinion audit report taken as an example to illustrate the contents and form of the audit report.

Example 7-1:

Report of Independent Auditors

To the Stockholders and Board of Directors of the Wrigley Company:

We have audited the accompanying consolidated balance sheet of the Wrigley Company as of December 31, 20X8 and the related consolidated statement of income, stockholders' equity and cash flows for the year then ended. These financial statements are the responsibility of the Company's management. Our responsibility is to express an opinion on these financial statements based on our audits.

We conducted our audits in accordance with auditing standards generally accepted in the United States. Those standards require that we plan and perform the audit to obtain reasonable assurance about whether the financial statements are free of material misstatement. An audit includes examining, on a test basis, evidence supporting the amounts and disclosures in the financial statements. An audit also includes assessing the accounting principles used and significant estimates made by management, as well as evaluating the overall financial statement presentation. We believe that our audits provide a reasonable basis for our opinion.

In our opinion, the financial statements referred to above present fairly, in all material respects, the consolidated financial position of the Company as of December 31, 20X8, and the consolidated results of their operations and their cash flows for the year then ended in conformity with accounting principles generally accepted in the United States.

Ernst & Young LLP
Chicago, Illinois
January 21, 20X9

Audit Opinion

The opinion expressed in the audit report may be one of four types: unqualified opinion, qualified opinion, adverse opinion or disclaimer of opinion.

1. Unqualified opinion

The auditor's unqualified report should be expressed when the auditor concludes that the financial statements give a true and fair view (or present fairly, in all material respects) in accordance with the identified financial reporting framework.

In an auditor's report on financial statements, an unqualified opinion is issued in a clear and affirmative manner when the auditor is satisfied in all material respects that:

- The financial information has been prepared using acceptable accounting policies, which have been consistently applied.

- The financial information complies with relevant regulations and statutory requirements.
- The view presented by the financial information as a whole is consistent with the auditor's knowledge of the business of the entity.
- There is adequate disclosure of all material matters relevant to the proper presentation of the financial information.

* **Unqualified opinion with an explanatory paragraph**

In certain circumstance, an audit report may be added by an explanatory paragraph (or an emphasis of matter paragraph) to highlight a matter affecting the financial statements.

Ordinarily, an auditor might write an emphasis of a matter paragraph:

- If there is a significant uncertainty which may affect the financial statements, the resolution of which is dependent upon future events. Examples of uncertainties that might be emphasized include the existence of related-party transactions, important accounting matters occurring subsequent to the balance sheet date, matters affecting the comparability of financial statements with those of previous years (e.g. change in accounting methods), the outcome of major litigation, and so on.
- To highlight a material matter regarding a going concern problem. For example, delinquency in loan repayment may be countered by management plans to reschedule loans, sale of assets, etc. If the going concern questions are not resolved, the auditor must adequately disclose in his report the principal conditions that raise doubt about the entity's ability to continue in operation in the foreseeable future.

It should be noted that the addition of an explanatory paragraph does not affect the auditor's opinion. However, if the matter is significant and material or not adequately disclosed in the financial statements, the auditor may wish to issue a qualified or an adverse opinion or a disclaimer.

Example 7-2:

...

In forming our opinion, we have considered the adequacy of the disclosures made in the financial statements concerning the possible outcome to litigation against B Limited, a subsidiary undertaking of the company, for an alleged breach of environmental regulations. The future settlement of this litigation could result in additional liabilities and the closure of B Limited's business, whose net assets included in the consolidated balance sheet total $XXX and whose profit before tax for the year is $ YYY. Details of the circumstances relating to this fundamental uncertainty are described in note 15. Our opinion is not qualified in this respect.

...

2. Qualified opinion

An auditor's report containing a qualified opinion is issued when the auditor concludes that an unqualified opinion cannot be expressed but that the effect of any disagreement with management, or limitation in scope, is not so material as to require an adverse opinion or disclaimer of opinion. A qualified opinion should be expressed as "fairly presenting the financial statements except for" the effects of the matter to which the qualification relates.

> **Example 7-3:**
>
> ...
>
> Included in the accounts receivable shown on the balance sheet is an amount of $XXX due from a company which has ceased trading. XYZ plc has no security for this debt. In our opinion the company is unlikely to receive any payment and full provision of $XXX should have been made, reducing profit before tax and net assets by that amount.
>
> Except for the absence of this provision, in our opinion the financial statements give a true and fair view of the state of the company's affairs as at December 31, 20X9 and of its profit (loss) for the year then ended and have been properly prepared in accordance with the Companies Act 20X5.
>
> ...

3. Adverse opinion

An adverse opinion is issued when the effect of a disagreement is so material and pervasive to the financial statements that the auditor concludes that a qualification report is not adequate to disclose the misleading or incomplete nature of the financial statements. Such reports are issued only after all attempts to persuade the client to adjust the financial statements have failed.

> **Example 7-4:**
>
> ...
>
> As more fully explained in note 8, no provision has been made for losses expected to arise on certain long-term contracts currently in progress, as the directors consider that such losses should be off-set against amounts recoverable on other long-term contracts. In our opinion, provision should be made for foreseeable losses on individual contracts as required by Statement of Standard Accounting Practice 9. If losses had been recognized, the effect would have been to reduce the profit before tax for the year and the contract work in progress at December 31, 20X9 by $XXXX.
>
> In view of the effect of the failure to provide for the losses referred to above, in our opinion, the financial statements do not give a true and fair view of the state of the company's affairs as at December 31, 20X9 and of its profit (loss) for the year then ended. In all other respects, in our opinion the financial statements have been properly prepared in accordance with the Companies Act 20X5.
>
> ...

4. Disclaimer of opinion

An auditor's report containing a disclaimer of opinion should be expressed when the possible effect of a limitation on scope is so material and pervasive that the auditor has not been able to obtain sufficient and appropriate audit evidence and therefore is unable to express an opinion on the financial statements.

> **Example 7-5:**
>
> ...
>
> However, the evidence available to us was limited because we were unable to carry out auditing procedures necessary to obtain adequate assurance regarding the quantities and condition of stock and work in progress, appearing in the balance sheet at $XXXXX. Any adjustment to this figure would have a consequential significant effect on the profit for the year.
>
> Because of the possible effect of the limitation in evidence available to us, we are unable to form an opinion as to whether the financial statements give a true and fair view of the state of the company's affairs as at December 31, 20X9 or of its profit (loss) for the year then ended. In all other respects, in our opinion the financial statements have been properly prepared in accordance with the Companies Act 20X5.
>
> ...

Circumstance that may result in other than an unqualified opinion:

There are at least two circumstances where the auditor may not be able to express an unqualified opinion:

- A limitation in scope (Scope limitation)

If the auditor is unable to obtain enough evidence to conclude whether the financial statements, in whole or in part, present fairly, a scope limitation exists. A limitation in scope of the auditor's work may sometimes be imposed by the entity (e.g. management's unwillingness to permit the auditor to confirm receivables with debtors) or may be imposed by circumstances (e.g. the auditor's appointment being too late to permit attendance at the annual physical inventory count). A scope limitation could also result from inadequate accounting records or an inability to carry out an audit procedure considered necessary by the auditor.

- A disagreement with management

If the financial statements, in whole or in part, have not been prepared according to generally accepted accounting principles, a GAAP departure exists. Based on enough evidence, the auditor would conclude that the financial statements as a whole or a portion thereof do not present a true and fair view. Such differences may be about the acceptability of accounting policies selected, the method of their application, or the adequacy of disclosures in the financial statements.

As portrayed in Table 7-2, scope limitation could lead to a qualified opinion or a disclaimer of opinion while disagreement with management could lead to a qualified opinion or an adverse opinion.

Table 7-2 Matrix of Audit Opinion

Materiality	GAAP departures	Scope limitations
Immaterial	Unqualified	Unqualified
Material	Qualified	Qualified
Highly material	Adverse	Disclaimer

Chapter Round-up

- An audit is an exercise whose objective is to enable auditors to express an opinion whether the financial statements give a true and fair view of the entity's affairs and have been properly prepared in accordance with the applicable reporting framework and statutory or other specific requirements.

- The purpose of an audit is to enable auditors to express an opinion as to whether the financial statements give a true and fair view.

- Audits are typically divided into three types: audits of financial statements, operational audits, and compliance audits. Accordingly, auditors mainly fall into two groups: independent external auditors and internal auditors.

- Audit risk has three components: inherent risk, control risk, and detection risk. Auditors have no control over IR and CR while they can control the level of DR.

- The auditor should plan the audit work so that the audit will be performed in an effective manner.

- The auditor should conclude whether sufficient appropriate audit evidence has been obtained to reduce to an acceptably low level the risk of material misstatement in the financial statements. The procedures for obtaining audit evidence include inquiry, observation, inspection, recalculation, re-performance, confirmation and analytic procedures.

- Tests of controls are audit procedures to test the effectiveness of control policies and procedures in support of a reduced control risk. Substantive procedures are tests performed to obtain audit evidence to detect material misstatements in the financial statements.

- The opinion expressed in the audit report may be classified into four types: unqualified opinion, qualified opinion, adverse opinion and disclaimer of opinion.

Glossary

assurance	n.	保证,担保
material	adj.	重要的
override	v.	凌驾,越权
contingent	adj.	偶然的,偶发的,不确定的
attestation	n.	鉴证,认证
integrity	n.	正直,诚实
confidentiality	n.	保密,保密性
limitation	n.	限制,限度
fraud	n.	舞弊
compliance	n.	顺从,服从
susceptibility	n.	敏感
memorandum	n.	备忘录,便笺
substantive test		实质性测试
confirmation	n.	确认,证实,证明
delinquency	n.	拖欠债款
unqualified opinion		无保留意见
qualified opinion		保留意见
adverse opinion		否定意见
disclaimer of opinion		无法发表意见

Review Questions

(1) What is the objective of an audit?

(2) What are the differences in audits of financial statements, compliance audits, and operational audits?

(3) What are the four phases of an audit process model? Briefly describe each.

(4) Why does the audit have some inherent limitations?

(5) What are the three components of audit risk? Define each of the three.

(6) What are the frequently used procedures for obtaining audit evidence? Briefly explain each.

(7) Define test of control and substantive procedures respectively.

(8) What are the four different opinions an auditor can issue? Briefly discuss each.

(9) What circumstances lead to adding an explanatory paragraph?

(10) What's the meaning of materiality in auditing? Why is it necessary to make the materiality assessment?

Exercises

1. True or false

(1) Auditing can provide absolute assurance as to the "truth and fairness" of financial statements.

(2) Audit risk is composed of inherent risk, control risk and detection risk, all of which cannot be controlled by the auditors.

(3) The observation and inspection procedures are similar to each other in process of obtaining audit evidence. Hence they are interchangeable.

(4) To check whether the company complies with applicable laws and regulations is one big section of auditing work.

(5) Internal auditing is an independent appraisal function within an organization to examine and evaluate its management.

(6) Independent auditors are external auditors who provide auditing services for government supervision purposes.

(7) Confidential client information may generally be disclosed only with the permission of the client.

(8) Auditors bear the responsibility of not disclosing any of the client's information without consent.

(9) A qualified opinion is given when the auditor decides that there is a material misstatement in the financial information disclosed.

(10) If there is an explanatory paragraph in the audit report, it indicates that the report must express an opinion other than an unqualified opinion.

2. Identification

Each of the following represents tasks that auditors frequently perform:

(1) Review of tax return of corporate president to determine whether she has included all taxable income.

(2) Review of the activities of the receiving department of a large manufacturing company, with special attention to the efficiency of the materials inspection.

(3) Examination of vacation records to determine whether employees followed company policy of two weeks' paid vacation annually.

(4) Audit of a small college to determine that the college had followed requirements of a bond indenture agreement.

(5) Examination of financial statements of a small business for use by stockholders.

(6) Audit of annual financial statements to be filed with the SEC.

(7) Audit of a statement of cash receipts and disbursements to be used by a creditor.

◆ **Required:**

For each of the above, identify the most likely type of auditor (independent, government, or internal) and the most likely type of audit (financial, compliance, or operational).

3. Expression of audit opinions

The following circumstances are mutually independent:

(1) Your client, XYZ Ltd, is being sued by one of its competitors for $20 million for an alleged patent infringement. Your client has assets of $50 million and a reported profit of $15 million. The client has disclosed adequately the lawsuit in a note to the accounts along with a statement indicating that they intend to vigorously defend the suit and are confident of winning the suit.

(2) Higgins Ltd has followed approved accounting standards but a note to the financial report indicates that the application of certain standards results in the financial report being materially misstated. The note details the reasons for this view. You do not concur with this view.

(3) You are unable to obtain sufficient evidence supporting Outback Ltd's investment in a foreign subsidiary which is considered material to the financial report.

(4) PM Trust is a reporting entity. Ms Peters, the financial director, refuses to adopt the account standard of "Related Party Disclosure" on the ground that it "requires confidential information to be disclosed to the public that should remain known only to the parties concerned". You are satisfied that the current financial report is materially correct in all other respects.

◆ **Required:**

Consider all facts given in each scenario, indicate the type of opinion you'd like to issue. Give reasons for your decisions.

 Group Activities

The following situation involves Kevin Trump, staff accountant with the local CPA firm of Jason, Leo, and Yong (JL&Y). The bookkeeper of Miracle Manufacturing Company resigned three months ago and has not yet been replaced. As a result, Miracle's transactions have not been recorded and the books are not up to date. Miracle must prepare interim financial statements to comply with terms of a loan agreement, but cannot do so until the books are posted. To help them with this matter, Miracle turns to JL&Y, their independent auditors. Miracle wants Kevin Trump to update their books because Kevin had audited them last year.

◆ **Required**:

① Identify the ethical issues that are involved.

② Discuss whether there has or has not been any violation of ethical conduct.

Supplementary Reading

Internal Control and Control Risk

Internal control is not only essential to maintaining the accounting and financial records of an organization, it is essential to managing the entity. For that reason, everyone from the external auditors to management to the board of directors to the stockholders of large public companies to government has an interest in internal controls. In many parts of the world, regulators have emphasized the importance of internal control by requiring management to make annual public statements about the effectiveness of internal controls.

Internal control, according to the Committee of Sponsoring Organizations of the Treadway Commission (COSO), is a process, effected by an entity's board of directors, management and other personnel, designed to provide reasonable assurance regarding the achievement of objectives in the following categories: effectiveness and efficiency of operations, reliability of financial reporting, compliance with applicable laws and regulations, and safeguarding of assets against unauthorized acquisition, use or disposition.

The reason a company establishes a system of control is to help achieve its performance and profitability goals and prevent loss of resources by fraud and other means. Internal control can also help to ensure reliable financial reporting and compliance with laws and regulations. The entity's internal control system consists of many specific policies and procedures designed to provide management with reasonable assurance that the goals and objectives it believes important to the company will be met. Controls are especially important in preventing fraud, supporting management objectives, insuring accuracy of transactions, and supporting assessment of the financial statements.

The internal control components are: the control environment, risk assessment, control activities, information, communication, and monitoring.

The control environment consists of the actions, policies, and procedures that reflect the overall attitudes of top management, directors, and owners. The control environment has a pervasive influence on the way business activities are structured, the way objectives are established, and the way risks are assessed. The control environment is influenced by the entity's history and culture. Effectively controlled companies set a positive "tone at the top" and establish appropriate policies and procedures. Elements of the control environment are: communication and enforcement of integrity and ethical values; commitment to competence; participation by those charged with governance—independence and integrity of the board of directors; management's philosophy and operating style—leadership via control by example; organizational structure; assignment of authority and responsibility; and human resource policies and practices.

All components of internal control, from control environment to monitoring, should be assessed for risk. Management's risk assessment differs from, but is closely related to, the auditor's risk assessment. Management assesses risks as part of designing and operating the internal control system to minimize errors and irregularities. Auditors assess risks to decide the evidence needed in the audit. The two risk assessment approaches are related in that if management effectively assesses and responds to risks, the auditor will typically need to accumulate less audit evidence than when management fails to, because control risk is lower.

Information is needed at all levels of the organization: financial information; operating information; compliance information; and information about external events, activities, and conditions. This information must be identified, captured, and communicated in a form and time frame that enables people to carry out their responsibilities. The information system controls should be tested because there are general IT and input risks that the accounting system does not produce sufficient audit evidence.

Control procedures (sometimes called "control activities") are policies and procedures that help ensure management directives are carried out. They help ensure that necessary actions are taken to address risks to the achievement of the entity's objectives for operations, financial reporting, or compliance. Generally, control procedures fall into four broad categories: performance reviews, information processing, physical controls, and segregation of duties.

Internal control systems need to be monitored. Monitoring is a process that deals with ongoing assessment of the quality of internal control performance over time. The process involves assessing the design of controls and their operation on a timely basis and taking necessary corrective actions. By monitoring, management can determine that internal controls are operating as intended and that they are modified as appropriate for changes in conditions.

To gain an understanding of the entity's internal control, the auditor is required to evaluate the design of controls and determine whether they have been implemented. Evaluating the design of a control involves considering whether the control is capable of effectively preventing, or detecting and correcting, material misstatements. It is especially important to evaluate the design of controls that address significant risks and controls for which substantive procedures alone are not sufficient.

Critical Thinking Questions:

(1) What are the five interrelated components of internal control? Briefly discuss them.

(2) Can evaluation of the control environment be a key element in determining the nature of the audit work? Why or why not?

Unit Eight
Accounting in Information Systems

Learning Objectives

When you have studied this chapter, you should be able to:

* evaluate the role played by the accounting information systems in a business and its relationship to other systems;

* describe the accounting systems supporting the business functions;

* explain how enterprise applications promote business integration and improve organizational performance;

* assess the challenges posed by accounting information systems in the enterprise and propose management solutions.

Warm-up: Dialogue

Jack: Hi, Peter. Can you tell me a little bit about your current job?
Peter: Certainly. What would you like to know?
Jack: First of all, what do you work as?
Peter: I work as a computer technician at Wansheng Insurance Co.
Jack: What are you responsible for?
Peter: I'm responsible for accounting information systems administration and in-house programming.
Jack: What sort of problems do you deal with on a day-to-do basis?
Peter: Oh, there are always lots of small system glitches. I also provide information on a need-to-know basis for employees.
Jack: What else does your job involve?
Peter: Well, as I said, for part of my job I have to develop in-house programs for special tasks from Wansheng's accounting and financial department.
Jack: Do you have to produce any reports?

Peter: No, I just have to make sure that everything is in good working order.
Jack: Do you ever attend meetings?
Peter: Yes, I attend organizational meetings at the end of the month.
Jack: Thanks for all the information, Peter. It seems that you have an interesting job.
Peter: Yes, it's very interesting, but stressful, too!

Text

Section 1 Accounting Information Systems—A Definition

An accounting information system (AIS) is a system of collecting, storing and processing financial and accounting data that are used by decision makers. An accounting information system is generally a computer-based method for tracking accounting activity in conjunction with information technology resources. The resulting financial reports can be used internally by management or externally by other interested parties including investors, creditors and tax authorities. Accounting information systems are designed to support all accounting functions and activities including auditing, financial accounting & reporting, management accounting and tax. The most widely adopted accounting information systems are auditing and financial reporting modules.

Traditionally, accounting is purely based on manual approach. Experience and skillfulness of an individual accountant are critical in accounting processes. Even using the manual approach can be ineffective and inefficient. Accounting information systems resolve many of above issues. AISs can support an automation of processing large amount of data and produce timely and accuracy of information.

Early accounting information systems were designed for payroll functions in 1970s. Initially, accounting information systems were predominantly developed "in-house" as legacy systems. Such solutions were expensive to develop and difficult to maintain. Therefore, many accounting practitioners preferred the manual approach rather than computer-based. Today, accounting information systems are more commonly sold as prebuilt software packages from large vendors such as Microsoft, SAP and Oracle where it is configured and customized to match the organization's business processes. Small businesses often use accounting lower costs software packages such as MYOB and Quickbooks. Large organizations would often choose enterprise resource planning (ERP) systems. As the need for connectivity and consolidation between other business systems increased, accounting information systems were merged with larger, more centralized systems known as ERP. In ERP, a system such as accounting information system is built as a module integrated into a suite of applications that can include manufacturing, supply chain, human resources. These modules are integrated together and are able to access the same data and execute complex business processes. Today, cloud-based accounting information systems are increasingly popular for both SMEs and large organizations for lower costs. With adoption of accounting information systems, many businesses have removed low skills, transactional and operational accounting roles.

Section 2 Accounting Information Systems and Their Role in Organizations

Information technology (IT) refers to the hardware and software used in computerized information systems and has been a major force in shaping our current society. The information age has important implications for accounting because that is what accountants are—knowledge workers. In fact, accountants have always been in the "information business" because their role has been, in part, to communicate accurate and relevant financial information to parties interested in how their organizations are performing. The information age also includes the increasing importance and growth of e-business, conducting business over the Internet or dedicated proprietary networks and e-commerce, a subset of e-business, which refers mostly to buying and selling transactions.

In many ways, accounting is itself an information system, i.e. a communicative process that collects, stores, processes, and distributes information to those who need it. For instance, corporate accountants develop financial statements for external parties and such other reports as accounts receivable aging analyses for internal managers. But users of accounting information sometimes criticize AISs for only capturing and reporting financial transactions, and that financial statements often ignore some of the most important activities that influence business entities.

Today, however, AISs are concerned with non-financial as well as financial data and information. Thus, our definition of an AIS as an enterprise-wide system views accounting as an organization's primary producer and distributor of many different types of information. The definition also considers the AIS as process focused. This matches the contemporary perspective that accounting systems are not primarily financial systems.

Accounting information systems have three basic functions:

The first function of an AIS is the efficient and effective collection and storage of data concerning an organization's financial activities, including getting the transaction data from source documents, recording the transactions in journals, and posting data from journals to ledgers.

The second function of an AIS is to supply information useful for making decisions, including producing managerial reports and financial statements.

The third function of an AIS is to make sure controls are in place to accurately record and process data.

Section 3 Components of an Accounting Information System

Accounting information systems generally consist of six main parts: people, procedures and instructions, data, software, information technology infrastructure and internal controls. Let's look at each component in detail.

I People

The people in an AIS are simply the system users. Professionals who may need to use an organization's AIS include accountants, consultants, business analysts, managers, chief financial officers and auditors.

With a well-designed AIS, everyone within an organization who is authorized to do so can access the same system and get the same information. An AIS also simplifies getting information to people outside of the organization when necessary. For example, consultants might use the information in an AIS to analyze the effectiveness of the company's pricing structure by looking at cost data, sales data and revenue. Also, auditors can use the data to assess a company's internal controls, financial condition and compliance with the Sarbanes-Oxley Act (SOX).

The AIS should be designed to meet the needs of the people who will be using it. The system should also be easy to use and should improve, not hinder, efficiency.

II Procedures and Instructions

The procedures and instructions of an AIS are the methods it uses for collecting, storing, retrieving and processing data. These methods will be both manual and automated, and the data can come from both internal sources (e.g. employees) and external sources (e.g. customers' online orders). The procedures and instructions will be coded into AIS software; they should also be "coded" into employees through documentation and training. The procedures and instructions must be followed consistently to be effective.

To store information, an AIS must have a database structure such as structured query language (SQL), a computer language commonly used for databases. The AIS will also need various input screens for the different types of system users and different types of data entry, as well as different output formats to meet the needs of different users and different types of information.

III Data

The data contained in an AIS is all the financial information pertinent to the organization's business practices. Any business data that impacts the company's finances should go into an AIS. The data included in an AIS will depend on the nature of the business, but it may consist of the following: sales orders, customer billing statements, sales analysis reports, purchase requisitions, vendor invoices, check registers, general ledger, inventory data, payroll information, timekeeping, and tax information.

This data can then be used to prepare accounting statements and reports such as accounts receivable ageing, depreciation/amortization schedules, trial balance, profit and loss, and so on. Having all this data in one place—in the AIS—facilitates a business's recordkeeping, reporting, analysis, auditing and decision-making activities. For the data to be useful, it must be complete, correct and relevant.

Ⅳ Software

The software component of an AIS is the computer programs used to store, retrieve, process and analyze the company's financial data. Before there were computers, AISs were manual, paper-based systems, but today, most companies are using computer software as the basis of the AISs. Small businesses might use Intuit's Quickbooks, Sage Peachtree Accounting, or Microsoft's Small Business Accounting but there are many others. Small to mid-sized businesses might use SAP's Business One. Mid-sized and large businesses might use Microsoft's Dynamics GP, Sage Group's MAS 90 or MAS 200, Oracle's Peoplesoft or Epicor Financial Management.

Quality, reliability and security are key components of effective AIS software. Managers rely on the information it outputs to make decisions for the company, and they need high-quality information to make sound decisions.

AIS software programs can be customized to meet the unique needs of different types of businesses. If an existing program does not meet a company's needs, software can also be developed in-house with substantial input from end users or can be developed by a third-party company specifically for the organization. The system could even be outsourced to a specialized company.

Ⅴ Information Technology Infrastructure

The information technology infrastructure is just a fancy name for the hardware used to operate the accounting information system. Perhaps most importantly, the hardware selected for an AIS must be compatible with the intended software. Ideally, it would be not just compatible, but optimal. One way in which businesses can easily meet hardware and software compatibility requirements is by purchasing a turnkey system that includes both the hardware and the software that the business needs. Purchasing a turnkey system means, theoretically, that the business will get an optimal combination of hardware and software for its AIS.

A good AIS should also include a plan for maintaining, servicing, replacing and upgrading components of the hardware system, as well as a plan for the disposal of broken and outdated hardware so that sensitive data is completely destroyed.

Ⅵ Internal Controls

The internal controls of an AIS are the security measures it contains to protect sensitive data. An AIS contains confidential information belonging not just to the company but also to its employees and customers. This data may include Social Security numbers, salary information, credit card numbers, and so on. All of the data in an AIS should be encrypted, and access to the system should be logged and surveilled. System activity should be traceable as well. An AIS also needs internal controls that protect it from computer viruses, hackers and other internal and external threats to network security. Furthermore, it must be protected from natural disasters and power surges that can cause data loss.

Because an AIS stores and provides such valuable business information, reliability is vitally important. The American Institute of CPAs (AICPA) and Canadian Institute of Chartered Accountants (CICA) have identified five basic principles important to AIS reliability:

(1) **Security**—Access to the system and its data is controlled and limited only to those authorized.

(2) **Confidentiality**—The protection of sensitive information from unauthorized disclosure.

(3) **Privacy**—The collection, use, and disclosure of personal information about customers is done in an appropriate manner.

(4) **Processing integrity**—The accurate, complete, and timely processing of data done with proper authorization.

(5) **Availability**—The system is available to meet operational and contractual obligations.

Chapter Round-up

- An accounting information system is a system of collecting, storing and processing financial and accounting data that are used by decision makers.
- Accounting information systems are designed to support all accounting functions and activities including auditing, financial accounting & reporting, management accounting and tax.
- An AIS is an enterprise-wide system viewing accounting as an organization's primary producer and distributor of many different types of information.
- Accounting information systems generally consist of six main parts: people, procedures and instructions, data, software, information technology infrastructure and internal controls.
- The American Institute of CPAs (AICPA) and Canadian Institute of Chartered Accountants (CICA) have identified five basic principles important to AIS reliability.

Glossary

module	n.	模块,组件
legacy system	n.	遗留系统
centralized system		集中式系统
cloud-based	adj.	基于云端的
procedure	n.	程序,步骤

instruction	n.	指令
infrastructure	n.	基础设施
component	n.	组件,部件
query	n.	询问
compatible	adj.	兼容的,相容的
unauthorized	adj.	未经授权的,未经许可的
encrypt	v.	加密,将……译成密码
surveil	vt.	对……实施监视(或监督)
traceable	adj.	可追踪的
virus	n.	病毒
hacker	n.	黑客
confidentiality	n.	机密性
integrity	n.	保存,健全
authorization	n.	授权,批准

Review Questions

(1) What is an accounting information system?

(2) Describe the role played by the accounting information systems in businesses.

(3) What are the different implementations of accounting information systems for small businesses and larger organizations?

(4) Describe the three basic functions of AISs.

(5) What are the six main parts of AISs?

(6) To whom do the professionals who need to use an organization's AISs refer?

(7) What's the meaning of procedures and instructions of an AIS?

(8) How to collect and use the data in an AIS?

(9) What are the five basic principles important to AIS reliability which have been identified by the AICPA and CICA?

Exercises

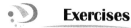

1. True or false

(1) An accounting information system is a system of storing and processing financial and accounting data that are used by decision makers.

(2) As the need for connectivity and consolidation between other business systems increased, accounting information systems were merged with larger, more centralized systems known as

cloud-based accounting information system.

(3) Large organizations often use accounting lower costs software packages such as MYOB and Quickbooks.

(4) In ERP, a system such as accounting information system is built as a module integrated into a suite of applications that can include manufacturing, supply chain, and human resources.

(5) AISs have two basic functions: The first function of an AIS is the efficient and effective collection and storage of data concerning an organization's financial activities. The second function of an AIS is to supply information useful for making decisions.

(6) Accounting information systems generally consist of six main parts: people, procedures and instructions, data, software, information technology infrastructure and internal controls.

(7) Today, cloud-based accounting information systems are increasingly popular for both SMEs and large organizations for lower costs.

(8) AIS software programs cannot be customized to meet the unique needs of different types of businesses.

(9) An AIS must prevent unauthorized file access by individuals who are allowed to access only select parts of the system.

(10) Access to the system and its data is controlled and limited to those authorized and some internal unauthorized.

2. Multiple choice

(1) Which of the following is NOT true about accounting information systems (AISs)?
   A. All AISs are computerized.
   B. AISs may report both financial and nonfinancial information.
   C. AISs, in addition to collecting and distributing large amounts of data and information, also organize and store data for future uses.
   D. A student who has an interest in both accounting and IT will find many job opportunities that combine these knowledge and skills areas.

(2) Which of the following is likely to be information rather than data?
   A. Sales price.
   B. Customer number.
   C. Net profit.
   D. Employees' name.

Group Activities

(1) Hiring an employee and taking a sales order are business activities but are not accounting transactions requiring journal entries. Make a list of some other business activities

that would not be captured as journal entries in a traditional AIS. Do you think managers or investors would be interested in knowing about these activities? Why or why not?

(2) Interview a sample of auditors from professional service firms in your area. Ask them whether or not they plan to offer any of the assurance services suggested by the AICPA. Also, find out if they offer services other than financial auditing and taxation. Discuss your findings in class.

Supplementary Reading

I The Annual Report (Communicating Accounting Information)

Many consider the annual report to be the single most important printed document that companies produce. In recent years, annual reports have become large documents. They now include such sections as letters to the stockholders, descriptions of the business, operating highlights, financial review, management discussion and analysis, segment reporting, and inflation data as well as the basic financial statements.

The expansion has been due in part to a general increase in the degree of sophistication and complexity in accounting standards and disclosure requirements for financial reporting. The expansion also reflects the change in the composition and level of sophistication of users. Current users include not only stockholders but financial and securities analysts, potential investors, lending institutions, stockbrokers, customers, employees, and (whether the reporting company likes it or not) competitors. Thus, a report that was originally designed as a device for communicating basic financial information now attempts to meet the diverse needs of an expanding audience.

Users hold conflicting views on the value of annual reports. Some argue that annual reports fail to provide enough information, whereas others believe that disclosures in annual reports have expanded to the point where they create information overload. The future of most companies depends on acceptance by the investing public and by their customers; therefore, companies should take this opportunity to communicate well-defined corporate strategies.

II Universal Concrete Products (Information for Performance Evaluation)

Jack Merritt is the controller for Universal Concrete Products (UCP), a manufacturing company with headquarters in Columbus, Ohio. UCP has seven concrete product plants located throughout the Midwest region of the United States. The company has recently switched to a decentralized organizational structure. In the past, the company did not try to measure profitability at each plant. Rather, all revenues and expenses were consolidated to produce just one income statement.

Under the new organizational structure, each concrete manufacturing plant is headed by a general manager, who has responsibility for operating the plant like a separate company. Jack has asked one of his accountants, Scott McDermott, to organize a small group to be in charge of performance analysis. This group is to prepare monthly reports on performance for each of the seven plants. These reports consist of budgeted and actual income statements. Written explanations and appraisals are to accompany variances. Each member of Scott's group has been assigned to one specific plant and is encouraged to interact with management and staff in that plant in order to become familiar with operations.

After a few months, the controller began receiving complaints from the general managers at several of the plants. Common to many of these complaints is the observation that Scott's staff members are interfering with operations and, in general, are "getting in the way". In addition, the managers worry that someone is constantly "looking over their shoulders" to see if they are operating in line with the budget. Two plant managers have pointed out that the work the performance analysis staff is trying to do should be done by them (i. e. explanation of variances). As Andrew Boord, one of the most vocal plant managers, stated, "How can these accountants explain the variances when they don't know anything about the industry? They don't know what's happening with our suppliers or our labor unions, and they haven't got a clue about our relationships with our customers."

The president of Universal Concrete Products, Hector Eschenbrenner, has also complained about the new system for performance evaluation reporting. He claims that he is unable to wade through the seven detailed income statements, variances, and narrative explanations of all variances each month. As he put it, "I don't have time for this and I think much of the information I am receiving is irrelevant!"

Critical Thinking Questions:

(1) The goal of preparing an annual report is to communicate information from a company to its targeted users.

① Identify and discuss the basic factors of communication that must be considered in the presentation of this information.

② Discuss the communication problems a company faces in preparing the annual report that result from the diversity of the users being addressed.

(2) Select two types of information found in an annual report, other than the financial statements and accompanying footnotes, and describe how they are useful to the users of annual reports.

(3) Discuss at least two advantages and two disadvantages of stating well-defined corporate strategies in the annual report.

(4) Do you think it is a good idea to have a special staff in charge of performance evaluation and analysis?

(5) In a decentralized organization such as UCP, what would seem to be the best approach to performance evaluation?

(6) What information would you include in a performance evaluation report for Mr. Eschenbrenner?

Translation

第一单元 会计概述

一、会计职业

会计发展成为一项职业已百年有余,并取得与律师、医生同等的社会地位。不同的国家有不同的会计专业组织,这些专业团体通过游说政府来表达成员的利益,并且提供行业自律的框架。国际上有一些重要的会计组织,比如美国注册公共会计师协会、特许公认会计师公会、加拿大注册会计师协会、澳大利亚注册会计师公会、(中国)香港会计师公会等。成为会计师公会会员必须满足特定条件。大部分情况下,成为会员要持有学位,完成专项学习或通过考试,并且有适当的工作经验。

会计师通常在三个领域供职:公共会计、商业会计和非营利组织会计。

公共会计向公众提供收费服务。由于当前企业结构日趋复杂,政府法规也不断增加,公共会计趋向于在四个领域提供专业化服务,包括审计、税务、管理咨询和破产。

还有许多会计师任职于企业。企业的高级会计主管,或者称为财务总管,全权负责其他会计人员的业务活动,包括总账、成本会计、预算、税务会计、内部审计和会计信息系统。

另一个领域是非营利组织会计。市政委员会、州政府和联邦政府每年收入并且支出巨额资金。政府会计致力于有效使用各项资源并且遵守市、州及联邦法律法规各项条款。其他非营利组织,如教会、慈善机构、医院和私立教育机构,也遵循与政府会计相似的程序。

作为现代社会的商业语言,会计应用于各种类型的经济主体,包括营利组织和非营利单位,这些组织和单位都需要利用经济资源,做出经济决策。

二、会计的定义

1. 定义

会计,常被称为商业语言,运用其独特的文字和符号向经济决策者,如经理人、股东、债权人等,传递财务信息。实际上,会计是一项向需要了解企业财务状况和经营业绩的人提供信息的服务。

会计被定义为确认、计量、记录和传递经济信息的活动,使用者根据会计提供的信息对经济事项做出判断和决策(图1-1)。

交易的确认指事项的确定,以及判断哪些事项体现与企业相关的经济活动。例如,向客户出售商品、提供服务,向员工发放工资,都是经济活动,会计称之为交易和事项。

在交易的影响被记录之前要进行交易的计量。经济社会中,经济活动以货币表示的价格来计量。货币的功能包括交换的介质和价值的衡量。因此,交易以元和分的货币单位来计量。

交易在确认和计量之后对企业产生影响,而记录是对所有交易进行记载的系统过程。因此,记录为企业提供经济活动的历史反映。技术上,所有记录的数据必须进行分类和汇总,从而有助于决策。

会计程序的最后一个步骤是传递信息,即编制财务报告并传达至潜在使用者的过程。如果包含在会计记录里的财务信息不能传递给潜在使用者,之前的确认、计量和记录就失去意义。信息使用者只有获得财务报告,才能分析和解释报告并做出相关经济决策。

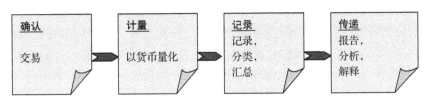

图1-1 会计程序

2. 会计信息使用者

会计的最终目标是向外部决策者和内部决策者(或外部使用者和内部使用者)以报告形式提供信息。

外部使用者指在企业之外但与企业有直接利益关系的个人或组织,如投资人、债权人、政府部门、供货商、客户和公众。他们的决策范围包括投资、授信、购买或出售商品及劳务、遵循税法及其他法律法规等。

内部使用者包括管理层和员工。其中,经理人必须使用财务数据来计划和控制企业经营。他们要思考如下问题:哪些资源可得?有多少债务?最有效的生产过程是怎样的?涨价或降价会有什么影响?等等。而员工也是财务信息的重要使用者,他们需要有关公司稳定性及营利性的信息。

3. 会计的分类

会计信息使用者在企业里有各不相同的经济利益,而现代会计为他们提供多样化的服务。因此,会计可分为两类:财务会计与管理会计。财务会计主要为企业外部使用者提供财务报告,而管理会计主要为内部管理层决策提供信息。

三、会计假设与基本原则

1. 企业组织结构

营利企业三种最为常见的组织形式是:个体经营或独资经营、合伙经营和公司。

独资经营指企业为个人所拥有。许多小型服务企业、零售商店以及诊所、律所等采用独资经营的形式。独资经营企业的所有者为企业提供现金和其他资产,获得全部利润,并且对企业的全部债务负有法律责任。但是,从会计的角度来看,个体经济体独立于其所有者,并且会计仅服务于企业事务而不是所有者的个人业务。

合伙经营指企业为两个或以上合伙人所拥有。成立合伙企业不需要特别的法律条件,但是合伙人之间必须要签订合约。尽管可以接受口头合约,但书面合约是优选,以有助于解决合伙人之间的分歧。此外,合伙人为企业提供资源并分享利润或分担损失。

合伙人不是独立的法律实体。因此,单个合伙人也对企业的债务负有个人责任。但是从会计的角度来看,必须将合伙企业区别于其所有者。与独资经营一样,合伙经营广泛运用于小型服务企业、零售业和诊所、律所等。

公司需遵循公司法成立,并且是独立的法律实体。其所有者称为股东,他们的所有者权利由他们在公司持有的股票所代表。由于公司是独立的法律实体,有限责任公司的股东,在持有的股票全部偿付之后,对公司剩余的债务不再承担责任。这个特征称为有限责任原则。

独立法律实体的身份使得公司可以以自己的名义从事各项事务,如同自然人一样。因此,公司可以购买、拥有或出售财产,可以以自己的名义起诉与被起诉,可以与他人签订合同。本质上,公司可以拥有与自然人一样的权利、义务和责任。股东可以在任何时间自由出售全部或部分股票。所有者权利转移的便利性,以及对公司债务负有的有限责任,大大增加了公司投资的吸引力。此外,利润以股利的形式分派给股东。

独资经营/合伙经营与公司(有限责任)的比较见表1-1。

表1-1 独资经营/合伙经营与公司(有限责任)的比较

	独资经营／合伙经营	公司(有限责任)
成立	方式简单,成本较低。	程序复杂,成本较高。
资本结构	* 仅所有者提供资本。 * 不发行股票,企业寿命通常为有限时间。 * 所有者对企业债务负有全责。	* 有潜在的大量股东为企业提供资本。 * 所有权可以通过出售来转移,公司寿命理论上是无限期的。 * 股东的责任限制于其对公司的投入。
管理	所有者自身参与企业管理。	首席执行官或职业经理人对日常经营负责。
盈利	利润只向所有者进行分配。	利润可以股利形式分配给股东,或者留存在企业内部。
纳税	纳税优势(纳税保护)。	双重纳税。

2. 会计假设

(1) 会计主体

如果要记录企业交易,并将其分类、汇总至财务报表,会计则必须清晰地界定主体的范围。在会计主体的假设下,主体的资产、负债和业务活动完全区别于所有者及其他主体的资产、负债和经济活动。每一个主体都有一套独立的会计记录,编制的报表也仅仅反映该主体的财务状况和经营业绩。

(2) 持续经营

持续经营的假设认为,企业在可预见的将来继续经营,没有意向对企业进行清算或者大规模地削减经营。如果管理层计划出售或者清算企业,持续经营假设和成本假设则不再有效,而财务报表也将基于预计的出售或清算价值来编制。这种情况发生的时候,财务报告必须清楚地界定价值确认的基础。

(3) 会计分期

财务信息的使用者需要及时的信息来进行决策。会计因此必须定期编制报告来反映企业经营业绩、财务状况、筹资及投资活动。法律也要求企业定期反映利润数据,比如出于纳税等目的。上述情况均需要将企业寿命人为划分为相等的时间间隔,也就是会计分期。在会计分期的前提下,利润的决定通常就是在同一个会计期间内将收入与费用进行配比的过程。

(4) 货币计量

货币计量要求会计记录只能包含可以用货币表示的事项。会计人员假定用货币表示的数据有助于经济决策,而且货币单位代表实际价值,可以计量净利润、财务状况以及财务状况的变动。任何不能用货币量化的事项均不能出现在会计信息系统里。然而,如果非货币信息与经济决策相关,则并不排斥将该信息反映在财务报告的注释中。

3. 其他会计原则

(1) 历史成本原则

历史成本原则要求资产以获得时的成本或发生的费用来记录,而不是以公允市价记录。这一原则确保提供可靠的信息,从而避免了提供主观市价的可能性,这种市价通常会有偏差。

(2) 权责发生制

权责发生制是指收入和费用在产生或发生的会计期间进行确认,尽管现金收支发生在其他时间甚至其他会计期间。由于大部分交易涉及的采购或销售通常与现金收支不发生在同一个时间点,因此权责发生制的使用使得收入与费用能进行正确的配比。

(3) 配比原则

配比原则要求当期因产生收入而发生的各项费用必须在该收入产生的期间扣除。也就是说,与当期收入相关的所有费用必须与当期收入相匹配,并且从收入中扣除以确定当期盈利。

(4) 充分披露原则

充分披露原则要求财务报表和报表附注或相关说明必须包括全部必要的信息,以防止误导任何理性有智的信息使用者。使用者理解财务报表所需要的全部信息必须要进行披露。例如,租赁准备金、大额采购保证金、悬而未决的法律诉讼或纠纷等都要在财务报表附注里进行披露。

4. 会计信息的质量要求

(1) 可靠性

如果使用者能够信赖信息反映的内容以及所发生交易的实质,如果信息完整、没有偏差和重大错报,如果信息是谨慎编制的,则信息就是可靠的。

(2) 相关性

提供的信息必须能够满足使用者的需要。以公司会计为例,企业必须提供广泛的信息以满足不同利益相关方的需求。

(3) 重要性

该原则指财务信息的重要性。信息的漏报、错报或者没有单独披露是否对某一特定报告使用者的经济决策产生潜在的负面影响,决定了信息的重要性。某一事项的重要性不仅取决于其金额,而且受制于其性质。例如,10 000美元的贿赂即使发生在大企业也是一个重要事项。会计人员基于对公司的了解以及过去的经验做出重要性的判断。财务报表的使用者通常信赖会计师的职业判断。

（4）实质重于形式

会计人员必须更多地关注交易的经济实质而不是法律形式。例如，某些租赁设备在会计处理上视同为购买的资产，而不是租赁的形式。实质上，这类交易在记录和报告时都视同为购得，尽管可能从未考虑过其法定所有权。

（5）可比性

信息必须建立在可持续的基础上，只有这样，不同会计期间的财务信息及不同来源的财务信息（比如，同行业其他企业的数据）才可以进行有效的比较。不同的实体只有使用相同的会计操作，包括同样的计量标准和报告准则，可比性才会更加有效。

（6）谨慎性

在选择会计程序及估值方法时，必须选择最能谨慎反映企业财务成果或财务状况的一种方式。也就是说，确定资产或收益的存在比确定负债或亏损的存在需要更多确凿的证据。

（7）可理解性

信息需要能够被使用者所理解，前提只是使用者具备一定的经济及会计知识，并且有意向较为认真地研读报告。

（8）及时性

如果信息很久之后才得以披露，或者报告的期间超过合理的间隔，信息的有用性将大为削弱。间隔的合理性取决于环境：公司管理层出于有效管理企业的目的，需要非常频繁的信息报告；而股东通常只需要年报即可。

第二单元　会计系统与会计程序

一、会计要素与会计等式

1. 会计要素

概念框架提出会计要素的定义是：对会计对象的基本分类及会计核算对象的细分，其目的是反映企业的财务状况与经营成果。会计要素可分为五大类：资产、负债、所有者权益、收入和费用。

资产指由过去的交易和事项所形成，由企业所控制并在将来能实现的经济利益。该定义明确了资产的三个重要特质：（1）必须存在将来的经济利益；（2）企业必须能控制该项利益，也就是企业能够在实现自身目标的同时受益于该资产，并且能够排斥或控制他人对该利益的接触；（3）使得企业控制该项利益的交易或实现必须已经发生。拥有某些资产并非等同于控制。例如，代理商持有委托销售的商品，但代理商对商品没有控制权，就不能将其视同为自己的资产进行处理。

资产可以细分为流动资产和非流动资产。通常，资产包括现金、应收账款、应收票据、存货、投资、设备、建筑物、交通工具、土地、专利、版权等。

负债指由于过去的交易和事项所产生的现时义务，该义务的履行将导致经济利益的流出。因此，一项负债必然会带来日后经济利益的牺牲，而企业几乎无法避免该利益的流出。义务必须在某一特定日期履行或者于某一特定事项发生之时履行。

负债也可以细分为两类:流动负债与长期负债,包括应付账款、应付票据、应付利息、应付职工薪酬、长期借款、长期应付款等。

所有者权益指资产减去负债后的剩余利益,主要包括两部分:实收资本(所有者投入)和留存收益(通过经营积累的收益)。企业的所有者对资产有最终索求权。

收入指经济利益的流入或增强,或者经济利益流出的减少,表现为资产的增加或负债的减少,但不包括所有者投入或其他导致权益增加的情况。收入主要来源于商品的销售、劳务的提供、财产的租赁以及借款的收益。任何收入的增加最终会带来所有者权益的增加。

费用指将来经济利益的消耗或损失,表现为资产的减少或负债的增加,但不包括所有者利益分配或其他导致权益减少的情况。费用包含销售成本、管理费用、销售费用、财务费用等。任何费用的增加最终会导致所有者权益的减少。

2. 会计等式

资产、负债、所有者权益及其相互关系反映了企业的财务状况。三者之间的平衡关系就称为会计等式,具体如下:

$$资产 = 负债 + 所有者权益$$

上述等式显示企业资产总额永远等于负债与所有者权益之和,也就是企业所有资源获得的两个渠道。交易会引起资产、负债和所有者权益的变化,即便如此,等式的平衡关系不会改变。

会计等式有两个要点:

(1)每笔交易至少影响等式的两个部分。这种双重记录的过程即为复式记账,这是大部分会计系统所使用的方法。

(2)交易记录之后,等式仍然保持平衡,也就是资产总和等于负债加上所有者权益。复式记账法中,这一点永远成立。

3. 会计循环

为了不断报告企业的进展,企业的生命被人为划分为相等的时长,也就是会计期间。这种等间距时长的划分被称为会计分期。

相等的会计期间使得报表使用者能对当期和前期的经营成果进行有意义的比较。在每一个会计期间里,都会采取有关步骤和程序以保证所有的交易都得以正确记录,并且能够在期末编制报表。这些以编制报表为终点的步骤和程序被称为会计循环。

会计循环始于企业交易的记录,止于正式财务报表的编制(图2-1),这些报表汇总了交易对企业资产、负债及所有者权益的影响。实务中,还有许多其他步骤或程序出现在记录交易和编制报表的过程中间。

会计循环的步骤	会计记录
(1)确认交易	原始凭证
(2)做日记账	普通日记账
(3)过账	总分类账
(4)编制试算平衡表	试算平衡表
(5)编制财务报表	财务报表

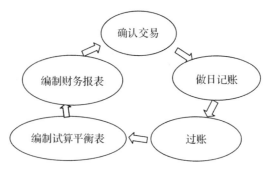

图 2-1 会计循环

二、总账会计与复式记账

1. 总分类账与 T 形账户

会计的功能之一是将交易的影响转变为会计要素的变化,并且将结果汇总在财务报表中。为了便于积累会计数据,交易被记录在分类账里。所谓账户是指用来记录财务报表项目增减变化的工具。由此,企业通常将对资产、负债、所有者权益、收入及费用的每一项内容进行账户的记录。企业为编制财务报表而进行登记的账户,统称为总分类账。

每个账户由三部分组成:(1)名称,用来描述所记录项目的属性;(2)记录增加额的部分;(3)记录减少额的部分。同时,账户通常有编号、交易日期及交易描述。基本的账户形式像字母 T,所以又叫 T 形账户。

T 形账户分为左边和右边,分别称作借方和贷方。借贷二词在会计上仅仅表示账户的左边和右边,而并没有其他的含义。当金额记录到账户的左边,就称为借记;记录到账户的右边,就称为贷记。交易记录完成后,即可计算账户余额。如果借方总额大于贷方总额,账户就有借方余额;反之,则为贷方余额。如果借方总额等于贷方总额,则账户余额为零。举个例子,现金账户的借方总额为 70 000 美元,贷方总额为 52 000 美元,则账户有借方余额 18 000 美元。

现金

借	贷
$70 000	$52 000
余额 $18 000	

T 形账户便于反映单独账户的交易影响,主要在教材以及课堂教学中使用。借贷记账的规则将在复式记账法中详细介绍。

2. 常用账户

如上所述,每一项报表中出现的要素,包括资产、负债、所有者权益、收入和费用都需要建立账户。账户的名称要能具体描述该项目的内容。部分最为常用的报表项目列示如下:

资产类账户

银行存款:该账户用来记录存入银行以及从银行提取的资金,是企业的银行账户,又称为往来账户或支票账户。

应收账款：应收账款指企业客户以赊账的方式接受其商品或劳务，从而款项暂欠。一项应收账款可以以口头的方式承诺，但更多地以出具发票来确认。应收账款也称作"Trade Debtors"或"Debtors"。

应收票据：该账户用来记录企业对另一方的索求权，通常以签字的票据为依据，如本票。应收票据比应收账款更加正式，含有另一方在将来的指定日期向企业支付确定金额款项的义务。

其他应收款：在会计期末，企业可能会发生源于各种交易的应收款。例如，预先支付给职工的现金垫款，未来所得商品或劳务的定金，仍未偿还的应收票据产生的利息收入，以及租户应缴的租金。企业通常为每一类债务人建立一个账户。

预付费用：预付费用指已经支付的款项，但尚未获得相关的商品或劳务，通常包括预先支付的租金或保险费用。每一类的预付费用都得要记录在单独的账户里，比如，预付租金和预付保险。

存货：存货表示生产制造企业所拥有的产品物资及其他企业用于经营销售的商品。

土地：该账户用于记录企业控制的土地。土地与其地上建筑物必须分开记录。

建筑物：该账户用于记录企业在日常生产经营中所用建筑物的购得或建造成本。

固定资产：企业里使用期限较长的有形资产记录在固定资产账户，一般包括任何非永久附着于土地或建筑物上的物体。固定资产通常包括：办公家具、工厂设备、机器设备、固定装置和交通运输工具。每一类型的装备都需要建立单独的账户，例如，办公家具或机器。

累计折旧：该账户反映固定资产购得后，分派及累计的费用。累计折旧又称为备抵账户，是针对相关账户的抵销或抵减。因此在资产负债表里，累计折旧账户抵减资产的原始成本，反映其账面价值。

无形资产：无形资产没有物理形态，但仍能为企业带来预期的经济利益。无形资产的价值来自所有者对资产的拥有和使用。和固定资产一样，无形资产最初以历史成本或其他可靠计量的成本入账，其价值在其后的有效使用期内进行摊销。无形资产包括专利、版权、特许经营权、品牌名称、商标等。

负债类账户

应付账款：应付账款指由于购买商品或劳务而向债权人支付款项的义务。该账户通常也称为"Trade Creditors"或者"Creditors"。

应付票据：应付票据是在指定日期向债权人支付特定金额款项的书面承诺。企业可以向贷款机构签发应收票据以换取现金，或者在赊购其他资产时签发应付票据。

预收款项：在尚未提供商品和劳务时客户提前支付的款项，不得记为收入，因为企业在提供商品和劳务之前对客户承担债务。一旦提供商品或劳务之后，金额将从预收款项转移到收入账户。收入意味着负债账户的减少。例如，从租户那里提前收取的房租，或者出版社提前2年收取的杂志订阅费用。

其他应付款：在任何特定的时间，企业都有可能对企业外部有关方面有所欠款。比如，许多企业都需要对出售的商品或提供的劳务缴纳税款，公司也可能欠缴所得税，季度的电话账单或许尚未支付，银行借款的利息或许也已到期。企业潜在的负债不能在此一一列举。重要的是，每一类这样的负债都需要建立一个单独的账户。

长期负债:长期负债指企业在下一年度无须偿还的债务。也就是说,不属于流动负债的部分就是长期负债。

所有者权益类账户

实收资本:实收资本是所有者投入企业以换取股份的现金或其他资产。不仅新创办的企业会产生实收资本,只要投资人或现任股东对企业投入资金,任何企业都会产生实收资本。简而言之,实收资本是所有者用以获取股份而投入或贡献的金额。

提取款项:该账户用于记录独资经营企业的所有者从企业取走资产,通常为现金。因此,该账户的记录意味着资产和所有者权益的同时减少。

留存收益:留存收益是企业净收益减去分派给股东的股利,并累积下来的部分。换言之,该部分是扣除各项费用与股利后企业剩余并累积的资金。

盈余公积:盈余公积指所有者权益项目中不是留存收益与实收资本的部分。很多盈余公积都从留存收益转出,企业会出于某种特定目的将所有者权益的一部分进行储备。

收入类账户

收入是企业经济利益的流入或者利益流出的减少,并且会导致所有者权益增加。收入通常来源于劳务的提供或者商品及其他资产的出售。收入账户包括服务收入、佣金收入、销售收入等。

费用类账户

费用包括劳务的成本、耗用或损失的经济利益,但不包括资本的减少。通常需要一些费用账户用来报告各种各样的费用项目。比如,工资费用、广告费用、折旧费用、利息费用等。

3. 会计科目表

如上所述,企业里所有账户的集合称为总账。总账里面账户按其在资产负债表和利润表里的先后顺序来排序,以便于查找和编制报表。会计科目表收录了完整的分类账账户名称及其编号,手工记账系统和计算机系统都有使用。

本教材为讲解会计程序而使用的部分账户,如表 2-1 所示。

表 2-1 会计科目简表

资产（100—199）		所有者权益（300—399）	
100	现金	300	实收资本
102	应收账款	310	提取款项
103	应收票据	320	盈余公积
110	预付保险		
111	办公用品	收入（400—499）	
113	存货	401	销售收入
150	土地	402	服务收入
160	建筑物	405	佣金收入
170	设备	407	利息收入
171	累计折旧		

续表

180 无形资产	费用（500—599）	
	501	工资费用
负债（200—299）	502	采购费用
200 应付账款	505	广告费用
210 应付职工薪酬	506	保险费用
214 应付票据	507	租金费用
215 应付利息	508	电气费用
220 预收款项	509	利息费用
230 应付抵押款	512	折旧费用

4．复式记账

如前所述，每笔交易会影响至少两个报表项目，且会计等式永远保持平衡。其核心思想就是每笔交易都有双重影响。因此，将每笔交易都记录至少两次的系统就称为复式记账。

复式记账的基本规则：有借必有贷，借贷必相等。

借贷记账户的增加或是减少取决于该账户是属于资产、负债、所有者权益、收入还是费用。借贷规则如图2-2所示：

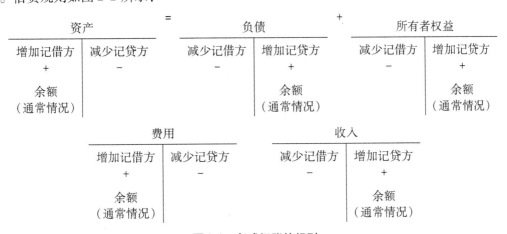

图 2-2　复式记账的规则

或者如表2-2所示：

表 2-2　复式记账的规则

账户类型	借	贷
资产	增加	减少
费用	增加	减少
负债	减少	增加
所有者权益	减少	增加
收入	减少	增加

重要的是,借记账户的增加还是减少,由相关账户类型决定,贷记亦如此。不能误以为借贷本身是增加或减少,仅仅表示T形账户左边和右边。

最后,举例说明如何使用复式记账法记录交易。可以按照以下步骤使用:(1)分析哪些账户受到影响;(2)判断该账户金额是增加还是减少;(3)决定将相应金额登记在借方还是贷方。

【例2-1】

1月份,泰德·特朗普律师事务所发生如下交易:

(1) 投入8 000美元开办事务所。
(2) 购买办公用品700美元。
(3) 从弗兰克家具公司赊购家具2 000美元。
(4) 收到当月的服务费3 500美元。
(5) 支付1月份房租600美元。
(6) 支付临时工工资800美元。
(7) 由于之前购买的家具,支付1 600美元给弗兰克公司。
(8) 提取470美元私用。

上述交易分析并记录如下:

(1) 投入8 000美元开办事务所。影响的账户是现金和实收资本。资产(现金)的增加记借方,所有者权益(实收资本)的增加记贷方。

现金		实收资本	
借	贷	借	贷
(1) 8 000			(1) 8 000

(2) 购买办公用品700美元。一项资产替代了另一项资产。办公用品增加,因此借记办公用品;而支付现金,因此贷记现金。

现金		办公用品	
借	贷	借	贷
	(2) 700	(2) 700	

(3) 从弗兰克家具公司赊购家具2 000美元。一项资产(家具)增加,因此借记家具。没有支付现金,但产生一项负债,因此负债(应付账款)增加。

家具		应付账款	
借	贷	借	贷
(3) 2 000			(3) 2 000

(4) 收到当月的服务费3 500美元。由于收到现金,现金账户增加3 500美元。因此,借记现金。并且使用一个新账户"服务费收入"贷记该账户。

现金		服务费收入	
借	贷	借	贷
(4) 3 500			(4) 3 500

(5)支付1月份房租600美元。由于支付现金,现金账户减少,因此贷记现金600美元。同时,建立一个新账户"租金费用"。600美元记在该账户的左边。

现金		租金费用	
借	贷	借	贷
	(5) 600	(5) 600	

(6)支付临时工工资800美元。支付现金,所以现金账户减少,贷记现金。资本由于费用的产生而减少,将建立一个新账户"工资费用"。借记该账户意味着费用的增加。

现金		工资费用	
借	贷	借	贷
	(6) 800	(6) 800	

(7)由于之前购买的家具,支付1 600美元给弗兰克公司。该笔交易使得现金账户减少,因此贷记现金。同时,负债账户应付账款也减少1 600美元,欠债减少。因此,借记应付账款。

现金		应付账款	
借	贷	借	贷
	(7) 1 600	(7) 1 600	

(8)提取470美元私用。提取现金意味着现金账户的减少。因此,贷记现金。所有者权益(实收资本)账户也减少470美元。建立一个新账户"提取款项"借记该账户来反映资本的减少。

现金		提取款项	
借	贷	借	贷
	(8) 470	(8) 470	

三、日记账、分类账和试算平衡表

1. 日记账

在会计循环中,做日记账是继分析交易与凭证后的第二个步骤,其过程是将交易记录在日记账里,并且用单独的分录登记每笔交易。

做日记账的过程描述如下:

(1)在日期一栏中登记交易日期。
(2)将借方账户的名称及金额登记在相应栏目里。

(3)将贷方账户的名称及金额登记在相应栏目里。
(4)将交易内容摘要记录在分录的下面。
(5)同时,将会计科目表里表示的账户编号登记在凭证号一栏里。

下面以例2-1为例,说明日记账的做法,如表2-3所示。

表2-3 例2-1的日记账

日期 20X7		账户及摘要	凭证号	借/$	贷/$
1月	4	现金	100	8 000	
		泰德·特朗普,实收资本	300		8 000
		记录投资于律师事务所的现金			
	5	办公用品	111	700	
		现金	100		700
		记录用现金购买办公用品			
	5	家具	130	2 000	
		应付账款	200		2 000
		记录赊购办公家具			
	29	现金	100	3 500	
		服务费收入	402		3 500
		记录收讫服务费收入			
	30	租金费用	507	600	
		现金	100		600
		记录当月支付的租金			
	30	工资费用	501	800	
		现金	100		800
		记录支付给临时工的工资			
	31	应付账款	200	1 600	
		现金	100		1 600
		记录支付以前购买的家具			
	31	泰德·特朗普,提取款项	310	470	
		现金	100		470
		记录所有者个人提取款项			

2. 过账

交易记录到日记账后,还要从日记账转移至分类账。将日记账的金额转移到分类账账户的过程叫作过账。其目的是将所有交易对每一项资产、负债、所有者权益、收入和费用类账户的影响进行分类。

在过账的过程中,日记账里每一笔借方或贷方的金额都分别被登记到分类账相应账户的借方或贷方里。

过账的具体步骤为:

(1) 找到分类账里即将登记借方的账户。
(2) 将日记账的页码写在分类账的凭证号一栏里。
(3) 将日记账里的借方金额登记到分类账的借方,贷方金额同样处理。
(4) 金额一旦登记到分类账,在日记账的凭证号一栏里写上账户编号。

继续用例2-1来演示从日记账到分类账的过账过程。

现金	
借/$	贷/$
1月4日　8 000	
5	700
29　3 500	
30	600
30	800
31	1 600
31	470
借方余额 7 330	

家具	
借/$	贷/$
1月5日　2 000	
借方余额 2 000	

办公用品	
借/$	贷/$
1月5日　700	
借方余额 700	

应付账款	
借/$	贷/$
1月5日	2 000
31　1 600	
	贷方余额 400

泰德·特朗普,实收资本	
借/$	贷/$
1月4日	8 000
	贷方余额 8 000

泰德·特朗普,提取款项	
借/$	贷/$
1月31日　470	
借方余额 470	

服务费收入	
借/$	贷/$
1月29日	3 500
	贷方余额 3 500

工资费用	
借/$	贷/$
1月30日　800	
借方余额 800	

租金费用	
借/$	贷/$
1月30日　600	
借方余额 600	

3. 试算平衡表

复式记账法要求每一笔交易都要以相等的金额记录到账户的借方和贷方。记录到分类账借方和贷方的金额是否相等将通过编制试算平衡表来检验。试算平衡表是一张将有余额的账户按照在总分类账中的顺序编排的列表。所有借方余额的账户列在一栏，所有贷方余额的账户列在另一栏。两栏各自的总额应该相等。如果这样的话，账户称为平衡。

继续以例2-1为例，泰德·特朗普律师事务所试算平衡表如表2-4所示。

表2-4 泰德·特朗普律师事务所试算平衡表

20X7年1月31日

账户名称	账户编号	借/$	贷/$
现金	100	7 330	
办公用品	111	700	
家具	130	2 000	
应付账款	200		400
泰德·特朗普，实收资本	300		8 000
泰德·特朗普，提取款项	310	470	
服务费收入	402		3 500
工资费用	501	800	
租金费用	507	600	
余额		11 900	11 900

试算平衡表仅能检验相等的借方和贷方已登记入账，并且账户余额计算正确。一张没有平衡的试算平衡表表明账户中至少有一个错误，或者编制试算平衡表时出现错误。但是，有一些错误不影响借方与贷方的平衡。例如，一笔金额被登记到错误的账户，一笔日记账可能遗漏，或者一笔错误的金额被同时记录到两个账户中。上述错误的存在更加强调在记录和登记交易的过程中必须格外仔细。

第三单元　财务会计

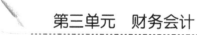

一、资产项目的会计核算

资产负债表里的资产能给企业带来预期的经济利益流入，并且成本或价值能可靠计量。资产通常分为流动资产与非流动资产。

流动资产指能够在一年内或超过一年的一个营业周期内变现或耗用的资产。流动资产通常包括现金、应收账款、应收票据、短期投资、预付款项、存货等。非流动资产通常指固定资产和无形资产。

1. 现金

现金是最重要且流动性最强的流动资产之一。一般来说,现金账户包括现金与现金等价物。

现金包括硬币、纸币、可转让票据,如支票、汇票,以及金融机构里随时可支付的存款。

现金等价物指流动性极高并且很快到期的投资,也就是可以快速变现,而且受价值变化风险的影响极小的项目。例如,银行汇票、货币市场即将到期的存款、银行透支及货币市场见票即付的资金等。根据一般的原则,三个月以内(包含三个月)的非交易性金融工具只要其价值变化的风险很小,都可以归属于现金等价物。

在大部分企业,涉及现金的交易数量大大超过其他类型的交易。同时,现金也是最易于被挪用的资产。因此,必须要有一个良好的内控系统来管理现金并记录现金交易,包括保护库存现金以及处理现金收支。现金的内控管理包括三个重要的方面:(1)现金处理和保管与现金记录的职责分离;(2)将每日的现金收入完好无损地存入银行;(3)用支票或者电子转账给其他个人或企业进行支付。

【例3-1】

斯卡特公司5月份发生了如下交易,要求做分录。

(1) 5月1日,所有者投入700 000美元。

(2) 5月6日,购买用品和设备120 000美元。

(3) 5月17日,向穆迪公司提供劳务,获得收入25 000美元。

答案:

(1) 借:现金 $700 000

      贷:实收资本 $700 000

(2) 借:用品与设备 $120 000

      贷:现金 $120 000

(3) 借:现金 $25 000

      贷:服务收入 $25 000

2. 应收账款

当前的经济实际上是信用经济。制造商、批发商和零售商常常将信用授予购买其商品或接受其劳务的客户以增加销量,也就是客户通常有一段指定时间,比如30或60天来进行支付。企业授予信用的意愿成为当代经济增长的一个重要因素。从而,应收账款应运而生。

应收账款是由于赊销而产生的到期款项,也称作"Trade Debtors"。有时候,企业只有获得像本票这样的正式法律文件,才可以授予信用。本票是债务人在指定日期支付某笔金额的书面承诺。这种情况下产生的应收账款就称为应收票据。应收票据比应收账款更加正式,原因是债务人以书面形式承诺来保证在将来指定日期支付款项。除了应收账款和应收票据,还有应收利息、应收股利等。

上述应收款的共同特点是:被视为高流动资产,并通常在短期内可以变现,因此在资产负债表里归类为流动资产。

【例3-2】

6月1日,斯卡特公司赊销50 000美元产品给速度公司。信用条件为2/10,n/30,速度公司在6月9日支付了款项。

答案：

6月1日	借：应收账款——速度公司	$50 000
	贷：销售收入	$50 000
6月9日	借：现金	$49 000
	销售折扣	$1 000
	贷：应收账款——速度公司	$50 000

不管在信用延展中多么小心谨慎，仍然会有一部分客户不能支付全部或部分账款。信贷部可能错误判断了客户的偿付能力，也有可能突发的财务问题导致了无法支付。决定赊销商品或劳务时，业务经理就明白一部分应收账款终将无法收回。这部分无法收回的账款称为坏账，视作信用基础上的业务成本。

会计实务的常规处理就是费用应该与收入配比，因此坏账也应该在产生赊销的期间进行确认。由于最终成为坏账的账款无法得知，在会计期末时，对坏账费用采用备抵法进行估算。例如，假设斯卡特公司20X8年赊销金额为400 000美元，在20X8年年底收回账款300 000美元。仔细复核应收账款后，管理层估计6 000美元账款将无法收回。20X8年12月31日，做一笔调整分录为：

借：坏账费用　　　　　　　　　　　　　$6 000
　　贷：坏账准备　　　　　　　　　　　　$6 000

坏账的估计金额通常基于过去的经营以及对将来经济和业务情况的预测，与个人判断有相当的关联。有两种方法普遍运用于坏账的估计。一种方法是在期末时将坏账确定为净赊销额的百分比。由于该方法将赊销额作为基数，因此又称为利润表法。另一种方法是分析每一个应收账款账户的账龄及收回的概率，因此称为账龄分析法。由于这种方法基于应收账款的分析，所以又称为资产负债表法。

以账龄法为例，该方法对坏账的估算基于账龄分析表。例如，假设过去会计记录的分析显示注销为坏账的比例，见表3-1。

表3-1　坏账比例分析

账龄分类	百分比/%
尚未到期	1
过期1—30天	5
过期31—60天	10
过期61—90天	20
过期91—180天	30
过期超出180天	60

斯卡特公司账龄分析结果见表3-2。

表 3-2 应收账款账龄分析表

20X8 年 12 月 31 日

单位：$

客户	余额	尚未到期	过期天数				
			1—30	31—60	61—90	91—180	超过 180
A 公司	680		680				
B 公司	335	335					
C 公司	590	240	350				
D 公司	860			420	440		
E 公司	470						470
F 公司	215					215	
G 公司	740	740					
H 公司	930	830			100		
…	…	…	…	…	…	…	…
合计	83 400	55 800	10 600	6 600	4 200	3 800	2 400

因此，用来抵销应收账款至可实现净值的坏账准备金额计算见表 3-3。

表 3-3 坏账准备金额的计算

账龄分类	金额/$	估计的坏账金额	
		百分比/%	金额/$
尚未到期	55 800	1	558
过期 1—30 天	10 600	5	530
过期 31—60 天	6 600	10	660
过期 61—90 天	4 200	20	840
过期 91—180 天	3 800	30	1 140
过期超出 180 天	2 400	60	1 440
合计	83 400		5 168

如表 3-3 所示，5 168 美元即为坏账准备的金额。一笔应收账款确定记为坏账时，借记坏账准备，贷记应收账款。有时候，一笔已经冲销的坏账日后重新部分或全部收回。如果这样，要重新建立应收账款账户以维持客户完整的活动历史记录。这一点对于将来客户信用评级非常重要。

3．短期投资

如果企业在经营中有闲置资金，通常会投资于短期有价证券，像债券和股票，用以获得资本利得、利息和股息。要建立一个短期投资账户来记录企业有价证券的购得与出售。对于交易性金融资产，账户借方记录证券最初的成本及按照市价进行价值重估时的增值部分。贷方记录出售证券时转出的账面价值及市价下跌时的减值部分。当期交易性金融资产产生的已收与应收利息和股息,以及出售证券的收益与其账面价值之间的差额,将通过投资收益的账户记入当期损益。

4. 存货

存货用来表示企业持有的商品或财产,未来在企业日常经营活动中将出售给客户,用于生产或耗用。存货通常包括商品、成品、在产品,以及各种原材料、燃料、包装物、低值易耗品等。作为企业最为活跃的资产之一,存货需要不断的获得、出售和替换。存货也是企业总资产的重要组成部分。

存货的会计处理包括记录购买存货的成本,确定成本的分配,包含分配到销售成本和期末存货的部分。两种截然不同的存货系统:永续盘存制与实地盘存制,将用来确定期末存货与销售成本的金额。其中,永续盘存制是目前企业最常使用的系统。

- 永续盘存制

该系统持续并详细地记录实际存货以及销售成本。新的交易发生时,永续盘存制会不断地计算最新的存货余额。

- 实地盘存制

通过实地盘点来确定实际存货,而销售成本则通过计算得出,也就是期初存货加上采购再减去期末存货。实地盘存制下,采购的项目会有持续的记录,但是出售的部分不进行记录。

比较:

永续盘存制与实地盘存制的基本区别表述如下:第一,在永续盘存制下,存货账户的余额提供持续并且最新的实际存货记录;第二,永续盘存制提供了期间内销售成本的累计过程。相比之下,实地盘存制下,需要实地盘点才能确定实际存货和销售成本;而永续盘存制下的盘点仅用来检验期末存货记录的正确性。

过去,企业经营的商品,如果数量巨大但单位成本缺较低的话,因为永续盘存制有高成本和耗时的特点,实际很难维持。这些企业通常包括药店、水果店、报亭、杂货店和五金店等。然而,随着计算机系统的使用,越来越多的企业得以使用永续盘存制。例如,大部分零售企业使用有扫描设备的收银机来读取产品的条形码。不仅可以记录销售价格,还可以将出售的商品录入存货记录。收银机实为计算机终端,将交易在发生时同时登记到会计记录和存货记录。

要计量销售成本的费用,必须将存货与销售成本之间的成本分配基于一定的成本流假设。无论是使用实地盘存制还是永续盘存制都是如此。基于不同的成本假设,用来分配成本的方法包括:(1)个别确认法;(2)先进先出法;(3)后进先出法;(4)加权平均或移动加权。针对某种存货,具体选择哪种成本方法取决于很多因素,比如每种方法对财务报表的影响、所得税法、管理层和报表使用者的信息需求、使用某种方法的办事成本,以及会计准则的要求。实际上,同样类型的存货可以有不止一种合适的方法。也就是说,会计准则并未规定针对某一种存货,哪一种成本方法"最好"。由管理层和会计来决定哪一种方法能为报表使用者提供最有用的信息。

非流动资产就是资产负债表里除了流动资产的部分。非流动资产基本包括长期投资、固定资产和无形资产等。

5. 固定资产

固定资产指有物理形态的非流动资产,持有期超过一个会计循环,企业获得固定资产是为了生产商品,提供服务或者管理,而不是出售给客户,包括土地、建筑物、设备、机器和交通运输工具。管理者使用这些资产的目的是在将来若干个会计期间内生产商品或提供劳务,这是区别于其他资产的主要因素。

(1) 固定资产的获得

固定资产的增加主要通过购买、建造和使用者投入。企业从外部获得固定资产时,获得成本以使得一切准备就绪的历史成本来入账,包括买价、交通运输费用、保险费、安装费、测试费、法律费用、税费、佣金费用等。

【例3-3】

斯卡特公司7月5日购得需要安装的设备一台。报价是25 000美元,包括10%的折扣。运输费总计800美元,安装费675美元。公司支付10 000美元现金,余款30天内支付。计算和分录如下:

设备报价	$25 000
减去:商业折扣	$2 500
净价	$22 500
加上:运费	$800
安装费	$675
采购费用	$23 975

分录:

7月5日	借:设备	$23 975
	贷:现金	$10 000
	应付账款	$13 975

企业建造资产作为自用时,采购费用包括所有直接用于建造的支出,包括人工、原材料和建造期的保险费用。建筑物的成本还包括建筑费用、工程费用、建筑许可和地基挖掘等费用。此外,还包括合理的电费、监管费用和机器的折旧费用。

至于使用者投入的固定资产,则以投资合同的协议价格或市价入账。

【例3-4】

斯卡特公司7月10日获得所有者投入机器一台,协议价是50 000美元,与市价一致。分录如下:

7月10日	借:机器	$50 000
	贷:实收资本	$50 000

购买土地时,土地成本包括支付给卖方的价格和中介的佣金,以及其他必要支出,比如产权调查费用、税费等。由于土地有无限期使用寿命,土地一般不折旧。

(2) 固定资产的折旧

折旧指由于固定资产过时和损耗而减少预期经济利益的情况,其价值的减少作为冲减收入的费用被登记入账。决定资产折旧金额的因素有成本、预期的使用期限和预计的残值。

使用期限指资产预期的经济利益能被企业使用的时长。资产的使用期限通常以时间来计算和表示。估算使用期限时,会计人员不仅需要考虑资产的物理损耗,还要考虑其技术期限、商业期限和法律期限。

残值指在使用期限末,企业处置资产时,对可收回部分净值的估算。资产的成本减去残值部分就是需要在资产使用期限内计入折旧费用的金额部分。如果资产的残值相比较于资产的成本,微乎其微,则计算折旧时,通常忽略不计残值。

至于折旧法,有几种方法可以用于在有效期限内分配资产的成本。最常用的四种方法是:直线法、余额递减法、年数总和法和工作量法。企业不必对所有的资产仅使用一种折旧法。所选择的方法要能反映未来资产的经济利益耗用或消失的方式,同时还要考虑其后的物理、技术、商业和法律因素。

以直线法为例来说明。

直线折旧法将等额的折旧费用在资产有效期限内分配到每一个会计期间。资产成本减去残值后,也就是折旧部分的金额,除以有效期限内的期间数,就得到每一期的折旧金额。

【例3-5】

假设一台机器成本22 000美元,残值2 000美元,有效期限4年。每年的折旧计算如下:

年折旧额 = (22 000 − 2 000)/4 = 5 000(美元)

当年的折旧分录为:

  借:折旧费用——机器 $5 000
   贷:累计折旧——机器 $5 000

即使资产的获得成本、残值和有效期限完全一样,不同的折旧方法会产生不同的折旧费用。直线法使得资产使用期内有统一的折旧费用,同时,资产的利益也假设为平均分配在整个使用期内。

6. 无形资产

无形资产指非货币性的非流动资产,没有物理形态且用于企业的日常经营。其价值来源于资产预期的经济利益,而企业最终控制其利益。无形资产可以进一步分类为可辨认的和不可辨认的无形资产。可辨认的无形资产指可以单独确认并且专门入账的资产。比如,专利、商标、品牌、特许经营、版权等通常为可辨认的无形资产。这些资产都是企业购得,并且以最初的买价入账。不可辨认的无形资产指商誉,与企业在客户中的良好声誉密切相关。商誉源自诸多因素,包括客户信心、高级管理水平、有利地理位置、生产效率、良好的雇员关系和市场渗透力等。成功的企业不断加强这些因素,但相关的支出无法单独识别。

将无形资产成本分配到各个收益期间的过程称为摊销。摊销类似于固定资产的折旧。任何购得的可辨认无形资产,其成本都要在预期的获益期间摊销。摊销计入费用。实务中,摊销通常使用直线法。

【例3-6】

斯卡特公司20X8年1月2日以现金购买一项专利20 000美元。专利预计有效期限为10年。相关分录如下:

1月2日 借:专利 $20 000
     贷:现金 $20 000
12月31日 借:摊销费用——专利 $2 000
      贷:累计摊销——专利 $2 000

二、负债与所有者权益的会计核算

负债定义为由过去的交易和事项形成的,预期会导致经济利益流出企业的现时义务。实际上,负债的分类基于预期经济利益流出的时间。因此,预期报告日后一年内偿还的债务称为流动负债,比如应付账款、应付票据、应付职工薪酬、预收款项、应付利息、应交税费等。流动负债通常通过流动资产或新的流动负债所形成的资金来偿还。非流动负债定义为报告日后超过一年时间偿还的债务,例如长期借款、应付抵押款、应付债券等。

所有者权益是企业所有者对资产负债表里资产的索求权。对独资经营和合伙企业而言,资本常常可以替代所有者权益。而对于公司而言,所有者权益通常由实收资本(股东的投资)和留存收益(企业经营的收益)组成。

1. 应付账款和应付票据

应付账款表示在企业经营周期中由于购买商品、物资和劳务而欠债权人的款项。没有像合同或票据这样的正式债务工具作为凭证,应付账款又称为开放式账户。赊购商品、物资或劳务的交易发生时,借记资产或费用,贷记应付账款。

应付票据常用来代替应付账款,是给予出借人有关义务的书面文件。应付票据可转变为可转让票据,其持有者能转让给其他人。应付票据通常要求借款人支付利息。债务发生时,借记资产,贷记应付票据。支付票据时,借记应付票据,贷记现金。

【例 3-7】

斯卡特公司 10 月 10 日购买一批原材料花费 5 000 美元,信用条件为 2/10,n/30。公司 9 天后支付款项。相关分录为:

10 月 10 日	借:原材料	$5 000
	贷:应付账款	$5 000
10 月 19 日	借:应付账款	$5 000
	贷:现金	$4 900
	采购折扣	$100

【例 3-8】

斯卡特公司 10 月 12 日购买存货花费 5 000 美元,签发一张年利率 6%,时间 30 天的票据。相关分录为:

10 月 12 日	借:存货	$5 000
	贷:应付票据	$5 000
11 月 10 日	借:应付票据	$5 000
	利息费用	$25
	贷:现金	$5 025

2. 应付债券

债券是一项负债的凭证,提供有关发行企业、面值、到期日和合同利率的信息。公司需要筹集大额的长期资本时,通常会向公众发行额外的股票或债券,使得许多不同的投资人可以参与贷款。

以不同于面值的价格发行债券的情况非常常见。根据发行价格与面值之间的差额,债券发行可分为三种:平价发行、溢价发行和折价发行。平价发行时,债券利率与市场利率一致。溢价发行时,发行价格高于面值,并且合约利率通常高于市场利率。折价发行时,发行价格低于面值,并且合约利率通常低于市场利率。

【例3-9】

斯卡特公司计划发行面值1 000 000美元,年利率10%的10年期债券。11月1日发行日,市场利率略高于10%,因此债券以市价950 000美元发行。有关该债券发行的分录如下:

11月1日	借:现金	$950 000
	应付债券折扣	$50 000
	贷:应付债券	$1 000 000

3. 长期借款

公司为了建造、研发或改造固定资产,常需要更长期限的借款。这样的借款实际上是偿还期超过一年的定期贷款。长期借款的结算包括本金和利息的偿还。

【例3-10】

斯卡特公司12月15日获得一项三年期借款1 500 000美元,年利率6%。借款存入银行,利率每年结算。三年末的时候,本金利息全部偿还。分录如下:

12月5日	借:现金	$1 500 000
	贷:长期借款	$1 500 000

第一年年末结算利息:

借:利息费用	$90 000
贷:应付利息	$90 000

第三年年末偿还本金和利息:

借:长期借款	$1 500 000
应付利息	$270 000
贷:现金	$1 770 000

4. 实收资本

公司的实收资本通常包括普通股、优先股和资本公积。普通股代表企业剩余的所有权,普通股股东是企业最终的所有者。在偿还负债及抵偿优先股权益之后,资产的剩余要求权归属于普通股股东。在破产或清算的情况下,负债和优先股权益可能超过资产在清算中的可变现净值,此时这种剩余要求权就毫无价值。大部分情况下,企业利润通常会超过债权人的要求权(利息)和优先股股东的要求权(优先股股息),则普通股股东能有所获益。值得一提的是,普通股股东的所有者价值没有上限。此外股东有公司董事会成员的选举权。

优先股作为实收资本的一种,不同于普通股,却有某些类似于负债的特征。大多数情况下,优先股没有投票权。其优先体现在股息支付和清算时资产要求权的优先获得。

需要总结并强调的是,公司的实收资本代表了所有者投入的部分,并表示所有者权益的来源。

5. 留存收益

留存收益账户反映企业累积的收益,并且这部分收益仅留作企业之用而不是作为股息分配给股东。最重要的是,留存收益意味着经营产生的净资产将留于企业并作为企业发展或其他需求之用。账户的贷方余额表明净资产整体上的增加,而借方余额的增加表明企业的亏损和股东的分配额大于经营产生的利润。这种情况说明企业的留存收益是赤字。

作为企业向股东分配的利益,股利被认为是留存收益的直接抵减。公司法中对股利的唯一要求是企业只有在盈利时才能支付股利。如果报表日在股利宣告日和支付日之间,资产负债表的流动负债部分将包含应付股利的账户内容。股利有现金股利和股票股利。如果支付现金股利,必须要满足几个条件:企业有留存收益,董事会必须宣告股利,并且公司要有足够的现金来支付股利。而股票股利则是按照现有股东当前持有的股票份额比例,向其发行额外的普通股。5%的股票股利表明按照之前已发行股票的5%再发行股票。

【例3-11】

斯卡特公司20X8年1月1日发行100 000份面值1美元的普通股,市价为10美元每股。其分录为:

1月1日　借:现金　　　　　　　　　　　$1 000 000
　　　　　　贷:实收资本　　　　　　　　　　$100 000
　　　　　　　　股票溢价　　　　　　　　　　$900 000

【例3-12】

20X8年12月30日,斯卡特公司董事长宣布100 000份面值10美元的普通股将分派每股40美分的股利,则股利为40 000美元(100 000×0.4)。其分录如下:

12月30日　借:已宣告股利　　　　　　　　$40 000
　　　　　　　贷:应付股利　　　　　　　　　$40 000

期末,股利账户将结账至留存收益账户。

12月31日　借:留存收益　　　　　　　　　$40 000
　　　　　　　贷:已宣告股利　　　　　　　　$40 000

20X9年1月10日,公司支付股利。

1月10日　借:应付股利　　　　　　　　　　$40 000
　　　　　　贷:现金　　　　　　　　　　　　$40 000

三、收入与费用的会计核算

收入的定义非常广。许多情况会引起预期经济利益的流入,比如提供商品或服务、投资或借款给其他企业、处置资产,以及接受津贴和捐赠等。若要形成收入,则经济利益的流入必须能够增加所有者权益,但是不包括所有者的资本投入。定义的另一个重点是,作为预期经济利益增加的结果,企业必须能控制这项增加。只有满足以下两个条件,才能确认收入:(1)经济利益流入可能性很大;(2)流入的经济利益能可靠计量。

同样,费用必然引起所有者权益的减少。例如,购买资产不会减少所有者权益,因此不发生费用。与收入的确认相似,只有满足下列条件,才能确认费用:(1)经济利益流出或耗用的可能性很大;(2)流出或耗用的经济利益能可靠计量。

费用分为三大类:销售费用、管理费用和财务费用。

销售费用通常来自交通运输、保险、租金、广告、销售服务等。管理费用指企业管理部门为组织和管理生产经营而发生的费用,通常包括董事会费用、咨询费用和其他费用。财务费用指筹资的财务管理活动中发生的费用,比如利息费用。上述费用又称为期间费用。

【例 3-13】

斯卡特公司 20X8 年 8 月 17 日向蜘蛛公司赊销商品 150 000 美元。分录如下:

8 月 17 日　借:应收账款　　　　　　　　　$150 000
　　　　　　贷:销售收入　　　　　　　　　　　　　$150 000

【例 3-14】

斯卡特公司 20X8 年 8 月 20 日向当地报纸支付现金 10 000 美元广告费用。分录如下:

8 月 20 日　借:广告费用　　　　　　　　　$10 000
　　　　　　贷:现金　　　　　　　　　　　　　　　$10 000

【例 3-15】

斯卡特公司 20X8 年 9 月 30 日支付利息 6 000 美元。分录如下:

9 月 30 日　借:利息费用　　　　　　　　　$6 000
　　　　　　贷:现金　　　　　　　　　　　　　　　$6 000

第四单元　财务报告和财务分析

一、财务报表

公众需要有用的信息来做出经济决策,管理层也需要向股东履行其管理职责,为此,企业必须向使用者提供年度财务报告。年报包含下列内容:一套财务报表、财务报表附注和董事长声明。此外,还有经营回顾、董事长报告、审计报告等。

包含在年报里的财务报表主要包括:

(1) 利润表;

(2) 资产负债表;

(3) 现金流量表。

本单元将简单介绍利润表和资产负债表的形式及作用。

1. 资产负债表

资产负债表通过资产、负债和所有者权益来反映企业在某一时间点的财务状况,就像一幅照片,捕捉某一时刻的静态画面。资产负债表的标题反映企业的名称、报告的名称和报告日期。此外,资产负债表分为三部分内容:资产、负债和所有者权益。会计等式构成资产负债表会计模式的基础:资产 = 负债 + 所有者权益。

资产负债表能提供有关信息来评估和预测企业的偿债能力与资本结构。偿债能力就是企业在债务到期时进行偿付的财务能力。一方面,资产负债表中的流动资产与流动负债有助于理解其短期偿债能力;另一方面,长期偿债能力由盈利能力与反映负债权益比的资本结构共同决定。通常,企业负债比例越高,债权人承担的风险越大,偿债能力就越弱;反之亦然(表 4-1)。

表 4-1　斯卡特有限公司资产负债表

20X7 年 12 月 31 日

资产	
银行存款	$16 700
应收账款	5 930
办公用品	4 900
设备	36 950
建筑物	20 000
土地	75 000
资产总额	159 480
负债	
应付账款	6 900
长期借款	67 000
负债总额	73 900
净资产	85 580
所有者权益	
斯卡特,实收资本	85 580
所有者权益总额	85 580

2. 利润表

利润表反映企业一段时期的经营成果,一段时期指一个月、半年或一年。净利润指一段时期收入超出费用的部分。如果费用大于收入,则发生亏损。利润表的标题表明报告的企业、报表名称及报告的时期。由于报告的时期反映了产生利润的时长,因此,时期的确认非常重要。

显而易见,利润表提供有关收入产生和费用发生的信息。尤为重要的是,会计信息能有助于使用者评估企业的盈利能力。通过比较和分析同一个企业在不同期间以及不同企业在同一个期间内的经营成果,我们能够知道企业在某一特定时期内是否有更好的盈利能力,使用者由此可以做出投资或贷款的决策(表4-2)。

表4-2　斯卡特有限公司利润表

20X8 年 12 月 31 日

收入	
销售收入	$800 000
服务收入	200 000
利息收入	20 000
收入总额	1 020 000
成本与费用	
销售成本	500 000
工资费用	180 000
租金费用	100 000
油气费用	5 000
其他费用	50 000
成本与费用总额	835 000
税前利润	185 000
所得税	55 500
税后利润（净利润）	129 500

3．现金流量表

另一张重要的报表就是现金流量表。事实上，企业的利润表仅反映收入和费用，并未报告企业的现金流。然而，收入与费用并非能反映现金流情况。因此，企业需要编制现金流量表来反映现金的流入与流出。这一点对于帮助使用者评估现金的来龙去脉和企业的偿付能力尤为重要，使用者可以由此做出有依据的决策。

现金流量表反映来自经营活动、投资活动和筹资活动的现金流。通过比较企业的现金流量表和利润表，可以了解经营活动产生的现金流如何反映经营所产生的利润（表4-3）。现金流量表还可以用于判断过去对现金流的预测是否准确，检验盈利能力与净现金流之间的关系，以及价格变化的影响。

表4-3　斯卡特有限公司现金流量表

20X9 年 12 月 31 日

经营活动产生的现金流：	
收到客户的现金	$141 600
向客户和雇员支付的现金	(113 000)
经营活动产生的现金净额	28 600
投资活动产生的现金流：	
购买土地和建筑物的现金	(104 000)
购买设备的现金	(36 900)
用于投资活动的现金净额	(140 900)
筹资活动产生的现金流：	
抵押贷款获得的现金	68 000
所有者投入的现金	78 100
所有者提取的现金	(15 000)
筹资活动的现金净额	131 100
现金增加（减少）净额	18 800
期初现金	—
期末现金	18 800

最后，如果企业是一家披露实体，则要求编制中期财务报表。中期报表就是一套半年的报表，包括利润表、资产负债表、现金流量表，以及部分报表注释。

二、财务报表解读

财务报表的解读是一个通过建立百分比、比率和趋势来重新分类和汇总财务数据的过程，从而解读企业的经营并理解其财务状况。

百分比分析和比率分析提供有效途径帮助决策者辨识报表里的重要关系及财务数据的趋势。计算比例和比率的目的是将财务数据简化至更加简洁、更易理解的程度，用以评价企业过去的经营以及预测将来的业绩。

1. 百分比分析

（1）横向分析

大部分报告实体在年报中包含最近两年的财务报表。对一个报表项目逐年变化的分析称为横向分析。横向分析时，报表里需要比较的单个项目或者项目群通常并列放在一起，然后，计算两年数据的差额，包括数量和百分比。计算差额时，前一年的数据作为基数。计算百分比时，用差额除以基年的金额。只有基年的数据为正数时，才能计算百分比，如果基年的数据是负数或者零，其变化不能表达为百分比。

百分比的增加或减少能揭示有重大变化的项目，并且分析者可以进一步调查其重要和不寻常的变化。调查的目的是确定变化的原因，判断该变化是有利还是不利，并且评估该趋势是否会继续。举例说明如下（表4-4和表4-5）：

表4-4 斯卡特有限公司比较资产负债表（横向变化，节选）

20X8年12月31日与20X9年12月31日

	年份		横向变化	
	20X9	20X8	$	%
资产				
流动资产				
银行存款	390	300	90	30.0
有价证券	380	440	(60)	(13.6)
应收账款	1 460	1 290	170	13.2
存货	2 010	1 770	240	13.6
预付费用	100	100	—	—
流动资产总额	4 340	3 900	440	11.3
…	…	…	…	…

表 4-5 斯卡特有限公司比较利润表（横向变化，节选）

20X8 年 12 月 31 日与 20X9 年 12 月 31 日

	年份		横向变化	
	20X9	20X8	$	%
销售收入(净额)	10 320	9 582	738	7.7
减去:销售成本	7 719	6 975	744	10.7
利润总额	2 601	2 607	(6)	(0.2)
销售费用	1 030	800	230	28.8
管理费用	567	620	(53)	(8.5)
财务费用	252	230	22	9.6
…	…	…	…	…

（2）纵向分析

横向分析比较了某一项目在相邻两个期间里变化的比例，而纵向分析是将报表里每一项的金额表达为某一特定项目的百分比。比如，资产负债表里，将每一个报表项目表达为资产总额或者负债和所有者权益总额的百分比。利润表里，则常常将净销售额或营业收入设为 100% 的基数，然后将每一个报表项目表达为基数的百分比。举例如下（表 4-6 和表 4-7）：

表 4-6 斯卡特有限公司比较资产负债表（纵向变化，节选）

20X8 年 12 月 31 日与 20X9 年 12 月 31 日

	年份		资产总额的百分比	
	20X9	20X8	20X9	20X8
资产				
流动资产				
银行存款	390	300	5.2	4.7
有价证券	380	440	5.1	7.0
应收账款	1 460	1 290	19.6	20.5
存货	2 010	1 770	27.1	28.1
预付费用	100	100	1.3	1.6
流动资产总额	4 340	3 900	58.3	61.9
…	…	…	…	…
资产总额	7 440	6 300	100.0	100.0

表 4-7　斯卡特有限公司比较利润表(纵向变化,节选)

20X8 年 12 月 31 日与 20X9 年 12 月 31 日

	年份		净收入的百分比	
	20X9	20X8	20X9	20X8
销售收入（净额）	10 320	9 582	100.0	100.0
减去:销售成本	7 719	6 975	74.8	72.8
利润总额	2 601	2 607	25.2	27.2
销售费用	1 030	800	10.0	8.4
管理费用	567	620	5.5	6.5
财务费用	252	230	2.4	2.4
…	…	…	…	…

（3）趋势分析

如果可获得三年或以上的财务数据,则常常用趋势分析来评估企业的成长前景。分析时,将最早的期间作为基数期间,随后所有的期间都与之比较。一般假设所选的基年对企业经营有代表意义。例如,销售收入(美元)和税后利润(美元)在过去连续 5 年的数据如表 4-8 所示(000 省略)：

表 4-8　连续 5 年的销售收入与税后利润

年份	20X5	20X6	20X7	20X8	20X9
销售收入	1 000	1 050	1 120	1 150	1 220
税后利润	200	206	218	220	232

显然,销售收入与税后利润的金额都在增加。如果这些变化用百分比表达的话,销售收入变化和税后利润变化的关系能得以更清楚的解释,也就是将每一年的数据除以基年（20X5）的金额,因此作表 4-9：

表 4-9　变化率

年份	20X5	20X6	20X7	20X8	20X9
销售收入	100%	105%	112%	115%	122%
税后利润	100%	103%	109%	111%	116%

可以发现,税后利润的增长远低于销售收入的增长。显然,应继续调查其他项目的趋势。可能的情况是,销售成本的增加大于销售价格的增长。关键在于,在对某一项目的重要性下结论前,需要复核其他相关数据。趋势分析的目标在于,评价各种相关的趋势,估算趋势是否有望延续。

2. 比率分析

比率分析作为最有用的比较方式,能够清楚并简单地表达很多数量之间的关系。相关数量关系存在于同一份报表的不同项目之间,也存在于不同报表的项目之间,因此,很多比率能够计算。分析者在选择比率之前需要细心考虑,以选择与关注方面最为相关的比率关系。因此,评价某一关系是否充分,必须要将该比率与其他标准,比如行业标准,进行比较。

作为决策工具,比率分析减少了对直觉因素的依赖,而是为理性且合理的判断建立基础。通过与同行业企业平均水平的比较,以及企业自身连续几年数据的比较,可以发现企业的竞争优势和弱势。比率可以有不同的分类方式,本单元将讨论三类比率,分别反映企业的盈利能力、流动性和财务稳定性。

(1) 盈利能力比率

盈利能力分析包括评估企业业绩的测试,其结果将和其他数据一起预测潜在的盈利能力。潜在利润对长期债权人和股东很重要,从长远来看,企业必须获得满意的利润才能生存。潜在利润对于像供货商和工会这样的报表使用者来说也非常重要,这些方面都着眼于与一个财务良好的企业维持稳定的关系。而财务是否良好取决于当前和将来的盈利能力。

① 资产回报率

$$资产回报率 = \frac{息税前利润}{总资产}$$

资产回报率衡量管理层经营的回报率。息税前利润指利息支付和税费缴纳之前的利润。分子中加进利息是为了反映资源的有效使用并未受到资产融资方式的影响。总之,资产回报率是衡量总资产盈利能力的公式。

② 利润率

$$利润率 = \frac{净收益}{销售净额}$$

利润率,又称为销售回报率,反映每一元的销售收入产生的净收益。计算方法是期间内的净收益除以销售净额。

③ 每股收益

$$每股收益 = \frac{税后利润 - 优先股股利}{发行的普通股股数}$$

每股收益衡量每一股普通股获得的净收益。该指标常常被媒体所使用,原因是股东特别关注财务年度里持有的股票获得多少收益。

④ 市盈率

$$市盈率 = \frac{每股市价}{每股盈利}$$

该比率反映投资者在市场上需要为每一元的收益支付多少金额。市盈率可以帮助使用者对不同企业股票的市价进行比较。

⑤ 股息收益率

$$股息收益率 = \frac{每股股利}{每股市价}$$

该比率通常被更多关注股利而不是股票价格升值的使用者所使用。股息收益率反映了投入资金的回报率,而且更易于和其他投资机会的收益率进行比较。该指标也常被新闻报纸作为证交所价格报告的一部分所引用。

(2) 流动性比率

流动性是财务报表的一个重要因素,不能履行短期义务的企业将迫于清算的压力。这方面分析的重点是营运资本或者营运资本的某些部分。

① 流动比

$$流动比 = \frac{流动资产}{流动负债}$$

流动比衡量企业偿还短期债务的能力，反映流动资产超过流动负债的数量。过低的比率可能表示在紧急情况下无法偿还短期债务。而过高的比率对债权人有利，但表示可能有过多的投资用于营运资本却未能产生利润。根据经验，分析者通常认为流动比至少应有2∶1。也就是，企业对每1元的负债都要维持2元的流动资产。

② 速动比

$$速动比 = \frac{流动资产 - 存货}{流动负债}$$

流动比的局限性在于分子中包含了存货，而存货的流动性不如现金、有价证券、应收票据和应收账款。在企业正常的经营中，现金的获得通常在存货出售和现金收回之后。因此，速动比用来补充流动比，为衡量流动性提供更为严密的方法。

③ 应收账款周转率

$$应收账款周转率 = \frac{净销售收入}{应收账款平均余额}$$

该比率反映应收账款的平均余额一年内可以变现多少次。同时，该指标也可以衡量信用授予和收账政策是否有效。比率越高，赊销与收回现金之间的时间越短。由于竞争的因素，企业的信用政策常常受到行业惯例的影响。将该指标与行业标准比较可以反映企业是否与其竞争者的经营成果有偏离。

④ 平均收账期

$$平均收账期 = \frac{365\ 天}{应收账款周转率}$$

365 天除以应收账款周转率可以得出从信用销售到收回账款的平均天数。

⑤ 库存周转率

$$库存周转率 = \frac{销售成本}{平均存货余额}$$

库存周转率衡量存货是否充足并且是否得到有效管理。控制好投入存货的资金是企业管理的一个重要方面。投入存货的资金规模和存货周转取决于许多因素，比如企业的类型和一年中的时间。超市比汽车销售商有更高的库存周转率，而一个季节性企业的存货水平通常会在某一时期高于一个营业周期中的其他时期。

（3）财务稳定性比率

该部分比率用于分析企业长期经营的能力、履行长期债务的能力，以及是否有足够的营运资本成功经营的能力。

① 资产负债比

$$资产负债比 = \frac{负债总额}{资产总额}$$

由债权人投入的资产所占比重对于长期投资人来说非常重要，原因是债权人在企业清算的情况下对资产有优先要求权——债务人要先于股东得到资产的分配。由股东投入的资产占比越大,对债权人的保护越大。

② 资产权益比

$$资产权益比 = \frac{所有者权益总额}{资产总额}$$

资产权益比意在估测企业的长期稳定性,该比率检验了所有者权益与总资产之间的关系。

③ 利息保障倍数

$$利息保障倍数 = \frac{息税前利润}{利息费用}$$

该比率反映企业能否用当期利润定期支付利息。分子中加进利息费用和所得税是因为该比率衡量企业可得的利润能否支付利息费用。

表4-10为财务比率汇总表。

表4-10　账务比率汇总表

比率	计算方法	含义
盈利能力		
资产回报率	$\dfrac{息税前利润}{总资产}$	衡量全部资产的收益率。
利润率	$\dfrac{净收益}{销售净额}$	衡量每一元销售额的盈利能力。
每股收益	$\dfrac{税后利润 - 优先股股利}{发行的普通股股数}$	衡量每一份普通股获得的利润。
市盈率	$\dfrac{每股市价}{每股盈利}$	衡量投资者对每一元盈利支付的价格。
股息收益率	$\dfrac{每股股利}{每股市价}$	衡量投资人基于当前市价的收益。
流动性		
流动比	$\dfrac{流动资产}{流动负债}$	衡量短期负债,反映企业用流动资产偿还短期负债的能力。
速动比	$\dfrac{流动资产 - 存货}{流动负债}$	衡量短期流动性的更严密的一个指标。反映企业用流动资产满足意外需要的能力。
应收账款周转率	$\dfrac{净销售收入}{应收账款平均余额}$	衡量收账方法是否有效。评估应收账款余额是否过剩。
平均收账期	$\dfrac{365\,天}{应收账款周转率}$	衡量企业收回账款的平均天数。

续表

比率	计算方法	含义
库存周转率	$\dfrac{\text{销售成本}}{\text{平均存货余额}}$	反映存货的流动性。衡量期间内,存货平均卖出的次数。
财务稳定性		
资产负债比	$\dfrac{\text{负债总额}}{\text{资产总额}}$	衡量债权人提供资产的占比以及使用杠杆的程度。
资产权益比	$\dfrac{\text{所有者权益总额}}{\text{资产总额}}$	衡量股东投入资产的占比以及使用杠杆的程度。
利息保障倍数	$\dfrac{\text{息税前利润}}{\text{利息费用}}$	衡量企业用当期利润支付利息费用的能力。

第五单元 财务资源管理

一、资金的来源

1. 企业融资

融资(筹资)可以简单定义为获得资金或资本。筹资活动指为企业的经营和投资活动筹集资金。筹资活动的例子包括发行股票融资、接受政府拨款、向银行或其他金融机构借款、借款的偿还,以及股东持股的回购。

资金可以从许多渠道获得(图 5-1)。从根本上来讲,债务资本和权益资本是融资的主要来源。权益资本很大程度上指用部分所有权换取资金的投入,主要包括股本和留存收益。也包括其他形式,例如风险资本、政府拨款、特许经营等。债务资本指向债权人借款,并且规定在将来的某一时间偿还本金和利息,主要包括银行借款、债券、应付账款、保理业务等。

图 5-1 不同的资金来源

实际上,企业资金的需求随企业类型和规模的不同而改变。因此,选择合适的资金来源和融资组合是每一位财务经理的重要挑战。而选择的过程需要对每一项资金来源做深入的分析,并需要理解其全部特点。

(1) 发行股票

股票的发行是指企业通过发行股票来筹集资金。主要有两种形式:普通股资本和优先股资本。

普通股股东是企业的所有者,享有回报也承担风险。通常,潜在投资人可以通过购买公司新发行的股票成为其所有者。大部分情况下,由于新股东的加入,发行新股能筹集大量资金却没有公司被收购的风险。然而,发行新股会产生相当的费用,并且常常引起现有股东控制权的稀释。

因此,上市公司常常选择配股的方式。配股指以低于市价的折扣价,按现有股东的持股比例,向其增发股票的方式。股东可以接受认购权,以特定的价格购得新股;也可以选择在市场出售认股权。

优先股股东能在普通股股东分派股利之前,获得固定比率的股利。和普通股股东一样,优先股股东只有在企业有利润可分配时才能获得支付。但是,优先股没有投票权,也就是优先股股东在企业经营中没有话语权。

(2)留存收益

留存收益代表没有分配给股东的收益。公司可以部分或全部保留其利润,为发展项目提供资金。将留存收益用于项目资金而不用来分派更高的股利,其原因如下:

① 很多公司的管理层认为将留存收益留作资金不会引起现金的流出。

② 公司的股利政策实则由董事长决定。他们认为留存收益用于项目投资不需要股东或外部方面的参与。

③ 留存收益的使用可以避免发行成本和银行费用。

④ 留存收益的使用可以避免增发新股引起的控制权变化。

公司必须限制以留存收益进行自我融资,原因是股东必须获得与预期相符的合理股利,哪怕董事长们乐意于保留资金进行再投资。

(3)风险投资

风险投资指个人或公司以股权投资的方式提供长期的资本。风险投资人以所有权份额为交换标的来提供资本。这种方式有很大风险会损失全部的投资,也可能需要很长的时间才能获利。但是,同样也可能获得高利润和高回报。风险投资人需要非常高的投资收益率来补偿高风险。通常,风投公司倾向于选择创始人有很大份额的权益投资,并且公司已经盈利的企业来进行投资。

企业董事若要寻求风险投资公司的资助,则必须认识到:

① 风险投资人将获得企业的所有权份额。

② 需要说服风险投资人企业能够成功。

③ 风险投资公司可能在企业董事会中安排代表委员,以照顾其利益。

(4)特许经营

特许经营是以更少的资金拓展企业的一种方式。在特许经营合约中,特许经营人支付费用给经销商以获得用经销商的名号在当地经营的权利。经销商也必须承担一定的成本(可能是装修费用、开办成本、法律费用、市场费用和其他服务开支),并且会向特许经营人收取一笔费用来支付开办的成本。费用取决于之后特许经营人盈利时的定期支付。

尽管特许经营店铺很大部分的初始投资成本由经销商支付,特许经营人自己也需要贡献一部分投资。对于经销商而言,特许经营的好处在于:

① 拓展业务所需的资金大幅度减少。

② 企业形象得以加强,原因是特许经营人有动力、有权力采取任何适合的行动提升经营成果。

③ 经销商免于维护分店网络和管理员工的责任。

对特许经营人而言,好处是能够获得合同约定年数的企业所有权,以及大机构在市场和经营方面的支持。由于经销商的事先培训和制订的发展计划,特许经营人可以避免许多小企业会犯的错误。

(5) 银行借款

很多人筹资时想到的第一件事情就是银行。银行借款实际上也是企业融资最主要的来源。大部分情况下,有两种方式借款。一是透支,二是正式的贷款。透支是非常有弹性的一种融资方式,只要公司有良好收入,透支可以比正式贷款更加快速地得到支付。企业必须将透支保持在银行设定的范围之内,并且透支部分会产生利息费用。

许多企业更喜欢定期借款,理由是定期的支付使得现金流预测和预算更加确定。同时,定期借款关系中的银行在整个贷款期对企业也更加投入。许多小额贷款不需要任何保证,但是大额资金需要某种形式的保证。通常做法是,企业所有者提供自己的房屋作为保证,但是很多风险抗拒型借款人不会这样做。

(6) 债券

债券常用于某种具体活动的筹资。作为一种特殊类型的债务融资,债务工具由企业自己发行。债券不同于其他债务融资工具,因为企业规定了利率以及公司何时支付本金(到期日期)。因此,企业不必在特定到期日之前支付本金(可能也不需要支付利息)。债券发行时的价格称为面值。

(7) 保理业务

保理是一种金融交易,是企业将其发票或应收款出售给第三方金融公司,即保理商的业务。保理商将向企业客户收回款项。企业选择保理的主要原因是需要快速获得现金,而不是等到应收账款到期,而客户常常会在 30~60 天内支付。

通常,企业会立即获得发票或应收款价格的 80%~95%。例如,企业赊销额为 100 000 美元,保理商会在 24 小时内支付发票金额的 85%(85 000 美元),但要收取佣金和提前支付额部分的利息。企业客户还款后或在约定时间,保理商会将余额部分支付给企业。

保理业务使得企业更加快捷和灵活地建立现金流,从而更加易于支付职工薪酬,处理客户订单或进行日常经营的融资。

2. 资金的成本

资金的几种主要来源的成本如下:

(1) 股本
- 股利

股利就是将一部分公司收益分配给股东的结果。如果公司当年盈利,则投资人大多期望公司以股利的形式给予回报,通常有现金股利或股票股利。

股利政策,即公司给予投资人多少回报的政策,通常由公司董事会在法律范围内决定。股利是投资人的收入,因此公司的股利政策对一部分投资人而言,是重要的考虑因素。对于公司领导层而言,股利政策也是一个重要的考虑内容,原因是公司领导通常就是最大的股东。管理层尤其要决定股利的数额、派送时间和各种其他影响股利支付的因素。股利还有非常复杂的纳税影响,包括对投资人和公司。

- 提供信息的成本

向股东提供有关公司业绩信息的成本是非常可观的。通常包括编制财务报告的成本、在风景宜人的地方召开年度股东大会的成本、审计费用,以及为满足法律和证交所要求向股东披露信息的管理费用。

- 发行新股的成本

发行新股会产生各种间接的成本,无论首次发行还是在整个管理过程,通常包括法律、会计、市场、管理和纳税方面的支出。比如,向公众发行股票的法律费用、招募投资人的市场费用、管理层的时间和努力等。实际上,发行新股非常昂贵、复杂并且耗时。

发行新的普通股还会发生另一些间接成本,围绕着所有权的稀释、公开财务报表的法律要求,以及对股票要求的不可靠性。

(2)借入资金

- 利息费用是主要成本。利率可以是固定的或变动的。变动利率通常是银行的基准利率(由政府经济政策所支配)加上额外的部分(溢价),银行因此可以获利。总的来说,企业倾向于固定利率贷款,这样他们能确定地知道预期的成本如何。当然,如果经济扩张和通货膨胀造成当前的市场利率上升的话,企业的利息成本也会水涨船高。
- 通常会有一笔最初的管理费用来支付出借方发放贷款的管理成本。
- 保理业务方面:保理商要收取佣金,并且在企业客户还款之前,向提前支付部分的金额收取利息费用。

二、投资与项目评估

用于获得产能的支出称为资本支出,通常都是长期投资。资本支出的例子有:置换设备、扩大生产能力、开设新的办公地点或店铺、提高产品质量、引进新的产品线及提高成本效率等。

资本预算是评估资本支出是否理性和系统的过程。资本预算的主要目的是选择与企业目标一致且收益率最高的资本支出项目,从而增加企业的价值。因此,资本支出的决策对于企业长期盈利能力是非常关键的。决策一旦实行,相关的产能必须跟上,管理层也必须确保效率和效果。

高级管理层必须审慎考虑资本预算的决定,其原因如下:

(1)预算涉及大量资金,企业的成败往往与该决定密切相关。

(2)投入的资源需要长期使用。

(3)决定很难反转,其投资已是沉落成本,只有有效使用相关资产才能收回成本。

(4)由于存在许多不确定因素,像经济状况、技术发展、客户偏好和社会责任等,长期项目通常伴随很大的风险。

理论和实践上,管理层可使用诸多方法评估资本支出或者资本项目。

1. 投资回报率法

资本投资项目可以通过计算投资回报率(又称为会计收益率)来评估,并且可以与预先设定的目标或其他投资项目的收益进行比较。作为对投资项目盈利能力的一个大致估算，其计算方法是项目的年平均税后净利除以平均投资，公式如下（使用直线折旧法）：

$$投资回报率法 = \frac{平均利润}{平均投资} \times 100\% = \frac{平均利润}{初始成本 + 残值} \times 100\%$$

该方法由于使用简单，便于理解，而且相关数据能通过会计信息获得，所以广为使用。与投资回收期法不同，投资回报率法考虑到投资项目有效期内的盈利能力。然而，该方法也有致命缺陷——没有考虑金钱的时间价值。

2. 投资回收期法

投资回收期指项目产生的现金流能收回成本所需要的时间。也就是投资项目能偿付自身成本的时间。公式如下：

$$投资回收期法 = \frac{项目初始成本}{年净现金流}$$

该方法计算简单，易于理解，在实践中也广泛使用。显然，较短的回收期有助于企业流动性，并且减少投资的风险，而不确定性往往随着时间而增加。不足是：该方法忽略了金钱的时间价值和项目总体的盈利能力。但是，用其他方法评估项目而得到相同结果时，很多企业会使用该方法做出最终选择。

3. 净现值法

净现值法和内部收益率法都属于贴现现金流法，该方法将投资项目的成本和项目将来产生的净现金流现值进行比较。实际上，贴现现金流法考虑到了金钱的时间价值。

金钱的时间价值可以用终值和现值来表达。假设年利率为12%，由于一年产生的利息，则 1 120 美元为 1 000 美元的终值。如果将终值折现到今天的货币，1 000 美元就是 1 120 美元的现值。将终值转变为现值的过程就是贴现，我们用贴现率表示现值的计算。其实，利率和贴现率在既定的终值-现值关系中是一回事。公式如下：

$$现值 = 终值 \times (1 + r)^{-n}$$

$$终值 = 现值 \times (1 + r)^{n}$$

r：利率（或贴现率）

n：时间期数

项目评估中，使用贴现现金流法，可以比较项目的现时成本和预期现金流的现值，而且两者只有在使用相同货币计量的前提下才能进行比较。通过将预期货币折现为现值，也就是将来的金额在今天的等额货币，我们就可以将二者进行比较。

净现值法就是将预期净现金流折算为现值，并与资本项目的成本进行比较。实际上，预期收益的现值和项目成本之间的差额就是净现值。如果净现值是正数，即收益的现值超过成本的现值，则项目可接受。如果净现值是负数，则项目基本不值得投资。

净现值法的主要优势是决策会使股东财富最大化。此外，该方法已考虑金钱的时间价值。

【例 5-1】

斯卡特公司考虑是否对项目投资 18 000 美元，该项目将在第一年产生 10 000 美元利润，第二年 8 000 美元利润，第三年 6 000 美元利润。资金的成本率是 10%，即项目的收益率至少为10%。要求用净现值法评估该项目。

答案：

年份	现金流/$	现值/$
0	(18 000)	(18 000)
1	10 000	9 090
2	8 000	6 608
3	6 000	4 506
		净现值：2 204

净值为正，代表该项目能获利10%以上，因此项目可接受。

4. 内部收益率法

内部收益率的定义是使投资项目的净现值等于零时的贴现率。换句话说，如果以内部收益率作为贴现率，则贴现的现金流入将与贴现的现金流出相等。项目的内部收益率大于资金成本率的话，则项目值得投资。公式如下：

$$\text{IRR} = A + \left[\frac{a}{a+b} \times (B-A)\right]$$

公式中：A 是净现值为正数的贴现率，

a 是正净现值的数额，

B 是净现值为负数的贴现率，

b 是负净现值的数额。

内部收益率法的优点是将项目的有关消息汇总为一个数字，并且也考虑到金钱的时间价值。然而，内部收益率法也存在不可避免的问题。例如，由于结果以百分比而不是货币数量表达，就有可能产生互相矛盾的结论，即出现相互排斥的项目。而且，手工计算内部收益率不是很简单，需要猜测和估计。实践中，财务计算器和电子表格都能快速准确地计算内部收益率。

第六单元　管理会计

一、什么是管理会计

1. 管理会计的定义

管理会计是会计的一个分支，向组织里所有级别的管理层提供财务信息和其他信息，使其能够履行计划、控制和决策的职责。管理会计在各种形式的组织里都会使用，包括营利企业、非营利组织和政府部门。

2. 管理会计与财务会计

管理会计和财务会计之间存在共性，都是处理企业的经济事项，并且有许多方面互相重叠，比如存货计价、成本核算等。但是，管理会计和财务会计在很多方面也存在差异：(1)信息的主要使用者;(2)报告的类型;(3)报告的频率;(4)外部验证。

(1) 信息的主要使用者

财务会计信息的使用者为外部使用者,比如股东、债权人、潜在投资人、客户和政府部门。而管理会计的使用者在企业内部——主要是管理层。

(2) 报告的类型

财务会计要符合外部使用者的信息要求,为其提供通用报告,包括利润表、资产负债表和现金流量表。通用报告大部分情况下是监管机构所需要的,并且要与相关会计准则一致,比如一般公认的会计准则(GAAP)。管理会计系统为内部使用者提供特殊目的的信息,通常是特定的财务和非财务信息,使用者据此做出经营决策。这种报告不需要遵循会计准则的要求,包括财务预算、销售预测、业绩报告、成本报告、增量分析报告等。此外,管理层可以了解作为通用报告编制基础的有关信息。

(3) 报告的频率

财务会计系统里,在每个报告期末,通常是会计年度末,编制报告。还需要编制详细程度稍低一些的半年报。报告需要定期编制,并且符合所得税法规和会计准则的要求。相比之下,管理会计根据管理层的需求编制报告——每天、每周、每月或定期。管理层必须根据最新信息做决策。

(4) 外部验证

企业编制的通用报告通常需要接受外部审计,来验证报告是否真实公允地反映企业财务状况和经营业绩。管理会计的特殊目的报告不需要审计,尽管管理层也可能需要内部审核。

二、成本分类

成本是经济资源的耗用,并以此换得产品或服务。根据成本分析的具体目的,成本可以有不同的分类方式,也就是不同的成本为不同的目的所用。此外,这些分类方式并非互相排斥,而是相互补充的。

1. 以利润计量为目的的分类:生产成本和期间费用

生产成本与期间费用对编制企业利润表非常重要。作为产品物理形态的必要部分,生产成本与产品密切相关。生产成本包含三类生产要素:直接原料、直接人工和制造费用。

(1) 直接原料

所有产品都需要原材料成分。生产面包的面粉、生产汽车的钢铁、生产家具的木材和生产手机的塑料都是直接原料的例子。原料在物理形态上转变为产成品的一部分,因此原料可以直接追溯到产品。可直接追溯并成为产成品一部分的原材料,其成本称为直接原料成本。直接原料不包括像润滑油、胶水、螺丝、钉子这样的杂项部分,这些原料被视为间接原料并包含在制造费用中。

(2) 直接人工

直接人工包括所有的人工成本,这种人工成本因具体的工作而产生,并且可以经济方便地追溯到产成品中。例如,支付给房屋建筑工匠的工资或支付给车间里流水线工人的工资。另外一些人工也是生产过程的必须支持,但不能直接追溯到产成品。比如,支付给维护人员和产品主管的工资,这些人工被归类为间接人工成本,包含在制造费用当中。

（3）制造费用

除去直接原料和直接人工之外的所有生产成本都属于制造费用。间接原料、间接人工、照明电力、维护、保险、租金与折旧等都是制造费用的项目。将制造费用成本追溯到产成品是不方便或不现实的。因此,需要计算制造费用的分配率,即用制造费用总额除以生产能力的计量基础（如直接人工的工时）。

期间费用在特定的期间里进行确认,且不是生产产品直接需要的部分。因此,期间费用直接在当期利润表里确认为费用。期间费用根据功能属性的不同,通常分为三大类：销售费用、管理费用和财务费用。比如,广告费用和总经理的薪酬都属于期间费用,利息费用也同样如此。

2. 以计划与控制为目的的分类：变动成本和固定成本

管理层通常必须评估销量或产量的变化对企业利润的影响。成本分类最为广泛使用的方式之一是根据成本性态来划分,也就是衡量成本如何随业务量水平的变化而改变,比如生产的单位数量、机器小时或人工小时等。在这个意义上,成本主要分为两类：变动成本和固定成本。

（1）变动成本

变动成本指与产量成正比关系变化的成本。直接原料、直接人工和某些制造费用,如机器运行所需的电力,都是变动成本。

（2）固定成本

固定成本指在一定的经营区间内,能保持相对不变,即不随产量变化而改变的成本。在一个制造企业,不管期间内完成多少生产单位,固定成本都没有变化。许多制造费用的项目都是固定成本,比如设备的折旧、厂房租金、生产主管的工资等。固定成本只有在一定的期间和一定的产能范围内才可以被称为"固定"。也就是说,产能改变时,短期内的固定成本在更长的时期内可能变为变动成本。

三、管理会计与决策

决策指在可供选择的行为中做出选择,而选出的结果通常基于对盈利能力或成本节约的计量。企业决策有关不断重复的常规程序,也有关复杂且不常发生的情况。企业决策的例子包括生产什么产品、如何生产、产品定价、如何销售、如何分配资源、购买何种设备及是否扩张产能等。

尽管管理层决策没有统一的方式,决策的过程通常包括以下步骤：确定目标和问题,收集可选行为的信息,评估其结果,然后做出决策。通常,决策质量很大程度取决于决策者获得的信息。企业里,管理会计提供决策所需要的大部分量化信息（收入、成本、投资和经营数据）。同时,定性因素也在决策中有重要的作用,比如管理层的直觉与经验、公众形象、社会责任、竞争等。

大部分情况下,企业经理会利用管理会计工具做决策。这些工具包括预算、本量利分析、成本性态分析等。

1. 预算

预算是详细的书面计划,反映资源预期如何获得、如何在特定时期内使用,以实现组织目标。预算期通常就是会计年度。年度预算常常细分为更短时期的预算,如月或者季度预算,从而实际结果和预算结果可以及时进行比较。编制预算的过程是有效管理企业的必要阶段。作为一项管理工具,预算基于企业设定的目标,针对企业预期的行为,为管理层提供正式的计划。

首先,预算编制确定财务和经营目标,为企业活动和交易提供方向。然后,实际行为发生时,出于控制的目的,行为将受到相关预算的监管与核实。若实际行为与计划行为之间发生明显的差异,则需要及时调查和纠正。因此,编制预算有如下好处:

- 可以迫使管理层系统地制订计划。
- 可以为管理层界定职责框架。
- 可以协调企业不同部门之间的行为,以最大程度朝共同目标整合努力。
- 可以作为沟通工具,各位经理人以此交流有关目标、想法和成就的信息。
- 可以增强管理层以及员工的动力,以实现目标。

总预算是一系列相互关联的预算,反映一段时期综合的行为计划。编制总预算时,企业通常逐个编制以下预算:

(1)销售预算。
(2)生产预算。
(3)直接原料预算。
(4)直接人工预算。
(5)制造费用预算。
(6)销售成本预算。
(7)销售费用预算。
(8)管理费用预算。
(9)财务费用预算。
(10)总预算。

【例6-1】 生产预算

斯卡特公司制造两种产品A和B,需要编制20X8年的预算。两种产品都由同样等级的人工——等级Q完成。公司库存目前有800单位A产品和1 200单位B产品。其中,B产品中有250单位发现质量已损坏,需要报废处理。A产品的销售预算是3 000单位,B产品是4 000单位,假设公司保持产成品库存量为三个月的销售量。

等级Q的工人最初预期能用2小时生产1单位A产品,3小时生产1单位B产品,时薪为5.50美元。但是,与工会谈判后,工人时薪要求增加0.5美元,而A、B产品的生产工时则缩减20%。

要求:编制20X8年的生产预算和直接人工预算。

答案:

A产品期末存货:$3/12 \times 3\,000 = 750$(单位)

B产品期末存货:$3/12 \times 4\,000 = 1\,000$(单位)

预期生产单位A产品的时间为$80\% \times 2 = 1.6$(时),B产品时间为2.4(时)。时薪为6美元。

(1) 生产预算

	产品 A/单位	产品 B/单位
预算销售	3 000	4 000
期末存货	750	1 000
期初存货	(800)	(1 200)
报废		250
产量	2 950	4 050

(2) 直接人工预算

	等级 Q/时	时薪/$	成本/$
2 950 个单位的 A 产品	4 720	6	28 320
4 050 个单位的 B 产品	9 720	6	58 320
合计	14 440		86 640

2. 本量利分析

本量利分析主要被管理层用来估算销售价格、销量和成本之间的关系,以计划制订可接受的利润水平。本量利分析在预算中对管理层尤为重要,因为管理者需要评价若干有关预期财务业绩的可选战略。本量利分析可用来解决下列问题:

(1) 公司的保本点是什么?
(2) 多少销售水平可以实现净利的既定目标?
(3) 如果销售价格提高或降低,对销量和保本点有何影响?
(4) 如果广告成本增加,对销量和利润会有何影响?
(5) 需要增加多少销量才能抵销采购成本的增加?
(6) 利润最大的销售组合是什么?

总之,管理层使用本量利分析确定所需的业务量水平来避免损失,实现目标利润,以及监督业绩。

保本分析实际上是本量利分析的起点。保本点指收入与总成本正好相等时的销量,没有盈利也没有亏损。销量超过保本点即可获利,反之则是亏损。尽管保本点因为没有利润,并非企业理想的业绩,但是保本点反映了企业避免亏损所需要的业务水平。

分别以产量和销售额计算的保本点,其公式如下:

$$保本点产量 = \frac{固定成本总额}{单位贡献率}$$

$$保本点销售额 = 保本点产量 \times 单位售价$$

在上述公式中,单位贡献率是单位销售价格与产品变动成本之间的差额。

保本点如图 6-1 所示。

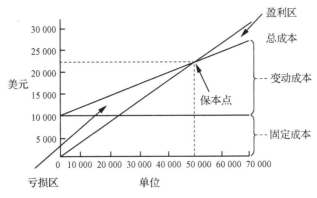

图 6-1　本量利分析图示

第七单元　审　计

一、定义和目的

1. 审计的定义

财务会计中,我们了解到企业发行财务报表的一个原因是向有关方面传递企业的财务状况与经营成果。财务报表的使用者可能是现在与将来的股东、债权人、政府、客户和供货商。由于这些使用者不能直接获得公司内部的信息,他们必须依赖于管理层的诚实来作保披露的财务信息没有重大错报。因此,审计的原因之一是减少财务报表提供虚假或误导信息的风险。此外,被证券交易管理委员会监管的公司要求具有年度独立审计。例如,主要的股票交易所(包括纽约证交所、纳斯达克、伦敦证交所、东京日经等)都有规定,要求全部上市公司审计年报。

审计定义为循证业务,契约中审计提供合理保证,也就是财务信息与既定的财务报告框架相比对,没有重大错报。

审计的目的是,就财务报表是否真实公允地反映企业事务,而且是否根据报告框架(例如,有关法律法规和会计准则)而编制,发表意见。

2. 行业准则与职业道德

(1) 行业准则

国际审计准则(ISA)由国际会计师联合会(IFAC)下的国际审计与鉴证准则理事会颁布,是执行财务信息审计业务的行业准则。国际审计准则涵盖审计的很多领域,比如审计目的、责任、审计计划、审计证据、内部控制和审计报告。

很多国家都颁布自己的审计准则,其中许多都早于国际准则的颁布。这些国家的行业或监管主体通常会提供两者之间的详细比较。需要注意的是,国际审计准则不会超越地方或国家的准则与规定。

(2) 职业道德

很多国家的职业会计与审计组织都有自己的道德规范和行业行为准则。一般用于规范审计师职责的道德准则包括：

- 独立性

独立性是从事公共业务的职业会计师的主要特征，是保持客观性的特定条件，在审计中有很多实现方式。例如，审计师向客户提供审计服务时，不得接受介绍费等。因此，审计师必须有一个立场，在执行审计测试、分析审计结果和鉴证审计报告时，提供没有偏差的意见。值得注意的是，审计师必须保持事实上和形式上的独立。

- 诚实与客观

会计师必须在所有的职业关系和业务关系中保持正直和诚实。客观的原则要求所有的会计师能够公平、理智而诚实，并且没有利益冲突。比如，职业会计师不得接受或提供礼物，原因是该行为有可能对他们的职业判断造成不合适的影响。

- 职业能力和职业审慎

职业会计师有持续的责任将专业知识和技能保持在所需的水平，以保证在当前实务、法律及技术发展的基础上，为客户提供有水平的专业服务。

- 保密

职业会计师必须对由职业关系和业务关系所获得的信息进行保密。除非有法律或职业权利，会计师不得未经适当和专门的授权，向第三方披露任何信息。

- 职业行为

会计师的行为必须与行业的良好声誉保持一致，并且不能进行任何可能破坏行业声誉的活动，包括对客户、第三方、会计行业的其他从业者、雇主及公众的责任影响。

- 技术标准

专业服务的提供必须遵循相关技术和行业准则，比如国际审计准则、会计师行业准则和相关法律法规。

3. 审计的局限性

对于财务报表是否真实和公允，审计能提供合理的但并非绝对的保证。原因如下：

（1）审计不是纯粹客观的活动。审计师需要做出主观判断，涉及主观估测。

（2）审计必须在成本—收益的关系上面表现合理。大量的交易和100%执行测验的潜在高额成本使得审计师要抽样，并在抽选样本中进行交易和余额的测试，得出结论。而结果就是抽样风险不可避免。

（3）会计和内控系统存在固有的缺陷。管理层超越控制的潜在可能与共谋行为破坏内控的可能性说明总有重大舞弊和差错发生的可能性。审计程序并非设计为100%识别这些舞弊或错误。

（4）审计证据是劝诱的，而非确定的。也就是，审计证据提示什么是可能的，而不是什么是确凿的。作为基础的事实是，账户中一些数字是估计值，一些则是主观判断。

因此，审计师仅能发表意见，而不能证明账户的完全正确性。

二、审计类型

审计通常分为三类：财务报表审计、经营审计与合规审计。

1. 财务报表审计(外部审计)

财务报表审计检查财务报表以确定报表是否真实公允地反映企业财务状况和经营成果,并且符合既定标准。

2. 经营审计(内部审计)

经营审计指考察企业某个具体单位的业绩。经营审计审核企业全部或部分经营程序以评估经营的效果和效率。具体包括内控审核、财务和经营信息审核、合规审核,以及任何企业认为需要评估的方面。相关建议通常会提供给管理层以做改进。

3. 合规审计

合规审计指对企业组织经营过程的审核以确定该组织是否遵循上级设定的特定程序、准则或规定。例如,审计某家银行是否遵守准备金的要求,审核纳税人是否遵守国家税法等。合规审计在非营利组织中非常常见,这些组织至少部分由政府出资。许多接受联邦政府资助的实体或非营利组织必须安排合规审计。

由此可见,审计师主要也分为两类:独立外部审计师和内部审计师。独立外部审计师的主要业务是报表审计,而内部审计师重点关注经营审计。政府审计主要针对合规审计,因此兼具外部审计和内部审计的职能。

外部审计和内部审计之间的协调合作能够最小化审计工作的重复,并且有助于审计问题和范围的广泛覆盖。协作包括定期会议讨论审计计划和相互利益的事宜,互相查阅审计程序和工作底稿,交换审计报告和管理建议书,以及审计技术的共同发展。

三、审计风险

1. 审计风险定义

近年来,审计有向风险导向型转变的趋势,主要指审计技术的发展能反映审计中的风险因素。审计经过判断来确定何种风险水平与客户系统的不同方面相关,并设计恰当的审计测试。这种方式确保最多的审计努力分配在风险最高的地方,由此,检测到错误的机会大大增加,并且在"安全的"领域不会花费太多的时间。不断增长的风险导向型审计反映两个事实:(1)日益复杂的企业环境增大舞弊和错报的危险;(2)来自客户的压力不断加大,使得审计必须降低收费水平却要提高服务水平。

实质上,审计风险指在报表有重大错报时,审计给出不恰当的意见。审计风险不可能完全避免。审计风险越高,需要搜集越多的审计证据,从而为发表审计意见取得充分的保证。审计风险由三部分组成:固有风险、控制风险和检查风险(图7-1)。

图7-1 审计风险构成

固有风险指在不考虑内部控制的前提下,账户或交易发生重大错报的可能性,无论是单独出现还是与其他账户和交易中的错报共同存在。

控制风险指客户的会计和内部控制系统没有及时阻止、检测和纠正重大错报的风险。

检查风险指审计师的实质性测试未能发现账户或交易中重大错报的风险。

2. 审计风险模型

三者之间的数学关系可以用下列模型表示：

$$审计风险 = 固有风险 \times 控制风险 \times 检查风险$$

其中,固有风险和控制风险独立于审计,且不受审计师控制。相比之下,检查风险与审计程序的性质、程度和时间密切相关,也就是审计师能够控制检查风险的水平。实际操作中,审计师确定可接受的审计风险值(基于审计师对经营风险的评估),加入估测的固有风险值和控制风险值(审计师无法改变二者),最后计算出检查风险,从而决定审计测试的工作量。

四、审计过程模型、审计证据和审计程序

1. 审计过程模型

审计过程模型提供现场工作中详细的审计步骤,以实现具体的审计目的。说明如下(表7-1)：

表 7-1　审计过程模型

	第一阶段：接受客户
目的	接受客户与被客户接受。确定接受新客户或者继续与老客户的关系,以及需要的工作人员类型及数量。
程序	(1) 评估客户背景及审计原因。 (2) 就该客户确定审计师是否符合职业道德要求。 (3) 确定其他的职业要求。 (4) 与前任审计师沟通。 (5) 准备客户建议。 (6) 选择执行审计的工作人员。 (7) 签订业务约定书。
	第二阶段：审计计划
目的	确定审计证据和审核需要的数量及类型,以确保报表没有重大错报。
程序	(1) 执行有关审计程序以了解企业及其环境,包括企业内控。 (2) 评估报表重大错报的风险。 (3) 确定重要性。 (4) 编写审计计划备忘录及审计计划,包括审计师对已识别风险的反应。
	第三阶段：测试和证据
目的	测试有关内控及报表公允性的证据。
程序	(1) 控制测试。 (2) 交易的实质性测试。 (3) 分析性程序。 (4) 账户余额测试。 (5) 寻找未记录的债务。

续表

第四阶段:评价和报告	
目的	完成审计程序,发表审计意见。
程序	(1) 评估公司治理有关证据。 (2) 执行有关程序,识别期后事项。 (3) 复核财务报表及其他报告材料。 (4) 执行结束程序。 (5) 编写合伙人注意事项。 (6) 向董事会报告。 (7) 编写审计报告。

2. 制定重要性

如果信息的漏报或者错报能够影响报表使用者的决策,则该信息是重要的。因此,重要性是一种门槛或者截止点,而并非信息必须有的基本性质特征。重要性指在考虑财务报表目的的前提下,尽管信息不准确或不精确,但仍能够接受的程度。

制定重要性标准是设计审计时使用的概念,审计师因而能够获得合理的保证,能确认有关重要数额或性质的错误。重要性水平越低,审计成本越高。如果任何小额的错误都必须发现,则审计将花费大量的时间;如果可以接受一定程度的不准确(较高的重要性水平),则情况相反。

实务中,重要性水平通常很难确定。但是,要考虑四个因素:项目的数额大小、项目的性质、环境和审计该项目的成本与收益。考虑所有的重要性因素,又该如何设定重要性水平?国际准则对此没有任何指导。实践中,每一家会计师事务所都有自己的设定标准或者经验,与报表基数相关,比如净收入、总收入等。实务中使用的经验包括:税前收入的 5% 至 10%,流动资产的 5% 至 10%,流动负债的 5% 至 10%,总资产的 0.5% 至 2%,等等。

举例说明如下:20X9 年年底前,50 000 美元设备修理的支出被错误记入设备账户而不是营业费用。结果是(忽略折旧),资产总额合计应为 1 490 000 美元,而不是 1 540 000 美元。税前收入应该是 58 000 美元,而不是 108 000 美元。问:财务报表是否公允,而且没有重大的误导?

分析:财务报表有重大错报,主要是净收入,一项重要性标准的重要基础,被高估86%。这种净收入的高估势必会改变报表使用者的决策,因而是重大的错报。

3. 审计证据和获得审计证据的审计程序

(1) 审计证据

管理层对报表的真实公允负责,因此报表基于使用的财务报告框架,反映企业的实质和经营情况。管理层用于编制报表的基础,如会计记录和其他信息,也是审计所使用的审计证据,例如,会议记录、第三方函证、分析报告、与竞争者的比较数据及控制手册等。

审计证据包括审计用来得出结论的全部信息,在此基础上,审计将发表审计意见。其中包含会计记录和其他作为报表基础的信息。审计师的责任是获得充分恰当的审计证据,以得出合理结论。其中,充分针对证据的数量,而恰当针对证据的质量。审计证据的充分和恰当事关审计的职业判断。

（2）获得审计证据的审计程序

审计通过以下技术方式获得审计证据。

询问。询问是最常用的证据搜集方式,包括向企业内部和外部的知情者获取信息。比如,审计过程中,针对某一问题,从客户方面获得的书面或口头信息。

观察。观察指观看他人正在执行的过程或程序。比如,观察企业职员对存货的记录,或者观察没有留下审计线索的内控程序。观察提供有关程序执行的证据。

检查。检查指审计查看客户的凭证和记录以证实包含在或应该包含在报表里的信息。例如,审核销售订单、销售发票、运单、银行对账单等。

重新计算。重新计算指检查原始凭证和会计记录的数字计算是否正确,或者执行独立的验算。

重新执行。重新执行指审计独立执行原本属于企业内控部分的程序,可以人工执行,也可以通过计算机辅助审计技术来执行。例如,重新执行应收账款的账龄分析程序。

函证。函证指获得第三方的问询回复以证实报表中的信息。比如,审计通过与债务人的直接沟通获得应收账款的确认。函证是审计从独立的第三方获得的书面或口头回复,以证实所需信息的正确性。

分析性程序。分析性程序指对重要比率和趋势的分析,包括对波动和与其他相关信息关系的相应调查。

4. 控制测试和实质性测试

恰当的审计方式需要设计并执行审计程序,而对已确认风险的评估为此奠定了基础。但风险评估本身并不提供充分恰当的审计证据来形成审计意见。风险评估必须伴随进一步的审计程序,即控制测试和实质性测试。有些情况下,审计师可能决定只有控制测试才合适,而另外一些情况,审计师可能决定只有实质性测试才是恰当的。通常情况下,两者会同时使用。

（1）控制测试

控制测试是测试控制方法和控制程序是否有效的过程,以证明较低的控制风险。关键的内控必须有控制风险评估。评估的控制风险越低,控制测试就要越广泛,以支持对内控的高度依赖。确定多少以及怎样的证据能够充分支持具体的控制风险程度,是一项职业判断。

审计证据的搜集技术通常有四种类型,而控制测试的实质就是使用其中的一个（或几个）,包括询问客户雇员、观察、检查（凭证的检查）和重新执行（或重新计算）。例如,审计师通过询问电脑管理员或者电脑系统的使用者,来确认未经授权的人员无法接触计算机文档。再如,通过观察执行人员按照管理者的书面授意进行存货的盘点,来确认存货盘点控制程序的有效性。

控制测试的评估水平直接影响到实质性测试的设计。控制风险的水平越低,审计师从实质性测试中需要的证据就越少。控制风险的评估会影响实质性测试的性质、时间与程度。即使审计师执行了控制测试,内控系统也存在先天的局限,包括管理层越权、人们犯错的可能,以及系统改变的影响等。因此,重要的交易、账户余额和披露都需要执行实质性测试,以获得充分恰当的审计证据。

（2）实质性测试

实质性测试是为获得报表中是否有重大错报的证据而执行的测试。实质性测试反映审计师对重大错报风险的评估。评估风险越高，实质性测试的程度就越深，程序执行的时间就越接近有关期间。实际上，实质性测试设计的目的是减少有关财务报表认定的检查风险（报表认定包括存在、完整、权利、估值等）。

测试的性质有两种类型：具体交易与余额的测试和分析性程序。通过会计系统检查特定类别交易的处理，这一审计程序称为交易测试。交易测试通常执行于下列账户：固定资产、长期负债和权益类账户。例如，搜查未记录的负债。

余额的测试或者为总账账户余额的有效性提供合理保证，或者确认账户中的错报。测试余额时，审计师关注报表项目是否高估或者低估。这些测试用来检查高流动性账户的详细内容，比如现金账户、应收账款、应付账款等。余额的测试很重要，因为审计的最终目的是对报表发表意见，而报表就是由账户余额组成。在审计小型企业时，审计师往往只依靠余额测试。

分析性程序指对重要比率和趋势的分析，包括由此产生的进一步调查，主要针对与其他相关信息或者推算金额不符的波动及关系。执行分析性程序的好处之一是，能够运用比较和关系分析来揭示账户余额或数据是否合理。如果分析性程序发现与其他相关信息或者推算金额不符的重大的波动及关系，审计师必须执行其他程序，比如调查并且获得充分的解释和恰当的确凿证据。

五、审计报告和审计意见

1. 审计报告

审计报告是外部审计对财务报表是否真实公允而发表意见的载体。因此，审计报告应该包含针对报表整体的清晰书面意见。

一份正式而且完整的审计报告应该包括以下基本要素：

- 标题
- 收件人
- 说明段
- 范围段
- 意见段
- 报告日期
- 审计师地址
- 审计师签名

以下是一份标准无保留意见的审计报告范例，来说明审计报告的内容与形式。

【例7-1】

审计报告

里格利公司的董事长和全体股东：

我们审计了后附的里格利公司的报表，包括20X8年12月31日的合并资产负债表、该年度的合并利润表、所有者权益变动表和现金流量表。财务报表的编制是公司管理层的责任，我们的责任是在实施审计工作的基础上，对财务报表发表审计意见。

我们根据美国一般公认的审计准则执行审计。准则要求我们计划并执行审计工作，以获得关于财务报表是否有重大错报的合理保证。审计在测试的基础上，检查有关支持财务报表金额与披露的证据。审计还包括评估企业使用的会计原则与管理层做出的重大会计估计，以及评估整个财务报表的列报。我们相信我们的审计为我们的意见提供合理的基础。

我们认为，公司财务报表已经按照美国一般公认会计原则的规定，在所有重要方面，公允反映了公司20X8年12月31日的合并财务状况，以及20X8年度的合并经营成果和现金流量。

安永会计师事务所
芝加哥，伊利诺伊州
20X9年1月21日

2. 审计意见

审计报告中的意见有四种类型：无保留意见、保留意见、否定意见和无法发表意见。

（1）无保留意见

审计师认为财务报表在所有重大方面真实公允，并且符合既定财务报告框架，则可以发表无保留意见。

如果审计师在以下所有重大方面都满意，审计报告中就可以清楚并肯定地发表无保留意见。

- 财务报表的编制使用了可以接受的会计方法，并且持续地使用该方法。
- 财务信息符合相关法律法规的要求。
- 财务信息整体上表达的观点与审计师对企业业务的理解相一致。
- 与报表报告相关的所有重大事项都有充分披露。

* 带解释段的无保留意见

在某些情况下，审计报告会增加一个解释段（或者事项强调段），以强调影响财务报表的有关事项。

通常，审计师会写下事项强调段落，如果：

- 发生重大的不确定事项，可能影响财务报表，且事项的解决取决于将来的事件。不确定事项包括：关联方交易、重要的期后事项、影响报表与之前年度可比性的事项（比如会计方法的变更）、重大诉讼的结果等。
- 需要强调有关持续经营的重要事项。例如，拖欠债务导致管理层计划的债务重组，资产的出售,等等。如果持续经营的问题未能解决,审计师必须在报告中充分披露使之产生怀疑的主要情况,即关于企业在可预见的将来是否有继续经营的能力。

需要注意的是,解释段的添加并不影响审计意见。不过,如果相关事项很重要,或者没有在报表里充分披露,审计师可能会出具保留意见、否定意见,或者无法发表意见。

【例 7-2】
……
　　形成意见时,我们考虑了报表中关于 B 公司诉讼结果的披露,B 公司是企业的子公司,涉嫌违反环境法规。该诉讼的结果可能导致 B 公司额外的债务及公司业务的关闭。B 公司在合并报表中的净资产总额为 XXX 美元,当年的税前利润是 YYY 美元。关于上述重大不确定事项的详细情况已在附注 15 中进行说明。我们的意见是,在这一方面无保留。
……

（2）保留意见

如果审计师认为不能发表无保留意见,但与管理层意见不一致或者审计范围受限的影响不足以发表否定意见或无法发表意见,则报告中将出具保留意见。保留意见应该这样表述:"报表真实公允,除了"相关事项的影响。

【例 7-3】
……
　　资产负债表显示,包含在应收账款中的一笔款项 XXX 美元已到期,该笔款项的欠款公司已经停止营业。XYZ 公司对这笔债务没有担保。我们认为,公司不可能收回款项,应该做出 XXX 美元的全额(坏账)准备,并且以该金额抵减税前利润和净资产。
　　除了该笔准备金的缺失,我们认为财务报表已经按照 20X5 年公司法的规定,真实公允地反映了 20X9 年 12 月 31 日的公司财务状况及该年度的损益情况。
……

（3）否定意见

如果审计师认为意见不一致对报表产生的影响非常重大或者普遍,保留意见不足以充分披露报表的误导性和不完整,审计师就会发表否定意见。只有在所有游说客户调整报表的努力都失败后,才能发表否定意见。

【例 7-4】

……

如附注 8 所述,对于某执行中的长期合同可能产生的损失,没有建立准备账户,原因是董事长认为其他长期合同收回的金额能够抵销这个损失。我们认为,根据会计准则第 9 条款陈述的要求,应该单独为每一个合同可能产生的损失建立准备账户。一旦确认损失,其结果应减少当年税前利润 XXXX 美元,以及减少 20X9 年 12 月 31 日履行中合同 XXXX 美元。

考虑到企业未能预备上述的损失,我们认为,财务报表没有真实公允地反映公司 20X9 年 12 月 31 日的财务状况及该年度的盈亏。其他方面,我们认为,财务报表已经按照 20X5 年公司法的规定编制。

……

(4) 无法发表意见

如果审计范围受限的影响非常重大而且普遍,审计师无法获得充分恰当的审计证据对报表发表意见,那么审计报告就会出具无法发表意见。

【例 7-5】

……

但是,由于我们未能执行必要的审计程序以获得有关存货及在产品数量和状态的充分保证,在资产负债表中的金额为 XXXXX 美元,因此我们能获得的证据有限。任何对该数据的调整将对该年度利润额带来相应的重大影响。

由于获得证据的限制造成的可能影响,我们对财务报表是否真实公允反映企业 20X9 年 12 月 31 日的财务状况和该年度的损益情况,无法发表意见。其他方面,我们认为,财务报表已经按照 20X5 年公司法的规定编制。

……

导致发表非无保留意见的情况如下：

至少在以下两种情况下,审计师不能发表无保留意见。

- 审计范围受限

如果审计师不能获得足够的证据来判断整体或者部分的财务报表是否真实公允,则存在审计范围受限。审计范围受限有时候由企业所造成(例如,管理层不允许审计师向债务人确认应收账款),有时候由客观条件所造成(比如,审计师到场太晚,未能参加年度的存货盘点)。审计范围受限也可能归因于会计记录的不足,或者不能执行审计师认为必要的审计程序。

- 与管理层意见不一致

如果整体或部分的财务报表编制,未能遵循公认的会计准则,则存在与公认的会计准则相背离。基于足够的证据,审计师认为财务报表,整体或部分,不真实公允。这样的分歧可能关于是否接纳所用的会计政策、使用的方法,或者报表是否充分披露。

如表 7-2 所示,审计范围受限可能导致保留意见或无法发表意见,而与管理层意见不一致可能导致保留意见或否定意见。

表 7-2　审计意见图示

重要性	与公认的会计准则相背离	审计范围受限
不重要	无保留意见	无保留意见
重要	保留意见	保留意见
非常重要	否定意见	无法发表意见

第八单元　会计信息系统

一、会计信息系统的概念

会计信息系统(AIS)是一种收集、存储和处理决策人员使用的财务和会计数据的系统。会计信息系统是一种以计算机为基础,结合信息技术资源来跟踪会计活动的方法。由此产生的财务报告可以提供内部管理层或外部的投资者、债权人和税务机关等其他利益方使用。会计信息系统的设计目的是支持所有的会计职能和活动,包括审计、财务会计和报告、管理会计和税收。最广泛应用的会计信息系统是审计和财务报告模块。

传统上,会计是完全基于手工处理的。会计个人的经验和技巧在会计处理中是至关重要的。实际上,使用手动方法也可能是无效且低效的。会计信息系统解决了许多问题,可以支持大量数据的自动化处理,并能及时准确地产生信息。

20 世纪 70 年代,早期的会计信息系统是为工资业务而设计的。最初,会计信息系统主要是由企业"内部"开发并成为遗留系统。这种解决方案的开发成本很高,很难维护。因此,许多会计从业人员更喜欢手工方法而不是基于计算机的方法。如今,会计信息系统通常被作为预先构建的软件包,从微软、SAP 和 Oracle 公司这样的大型供应商那里销售,它们被配置和定制以匹配不同组织的业务过程。小型企业经常使用会计低成本软件,如 MYOB 和 Quickbooks。大型组织通常会选择企业资源计划系统(ERP),即随着与其他业务系统之间的连接和整合的需求增加,会计信息系统与更大、更集中的系统合并,成为 ERP 系统。在 ERP 系统中,像会计信息系统这样的系统被构建成一个模块,与一系列应用程序集成,这些应用程序可以包括制造、供应链和人力资源。这些模块集成在一起,能够访问相同的数据并执行复杂的业务流程。如今,基于云计算的会计信息系统在中小型企业和大型机构中日益流行,以降低成本。随着会计信息系统的采用,许多企业已经移除了低技能、事务性和运营会计的角色。

二、会计信息系统及其在组织中的作用

信息技术(IT)指计算机信息系统中使用的硬件和软件,是当前社会发展的主要推力。信息时代对会计有着重要的影响,因为会计是知识工作者。事实上,会计人员一直从事"信息业务",因为他们的角色在某种程度上是为了向对他们的组织表现感兴趣的各方传达准确和相关财务信息的。信息时代还包括电子商务的日益重要和繁荣增长,通过因特网或专用

的专用网络进行业务和电子商业——这是电子商务的一个子集,主要指买卖交易。

在许多方面,会计本身就是一个信息系统,是一种交流的过程,它收集、存储、处理和分配信息给需要它的人。例如,公司会计为外部当事人编制财务报表,其他报告如应收账款账龄分析则是给内部经理的。但会计信息的使用者有时会批评AISs只获取和报告财务交易,而财务报表往往忽略了影响业务实体的一些最重要的活动。

然而,今天,会计信息系统关注的是非财务及财务数据和信息。因此,我们将AIS定义为企业范围的系统,将会计作为组织的许多不同类型信息的主要生产者和分发者。该定义还将AIS视为是聚焦过程的。这与当代的会计系统并不主要是财务系统观点相匹配。

会计信息系统有三个基本功能:

AIS的第一个功能是高效、有效地收集和存储有关组织财务活动的数据,包括从原始凭证获取交易数据、在日记账中记录交易,以及将数据从日志中发布到分类账。

AIS的第二个功能是为决策提供有用的信息,包括产生管理报告和财务报表。

AIS的第三个功能是确保准确地记录和处理数据。

三、会计信息系统的组成部分

会计信息系统一般包括六个主要部分:人员、程序与指导、数据、软件、信息技术基础设施和内部控制。下面让我们详细了解每个组成。

1. 人员

AIS的人员指的是系统用户。可能需要使用公司AIS的专业人员包括会计师、顾问、业务分析师、经理、首席财务官和审计师。

有了一个精心设计的AIS,每个被授权的组织里的人都可以访问同样的系统获得同样的信息。AIS还可以在必要时将信息传递给组织以外的人。例如,咨询师可能会使用AIS的信息,通过查看成本数据、销售数据和收入来分析公司定价结构的有效性。同时,审计师可以利用这些数据来评估公司的内部控制、财务状况及对萨班斯—奥克斯利法案的遵守。

AIS系统的设计应符合用户的需要。该系统也应该易于使用和改进,而不是妨碍效率。

2. 程序与指导

AIS的程序与指导是它用来收集、存储、检索和处理数据的方法。这些方法既可以是手动的也可以是自动的,数据可以来自内部资源(例如,雇员)和外部资源(例如,客户在线订单)。程序与指导将被编码到AIS软件中,还应该通过文档和培训对员工进行"编码"。必须遵循始终有效的程序和说明。

为了存储信息,AIS必须有一个数据库结构,如结构化查询语言(SQL),这是一种常用于数据库的计算机语言。AIS还需要为不同类型的系统用户和不同类型的数据输入提供不同的输入界面,以及不同的输出格式,以满足不同用户和不同类型信息的需要。

3. 数据

AIS中包含的数据是与该组织业务实践相关的所有财务信息。任何影响公司财务的商业数据都应该纳入AIS系统。AIS的数据将取决于业务的性质,它可能包括以下几个方面:销售订单、客户账单报表、销售分析报告、采购需求、供应商发票、支票登记簿、总账、库存数据、工资信息、计时、税务信息。

这些数据可以用来编制会计报表和报告,如应收账款账龄分析、折旧/摊销表、试算平衡表、损益表等。把所有这些数据放在一个地方——AIS 中,可以促进企业的记录、报告、分析、审计和决策等活动。为了使数据有用,它必须是完整的、正确的并且相关的。

4. 软件

AIS 的软件组件是用于存储、检索、处理和分析公司财务数据的计算机程序。在有计算机之前,AIS 是手工的、基于纸张的系统,但是今天,大多数公司都使用计算机软件作为 AIS 的基础。小型企业可能会使用 Intuit 的 Quickbooks、Sage Peachtree Accounting,或者微软的小企业会计,还有一些其他的软件产品。中小型企业可能会使用 SAP 的 Business One。中型和大型企业可能会使用微软的动态 GP、Sage 集团的 MAS 90 或 MAS 200、甲骨文的 Peoplesoft 或 Epicor 财务管理。

质量、可靠性和安全性是有效 AIS 软件的关键要素。经理们依靠信息输出来为公司做出决策,他们需要高质量的信息来做出正确的决策。

AIS 软件可以定制,以满足不同类型企业的独特需求。如果一个现成的软件程序不满足公司的需要,软件也可以在内部开发,由终端用户提供输入,或者由第三方公司专门为组织开发。该系统甚至可以外包给一家专业公司来完成。

5. 信息技术基础设施

信息技术基础设施只是指代运行会计信息系统的硬件的一个专门名称。也许最重要的是,为 AIS 选择的硬件必须与预装的软件相兼容。理想情况下,它不仅要兼容,而且要最优。企业可以轻松地满足硬件和软件兼容性需求的一种方式是购买一个包含硬件和软件的交钥匙系统。理论上讲,购买一个交钥匙系统意味着,该公司可以获得其 AIS 硬件和软件的最佳组合。

一个好的 AIS 系统还应该包括一个维护、维修、更换和升级硬件系统组件的计划,以及一个处理破损和过时硬件的计划,以便彻底销毁敏感数据。

6. 内部控制

AIS 的内部控制是用来保护敏感数据的安全措施。AIS 包含的机密信息不仅属于公司,也包括员工和客户。这些数据可能包括社会保障号码、工资信息、信用卡号码等。AIS 系统中的所有数据都必须加密,系统的访问要被记录和监视。系统活动也要是可追踪的。AIS 还需要内部控制,以防止计算机病毒、黑客和其他来自内部和外部的网络安全威胁。此外,它必须预防可能导致数据丢失的自然灾害和电力故障等危害。

由于 AIS 存储并提供这种有价值的业务信息,可靠性至关重要。美国注册会计师协会(AICPA)和加拿大特许会计师协会(CICA)已经确定了保障 AIS 可靠性的五个基本原则:

(1)安全——对系统及其数据的访问仅限于被授权的人。

(2)保密——保护敏感信息不受未经授权的披露。

(3)隐私——用合规方式收集、使用和披露有关客户的个人信息。

(4)处理完整性——在正式授权下,准确、完整、实时地处理数据。

(5)可用性——系统可以满足操作和合同的义务。

Glossary

Account: A device used to record increases and decreases for each item that appears in a financial statement.

Accounting: The process of identifying, measuring, recording and communicating economic information to permit informed judgments and economic decisions by users of the information.

Accounting cycle: The sequence of accounting procedures from transactions to financial statements that takes place during each accounting period.

Accounting entity assumption: The assumption that a business entity is separate and distinct from its owners and from other business entities.

Accounting equation: An algebraic expression of the equality of assets to liabilities and owner's equity: Assets = Liabilities + Owner's equity.

Accounting information system: A system of collecting, storing and processing financial and accounting data that are used by decision makers.

Accounting period: A period of time covered by a set of financial statements.

Accounts payable: Amounts owed to creditors for the purchase of merchandise, supplies and services in the normal course of business; also commonly referred to as creditors or trade creditors.

Accounts receivable: Amounts due from customers for the sale of goods or services; also referred to as debtors, trade debtors or book debts.

Accumulated depreciation: The amount of depreciation that has been recorded and accumulated on an asset since it was acquired.

Adverse opinion: An adverse opinion is expressed when the effect of a disagreement is so material and pervasive to the financial statements that the auditor concludes that a qualification of the report is not adequate to disclose the misleading or incomplete nature of the financial statements.

Ageing of accounts receivable: The process of classifying accounts receivable on the basis of the length of time they have been outstanding; also a basis for determining the amount of the allowance for doubtful debts.

Analytical procedures: The analysis of significant ratios and trends including the resulting investigation of fluctuations and relationships that are inconsistent with other relevant information or deviate from predictable amounts.

Assertions: Assertions are representations by management, explicit or otherwise, that are embodied in the financial statements. Sometimes called "financial statements assertions", they can be categorized as follows: existence, rights and obligations, occurrence, completeness, valuation, accuracy cutoff, classification, understandability, measurement, and presentation and disclosure.

Assets: Assets are future economic benefits controlled by the entity as a result of past transactions or other events.

Attestation: A professional opinion in report form on compliance of the responsible party with some specific criteria.

Audit: The objective of an audit of financial statements is to enable the auditor to express an opinion whether the financial statements are prepared, in all material respects, in accordance with an identified financial reporting framework. The phrases used to express the auditor's opinion are "give a true and fair view" or "present fairly, in all material respects", which are equivalent terms. A similar objective applies to the audit of financial or other information prepared in accordance with appropriate criteria.

Audit assurance: The expression of a conclusion by an auditor that is designed to enhance the degree of confidence intended users can have about the evaluation or measurement of historical financial statements that is the responsibility of the auditee against the criteria of International Financial Reporting Standards or other national accounting standards.

Audit evidence: The information obtained by the auditor in arriving at the conclusions on which the audit opinion is based. Audit evidence will comprise source documents and accounting records underlying the financial statements and corroborating information from other sources.

Audit risk: Audit risk is the risk that the auditor gives an inappropriate audit opinion when the financial statements are materially misstated. Audit risk has three components: inherent risk, control risk and detection risk.

Balance sheet: A financial report listing the assets, liabilities and owner's equity of a business entity as at a specific date.

Break-even point: The sales volume at which revenues and total costs are equal resulting in no net profit or loss.

Budgeting: Preparing a plan for the future operating, activities of a business entity.

Cash: Money and any negotiable instrument such as a check, postal note, credit card duplicate or electronic transfer that a bank will accept for immediate deposit in a bank account.

Cash equivalents: Highly liquid investments which are readily convertible to cash at an entity's option and which are subject to an insignificant risk of changes in value, and borrowings which are integral to the entity's cash management function and which are not subject to a term facility.

Company (or corporation): A form of business structure incorporated to operate as a business entity under the Corporations Law.

Compliance auditing: A review of an organization's procedures to determine whether the organization is following a specific set of criteria (e. g. government regulation, commercial contract, and lease).

Contribution margin: The sales revenue less all variable costs (or unit selling price less unit variable cost).

Control risk: The risk that a misstatement that could occur in an account balance or class of transactions and that could be material, individually or when aggregated with misstatements in other balances or classes, will not be prevented or detected and corrected on a timely basis by the accounting and internal control systems.

Cost: An economic sacrifice of resources made in exchange for a product or service.

Cost behavior: How a cost responds to changes in the level of activity.

Cost-volume-profit (CVP) analysis: A management accounting technique used to evaluate how costs and profits are affected by changes in the level of business activity.

Current assets: Cash and other forms of assets that are reasonably expected to be converted to cash, sold or consumed within 1 year of the balance sheet date.

Depreciation: That portion of the cost of a non-current asset that is assigned to expense over time.

Detection risk: The risk that an auditor's substantive procedures will not detect a misstatement that exists in an account balance or class of transactions that could be material, individually or when aggregated with misstatements in other balances or classes.

Disclaimer of opinion: A disclaimer of opinion is expressed when the possible effect of a limitation on scope is so material and pervasive that the auditor has not been able to obtain sufficient appropriate audit evidence and accordingly is unable to express an opinion on the financial statements.

Dividend: A distribution of profit by a company to its shareholders, usually in the form of cash.

Double-entry accounting: The accounting system where every transaction affects two (or more) components of the accounting equation.

Due professional care: The activities of a professional fulfilling his duties diligently and carefully. Due care for an auditor includes the completeness of the working papers, the sufficiency of the audit evidence, and the appropriateness of the audit report.

Estimated useful life: The period of time a non-current asset is expected to be used by the entity.

Expenses: Decreases in owner's equity (apart from drawings) representing the consumption or loss of economic benefits in the form of reductions in assets or increases in liabilities.

Financial position: The economic condition of a reporting entity, having regard to its control over economic resources, financial structure, capacity for adaptation, and solvency.

Fixed cost: A production cost that remains relatively constant in total amount over a wide range of production levels.

Fraud: Refers to an intentional act by one or more individuals among management, employees, or third parties, which results in a misrepresentation of financial statements.

General journal: A book containing a chronological listing of transactions.

General ledger: A collection of accounts maintained by an entity to enable the preparation of that entity's financial statements.

Going concern assumption: The assumption that an entity will continue in the future and use its assets in operations rather than sell them.

Horizontal analysis: That part of an analysis based on the comparison of amounts reported for the same item in two or more comparative statements with an emphasis on the change from year to year.

Inherent risk: A component of audit risk. It is the susceptibility of an account balance or class of transactions to misstatement that could be material, individually or when aggregated with misstatements in other balances of classes, assuming that there were no related internal controls.

Intangible assets: Assets that usually do not have a physical existence and derive value.

Internal control system: The overall procedures adopted by a business to safeguard its assets, promote the reliability of accounting data, and encourage compliance with management policies.

Internal rate of return (IRR): The interest rate that discounts the net cash flows from an investment so their present value is equal to the cost of the investment.

Inventory: Goods or property acquired by a merchandising business for the purposes of resale in the ordinary course of operations.

Journal: A record in which transactions are initially recorded.

Liabilities: Future sacrifices of economic benefits that an entity is presently obliged to make to other entities as a result of past transactions or other events.

Liquidity: The ability of an entity to satisfy its short-term financial obligations; also refers to the average length of time it takes to convert a non-cash asset into cash.

Management accounting: A branch of accounting that provides information to management for planning, controlling and decision making.

Master budget: A set of interrelated budgets representing a comprehensive plan of action for a specified time period.

Materiality: Information is material if its omission or misstatement could influence the economic decisions of users taken on the basis of the financial statements. Materiality depends on the size of the item or error judged in the particular circumstances of its omission or misstatement. Thus, materiality provides a threshold or cutoff point rather than being a primary qualitative characteristic which information must have if it is to be useful.

Monetary unit assumption: Only those things that can be expressed in money are included in the accounting records.

Net present value (NPV) method: A capital budgeting method used to discount future net cash flows into present value terms with the entity's cost of capital.

Net profit: The excess of revenues over expenses.

Non-current liabilities: Obligations of the entity that do not require payment within 1 year of the balance sheet date.

Operating cycle: The average period of time it takes for an entity to purchase inventory and then receive cash from its sale.

Operational auditing: A study of a specific unit of an organization for the purpose of measuring its performance.

Ordinary shares: A class of share that has no preferences relative to other classes.

Owner's equity: The residual interest in the assets (less liabilities) of an entity.

Partnership: A form of business structure under which a business entity is owned by two or more people as partners sharing profits and losses.

Payback period (PBP): The length of time required to recover the cost of an investment from the net cash flows it generates.

Period assumption: The assumption that the life of an entity can be divided into arbitrary equal time intervals for reporting purposes.

Period costs: Costs charged to the profit and loss statement of the period in which they are incurred rather than being cost to inventories as product costs.

Periodic inventory system: A system of accounting for inventory in which the goods on hand are determined by a physical count and the cost of goods sold is equal to the beginning inventory plus net purchases less ending inventory.

Perpetual inventory system: A system of accounting for inventory that provides a continuous and detailed record of the goods on hand and the cost of goods sold.

Posting: The process of transferring information recorded in a journal to the individual accounts in the ledger.

Preference shares: Shares which receive preferential treatment over ordinary shares such as a preference in dividend distributions, and/or a preference in asset distributions if the company is wound up.

Product costs: Costs assigned to inventories during production and charged to the profit and loss statement when the related finished goods are sold.

Qualified opinion: A qualified opinion is expressed when the auditor concludes that an unqualified opinion cannot be expressed but that the effect of any disagreement with management, or limitation on scope, is not so material and pervasive as to require an adverse opinion or a disclaimer of opinion.

Ratio analysis: The comparison of relationships between financial statement accounts, the comparison of an account with non-financial data, or the comparison of relationships between firms in an industry.

Retained profits: Profits of a company that have been retained in the business rather than distributed to shareholders.

Return on investment (ROI) analysis: A technique used to evaluate the profitability of segments of a business.

Revenue: The inflows or savings in outflows of economic benefits that result in an increase in owner's equity during the reporting period (excluding capital contributions by owners).

Single proprietorship (sole trader): A form of business structure in which the business entity is owned by an individual.

Solvency: The ability of an entity to pay its debts as and when they fall due.

Special journals: Books of original entry used for such repetitive transactions as sales, purchases, cash receipts and cash payment.

Subsidiary ledger: A group of individual accounts, the total of which should equal the balance of a related control account in the general ledger.

Substantive procedures: Substantive procedures are tests performed to obtain audit evidence to detect material misstatements in the financial statements, and are of two types: (a) tests of details of transactions and balances; and (b) analytical procedures.

Sufficient appropriate audit evidence: Sufficiency is the measure of the quantity (amount) of audit evidence. Appropriateness is the measure of the quality of audit evidence and its relevance to a particular assertion and its reliability.

T-account: An account format shaped like the letter T, in which the left-hand side of the account is the debit side and the right-hand side is the credit side.

Tests of control: Tests of control are performed to obtain audit evidence about the effectiveness of the: (a) Design of the accounting and internal control systems, that is, whether they are suitably designed to prevent or detect and correct material misstatements; (b) Operation of the internal controls throughout the period.

Trial balance: A statement listing all of the accounts in the general ledger and their debit or credit balances. A trial balance is prepared to verify the equality of debits, and credits made to the accounts.

Unqualified opinion: An audit opinion expressed when the auditor concludes that the financial statements give a true and fair view (or are presented fairly, in all material respects) in accordance with the identified financial reporting framework.

Variable cost: A production cost that varies in total amount directly with the volume of production.

Vertical analysis: That part of an analysis in which the focus of the study is on the proportion of individual items expressed as a percentage of some specific item reported in the same statement.

References

DEEGAN C, 2000. Australian financial accounting [M]. 3rd ed. Sydney: McGraw-Hill Australia Pty Limited.

DYSON J R, 2007. Accounting for non-accounting students [M]. 7th ed. London: Pearson Education Limited.

HAYES R, DASSEN R, SCHILDER A, et al., 2005. Principles of auditing: an introduction to international standards on auditing [M]. 2nd ed. London: Pearson Education Limited.

HOGGETT J, EDWARDS L, 2000. Accounting in Australia [M]. 4th ed. Brisbane: John Wiley & Sons Australia Ltd.

LAUDON K C, LAUDON J P, 2015. Management information systems: managing the digital firm [M]. 14th ed. London: Pearson Education Limited.

MAUFFETTE-LEENDERS L A, ERSKINE J A, LEENDERS M R, 2007. Learning with cases [M]. 4th ed. London: Ivey Publishing.

VAN HORNE J C, WACHOWICZ JR J M, 2005. 财务管理基础[M]. 11版. 北京: 清华大学出版社.

龚菊明, 2007. 基础会计[M]. 上海: 复旦大学出版社.

刘建华, 白鸥, 黑岚, 2009. 会计英语[M]. 北京: 清华大学出版社.

沈勤, 张建明, 2010. 会计英语[M]. 苏州: 苏州大学出版社.